PRESENTED TO

BY

DATE

THE Love Dare

DAY BY DAY

ISBN: 978-1-4336-8137-0
B&H Publishing Group
Nashville, Tennessee
BHPublishingGroup.com

Unless otherwise noted, all Scripture quotations are taken
from the Holman Christian Standard Bible®, Copyright ©
1999, 2000, 2002, 2003, 2009 by Holman Bible Publishers.

The New American Standard Bible (NASB), Copyright ©
1960, 1962, 1963, 1968, 1971, 1972, 1973, 1975, 1977, 1995 by
The Lockman Foundation. Used by permission

The Holy Bible, New International Version (NIV), Copyright
© 1973, 1978, 1984 International Bible Society. Used by permission of Zondervan. All rights reserved

The New King James Version (NKJV), copyright © 1979,
1980, 1982, Thomas Nelson, Inc., Publishers

Dewey Decimal Classification: 242.2
Devotional Literature \ Love \ Marriage

Printed in China
3 4 5 6 7 8 9 10 • 18 17 16 15 14

THE
Love Dare

DAY BY DAY

A YEAR OF DEVOTIONS
FOR COUPLES

STEPHEN & ALEX
KENDRICK
WITH LAWRENCE KIMBROUGH

B&H
PUBLISHING GROUP
NASHVILLE, TENNESSEE

This Will Be a Challenge.

This one-year journey will take courage and endurance. At times it will seem challenging and difficult, and at other times it will be incredibly fulfilling.

To take this dare requires a resolute mind and a steadfast determination. It is meant to enrich your relationship with God and your spouse through a daily time of prayer, devotion, and action.

Don't quit early, for those who do will forfeit the greatest benefits. If you will commit to a day at a time for one year, the results could change your life and your marriage.

Consider it a dare, from others who have done it before you.

This one-year devotional journey contains the foundational principles of the original book, *The Love Dare*, while also providing fresh content and deeper studies.

A daily time of devotion is part of a living, loving relationship between you and God. Whether you read this alone or with your spouse, you should begin every day in prayer asking God to speak to you. This devotional should never be a substitute for your time in the Scriptures. It is meant to increase your understanding of biblical principles and awaken your appetite to search the Scriptures more deeply for yourself.

You are about to learn some things about yourself and your marriage. Some will be encouraging and some convicting. In either case, they will call for an honest view of where you are with your marriage and with God.

God uses the gift of marriage to help us eliminate loneliness, multiply our effectiveness, establish families, raise children, enjoy life, and bless us with relational intimacy. Marriage also shows us our need to grow and deal with our own issues and self-centeredness through the help of a lifelong partner. If we are teachable, we will learn to do the one thing most important in life—to love. This powerful union provides the path for you to learn how to love another imperfect person unconditionally. It is wonderful. It is difficult. It is life-changing.

This book is about love. It's about learning and daring to do whatever it takes to strengthen and reinforce God's purpose for marriage. If you accept this dare, you must take the view that instead of following your heart, you are *choosing to lead it*. The Bible says that "the heart is more deceitful than anything else" (Jeremiah 17:9), and it will pursue what feels right at the moment. We dare you to think differently, and choose to *lead your heart* toward what is best in the long run.

This journey is not a process of trying to change your spouse to be the person you want them to be. Rather, this is a journey of exploring and demonstrating genuine love, even when your desire is dry and your motives are low. The truth is, love is a decision, not just a feeling. It is selfless, sacrificial, and transformational. When love is truly demonstrated as it was intended, your relationship is more likely to change for the better.

During your daily devotions, you will learn more about the nature of love, as well as the character of God Himself. Read each day carefully and be open to a new understanding of what it means to genuinely love someone. (For more on how to have a daily devotion time, see page 378 in the appendix.)

You will be given a weekly dare to do for your spouse. Some will be easy, and some very challenging. But take each dare seriously, and be creative and courageous enough to attempt it. Don't be discouraged if outside situations prevent you from accomplishing a specific dare. Just pick back up as soon as it is within your ability and proceed with the journey.

Finally, you are encouraged to get a journal to record your personal thoughts and experiences as you put these truths into practice. It is important that you capture what is happening to both you and your mate during the journey. These notes will provide a record of your progress and should become priceless to you in the future.

Remember, *you* have the responsibility to protect and guide your heart. Don't give up and don't get discouraged. Resolve to lead your heart and to make it through to the end. Learning to truly love is one of the most important things you will ever do. May God bless you as you take this dare!

NOW THESE THREE REMAIN: FAITH, HOPE, AND LOVE.
BUT THE GREATEST OF THESE IS LOVE.
1 Corinthians 13:13

If I speak with the tongues
of men and of angels,
but do not have love,
I have become a noisy gong
or a clanging cymbal.

If I have the gift of prophecy,
and know all mysteries and
all knowledge; and if I have
all faith, so as to remove mountains,
but do not have love, I am nothing.

And if I give all my possessions
to feed the poor, and if I surrender
my body to be burned, but do not
have love, it profits me nothing.

1 Corinthians 13:1–3 (NASB)

DAY 1
Love is the greatest of these

If I have all faith, so that I can move mountains,
but do not have love, I am nothing.

1 Corinthians 13:2

Loving God and others is what life is really about. No matter who you are or what you do, it comes down to whether you'll live a life of love or not. And there is a vast difference between the two. One is priceless . . . and one meaningless.

Love is the most important ingredient to any meaningful relationship. It is fundamental to true significance. Your quality of life is directly tied to the amount of love flowing in you and through you to others. Though it's often overlooked, love is infinitely more valuable than riches, fame, or honor. They will pass away, but love remains. You can be fulfilled without these, but not without love.

The absence of love leaves a devastating void. When it is not present, your spirituality becomes superficial, your benevolent deeds self-centered, and your sacrifices insincere. In any relationship where love is not your motivation, you can expect it to feel bland and unfulfilling—if not meaningless. When asked to identify life's greatest command, Jesus summed it up this way: to love God with all you are and to love your neighbor as yourself. Will you embrace a life of love?

❧ THIS WEEK'S DARE ❧

Begin praying this week: "Lord, teach me what real love is and make me a loving person."

DAY 2
Love is life's motivator

For Christ's love compels us . . .

2 Corinthians 5:14

Anger can fuel hatred in a man's heart until he feels like attacking his enemy. But love can spark kindness in his heart so he lays down his life for his friend. Selfishness can drive a woman to tighten her grip and hoard her resources. But love can inspire her to open her hands and give sacrificially. Love is the purest and most powerful motivator. It gives courage to a coward, wisdom to a fool.

When love invades your heart, you are empowered to endure deeper pain, willingly pay a greater cost, and run risks to your reputation for the sake of another. Love causes a soldier to lay down his life for his country, a mother to pray relentlessly for her child, and a gracious God to send His only Son to die for our sins. Love is that powerful.

Paul the apostle endured beatings, intense persecution, and hardship throughout his life. He did it for one reason alone: "Christ's love" compelled him. If love began fueling your decisions, what would it drive you to do for your marriage?

﹌﹍ GO DEEPER ﹌﹍

Read 1 Corinthians 13. After you have read it, read verses 4–7 again. This time, replace the words "love" or "it" with your first name. Then close in prayer and ask God to help make this a reality in your life.

DAY 3
Love is the key

Now these three remain: faith, hope, and love.
But the greatest of these is love.

1 Corinthians 13:13

Love is fundamental to the success of your marriage. Not your current feelings of romance or sexual satisfaction. Not a stronger financial standing or even your spouse's behavior. All of these can circumstantially change, and they will. But when storms rise and conditions worsen, love-driven marriages endure and work through even the toughest issues without giving up.

When marriages crumble, couples often claim that it was due to their irreconcilable differences. But genuine love is a master at reconciliation. When love takes over, it compels us to humbly apologize and take full responsibility for our failures, then to fully forgive where our spouse has failed us. Over and over again.

Resilient marriages are built on honesty, respect, commitment, forgiveness, and endurance. And love constantly inspires all of these things to grow and thrive within us. Though love reaches far beyond marriage, it is a God-given key to its success. You can strip away most of the pleasures you and your spouse hold together, but your marriage hinges on love.

❧ THIS WEEK'S DARE ❧

Keep praying this week: "Lord, teach me what real love is and make me a loving person."

DAY 4
Love simplifies

*Do not owe anyone anything, except to love one another,
for the one who loves another has fulfilled the law.*

Romans 13:8

Love ultimately fulfills every law of God. It persuades
us to live out all that is good and forbids us from doing all
that is evil. Every act of hatred, subtle deception, or plot of
unfaithfulness is vetoed when love takes command in our
hearts. Love toward God leads us to obey Him and uphold
His rightful place of honor in our lives. If we do so, we will
by default not sin against His name. Love toward others
transforms our behavior for the better and defuses evil intentions like light dispels darkness.

Men who lead by love won't deceive or degrade their
wives or their neighbors. When love fills a woman's mouth,
she encourages her family instead of tearing them down.
When you're focused on love, you will naturally demonstrate
patience, tenderness, and kindness. Rather than trying to
manufacture right actions and attitudes, let love become
your first response and your default position. Then you're set
to launch into any circumstance graciously and to land with
no regrets.

❧ GO DEEPER ❧

Read Romans 13:8–10 and study Paul's explanation of
how love fulfills all of God's law.

DAY 5

Love is the business of men

*God has not given us a spirit of fearfulness,
but one of power, love, and sound judgment.*

2 Timothy 1:7

When a movie is marketed as a love story, we assume it's primarily for an audience of women. If plots don't contain fighting, bleeding, or exploding, men will gladly avoid them. But real love is not merely women's work. It's at the core of manhood, transforming men to be strong and courageous.

Love makes a husband put away childish things and embrace his responsibilities to lead his family. It drives him to defend his wife, provide for his children, and even lay down his life if they become endangered. Love motivates a man to confront injustice and take passionate stands for what he believes in, like crossing an ocean to fight for his country.

Jesus was the most loving man ever to walk the earth and remains the perfect example of manhood. With passion, He confronted evil, cast out demons, and rebuked religious hypocrites. Out of love, He served sacrificially, rescued the brokenhearted, and willingly died for the sins of the world. Real men embrace this love as the driving force to boldly do what boys merely dream of.

⤜ THIS WEEK'S DARE ⤐

Keep praying this week: "Lord, teach me what real love is and make me a loving person."

Day 6
Love is your job description

*This is the message you have heard from the beginning:
we should love one another.*

1 John 3:11

People from every nation, tribe, and tongue have it in common—everyone is longing to be loved. It's inbred, God-given, lifelong, and deeply felt. "Would someone please love me?" is the unspoken cry from billboards, television shows, magazines, and T-shirts. We work constantly to get others to notice our worth and validate us with their attention. We will even give ourselves to someone with hopes of receiving love in return. But ironically, people rarely take their focus off themselves so they can meet this need in others. Selfishly, we may even overlook our own spouse. But he or she needs it just the same.

Love, however, is your primary responsibility in marriage. Did you not vow to a lifelong love at the altar? Are you not the one God has privileged to fill your mate's love tank? And remember this: when your spouse deserves your love the least, that is when they need it the most. No one on Earth is more strategically positioned, commanded, and called on to love your mate than you are.

❧ PRAYER ❧

"Lord, I thank You for the spouse You have given me. Teach me to love them in a way that meets their needs and honors You. In Jesus' name, amen."

DAY 7
Love is fertile soil

. . . that you being rooted and grounded in love . . .
Ephesians 3:17 NASB

When we plant a living seed into healthy soil, we expect it to blossom. And just as flowers in a greenhouse are supplied with an ideal environment for growth, so a home filled with love provides the ideal atmosphere for people to bloom.

We know that children who grow up in loving families tend to sleep deeper, stand taller, and venture farther than those who are never secure in their parents' love. Likewise, when you provide safe, loving soil for your spouse to grow in, they will be more likely to flourish with confidence, knowing they are valued and secure.

What happens when someone is loved over the years? Their needs are met, dreams encouraged, opinions heard, and successes praised. They're assured of your patience and forgiveness when they fail, and free to express themselves honestly without fear of your judgment. They'll even weather intense seasons of disappointment with the stability your love supplies. Admit it—we'd all love to be loved like that.

✎ QUESTIONS ✎

How will your mate be affected by living with you in the future? Will they become radiant or saddened? Confident or angry? Will you dare to create a loving environment for your spouse to grow in?

DAY 8

Love is best when God is first

"You shall love the Lord your God with all your heart."

Matthew 22:37 NASB

Loving your spouse more than you love God is a form of idolatry. Far too many marriages suffer from this inversion. It places a created thing higher than the Creator. God should always be the first and primary object of our affection. He created us to love Him, and something unexplainably beautiful happens when we direct all of who we are at delighting in all of who He is. It is proper worship of the One who is worthy.

If love is the greatest thing you can do, then loving with all you are is the greatest expression you could ever make. Furthermore, if God is the greatest object of love, then awaken to the priceless purpose you have been given. You are wired, commanded, and invited to do the greatest thing in the greatest way for the greatest One. There is no higher calling. Yours is the most important over all of creation because you have been made in His image and are uniquely designed to express love in ways the rest of nature cannot.

Embrace this eternal privilege. Let every breath be an opportunity to learn how to better love the God who first loved you.

ᴥ☙ THIS WEEK'S DARE ☙ᴥ

Commit this week to prioritize a few minutes with God every day. Include prayer and Scripture reading.

DAY 9
Love is most when God is first

By this we know that we love the children of God,
when we love God and observe His commandments.

1 John 5:1–2 NASB

Keeping God first blesses your marriage more than any other practice. Everything in life takes on new value and meaning when it becomes an instrument for you to live out your love for God. Rather than placing yourself at the center of your relationships, all your energies and assets should be tools for worshipping Him. A husband might think his marriage would suffer from making God his greatest delight. On the contrary, it will flourish as he draws closer to the One who created marriage and loves his wife infinitely more than he does. God understands more than anyone what your marriage needs.

As you abide in Christ's love, the love you have for your spouse will increase in the overflow. Drinking His love in daily and expressing it back to Him fulfills you in ways your spouse cannot. This enables you to cherish your bride or groom like never before. The closer you get to Him, the more you will be like Him, think like Him, and passionately love your mate like He does.

GO DEEPER

Read 1 John 4:19–21. According to this passage, why do we love in the first place? Look at how God's Word repeatedly calls us to love others.

DAY 10
Love keeps God's commands

*"The one who has My commands
and keeps them is the one who loves me."*

John 14:21

Loving God is a wholehearted, lifelong adventure. It's not a part-time job or Sunday-only affair but a complete devotion of ourselves to seeking and treasuring who God is. Every thought, value, and action can become another way to say "I love You" to God. And loving Him is the perfect *why* behind *what* we do. It begins by confessing our faith in His Son Jesus (1 John 4:15; 5:1), and then is fueled by an ongoing obedience to Him—in everything (John 14:21). But our love makes following Him a relational delight rather than a religious chore (1 John 5:13). And as we daily abandon sin and do what He says, the peace and joy we derive makes us love Him even more.

God's Word says we also love Him through the ways we treat, serve, and love others (1 John 3:17; 4:11–21). So every conversation and interaction in your marriage is a new opportunity to bless your spouse and to demonstrate your love for God as well. Ultimately, how you love and respect your mate reveals every day the sincerity of your love and respect for God.

THIS WEEK'S DARE

Commit this week to prioritize a few minutes with God every day. Include prayer and Scripture reading.

Love walks with God

*"By this all people will know that you are My disciples,
if you have love for one another."*

John 13:35

Good disciples of Christ also tend to make good spouses. Your role as husband or wife is greatly enhanced by being a faithful and growing Christian. People who are not pursuing an intimate relationship with God are significantly limited, left to rely on their own feelings, thoughts, and efforts. When we refuse to obey Christ's commands, our spouses are left to deal with the fallout.

Only those living in fellowship with Christ are able to access His toolbox for marriage. His Word will nourish you spiritually and equip you for every good work. His counsel can guide your decisions with divine wisdom. Rather than your spouse having to depend on their own influence to change you, they know the Holy Spirit is already busy working on you and maturing you from the inside out.

It's romantic for a woman to see her strong husband humbling himself before God. It's inspiring for a man to see his wife living with deep conviction and passion. Walking with God is better than a thousand marriage books or counseling sessions.

✥ QUESTIONS ✥

What are your priorities for your marriage? How important is your walk with God to you? Are you helping your marriage in this area, or hindering it?

Love offers companionship

Then the LORD God said, "It is not good for the man to be alone."

Genesis 2:18

The repeated phrase during the Creation account is: "It was good." Water, sky, plants, and animals—everything God made was declared by the Creator Himself to be "good." But when God gazed on His perfect creation, He saw one thing that was "not good"—the man was alone. Adam deeply needed companionship. God's loving solution was the creation of a lifelong, intimate relationship: *marriage*. Truly, "a man who finds a wife finds a good thing" (Proverbs 18:22).

Among the truths we learn from the Trinity is that God, though One, maintains constant fellowship within the three Persons of the Godhead. Father, Son, and Holy Spirit enjoy one another in unbroken companionship. None is ever alone. This mysterious communion is also intended in marriage. Between a husband and wife, God offers the most intimate companionship a person can know with another individual on Earth.

You have the opportunity and responsibility each day to eliminate the sense of loneliness inherent in your spouse. It is not good enough to live together but remain emotionally distant. Loneliness should be absent. Love builds bridges between lonely hearts to make you close companions for life.

❧ THIS WEEK'S DARE ❧

Commit this week to prioritize a few minutes with God every day. Include prayer and Scripture reading.

DAY 13
Love brings completeness

"A man leaves his father and mother and bonds
with his wife, and they become one flesh."

Genesis 2:24

In the finale of God's creation, He made the first marriage by taking one man, removing part of him, and fashioning another person. Then, in the mystery of matrimony, two could come together and become one. Adam, though complete with God alone, found his God-given needs met even more fully with Eve, his complement, in life. This is true in your marriage. The Lord knew before you were born that you would one day marry your mate. And in His design of your gender differences and uniqueness, God intentionally created needs in both of you that the other would be exclusively designed to help meet.

The devil's desire is to use your distinctiveness to push you apart—to operate independently—as though what your spouse brings to you is unnecessary. But marriage has made you "one flesh." Now neither of you should live without the other. Though distinct in personality and ability, you have been designed to experience oneness in your diversity. You are no longer just you. You are so intimately combined with your mate that together you are to live as one complete person.

PRAYER

"Lord Jesus, bond our hearts together in marriage.
Teach us what it means to live as one. In Your name
we pray, amen."

DAY 14
Love extends help

"I will make him a helper suitable for him."

Genesis 2:18 NASB

Let's be honest—men need help. They try to function alone, but consistently fall short. God assigned Adam to a specific work, but knew he needed a helper to succeed. A wife's title as "helper" to her husband is a high compliment, not a criticism. In fact, God Himself is referred to as our Helper (Psalm 124:8). Jesus called His Spirit a Helper. A husband who has a wife willing to help him fulfill God's assignments for his life has a priceless treasure.

Marriage is one of God's unique ways of showing both men and women that we're not all-sufficient in ourselves. We both need our spouse and cannot fulfill God's plans for us without their help. This is why a single mother or father struggles so desperately—though often courageously—to be what their children need. Each role is dependent on the other's help, and it becomes impossible (without God's provision) for one person to perform both jobs alone.

God made it that way. He intended for you to assist your spouse as a primary purpose in your marriage. It even meets a need in you to know that you are needed.

QUESTIONS

Do you think in terms of being a helper for your spouse? How could you be a blessing today in an area where they could use your help?

DAY 15
Love multiplies itself

Two are better than one, because they have a
good return for their work. . . . Though one may
be overpowered, two can defend themselves.

Ecclesiastes 4:9, 12

Marriage is not as simple as one plus one. Because marriage is a God-ordained design that reflects His boundless nature, the union of a husband and wife produces much more than the sum of its parts. We don't merely add to one another's life; we multiply one another's effectiveness.

A person hopping on one leg cannot get very far, very fast. But two legs joining together become the action of running—making you faster and taking you farther. Two wings don't merely create balance; they enable the other to fly. What's generated by shared momentum creates an exponential increase in what's accomplished. A husband and wife working together offer a solid defense for their families against the influence of a godless culture.

Likewise, a man and wife praying together form a spiritual bond as God joins them in single-minded purpose (Matthew 18:19–20). By uniting in His name and agreeing in prayer, their intercession goes to another level. That's when one united with one has won.

⤳ THIS WEEK'S DARE ⤳

Find a family project that needs attention and work on it together. Do whatever you can to operate as a team from beginning to completion. Purpose to encourage each other along the way.

DAY 16
Love builds families

God blessed them, and God said to them,
"Be fruitful, multiply, fill the earth, and subdue it."

Genesis 1:28

God lovingly created and highly honors the institution of *family*—both physically and spiritually. He has uniquely designed marriage with all the elements for adding and multiplying families. One of His great purposes of marriage is the leaving and cleaving that forms a new family unit, forged by the union of a man and woman from two different homes. Marriage is also the God-ordained environment to multiply and reproduce life through the bearing and raising of children.

Married love comes with built-in construction and expansion plans, initiated by the One who desires for us to give Him "godly offspring" through our love for one another (Malachi 2:15). This new family you've originated in marriage is not simply a foundational building block of society. Your union and your children are a testimony to the living God, who continues to add and multiply His blessings on earthly families that will expand His heavenly family.

🙞 GO DEEPER 🙜

Read Genesis 1:26–28 and see what God's first commandment was to men and women. Do you see your marriage and children as a living witness of God's goodness? Has He not given you life itself? Does your worldview need to be altered to reflect the value He has given to you and your family?

DAY 17
Love unites families

"May the LORD make the woman who is coming into your home like Rachel and Leah, who together built up the house of Israel."... Boaz took Ruth and she became his wife.

Ruth 4:11–13 NIV

Marriage connects entire families. Your relationship is not only a union between you and your mate, but also a bridge builder between you and a new set of parents, siblings, grandparents, and cousins—all who may possess little in common with you except for the kinship your marriage creates.

But consider that this bond has the potential to bring the best of the fellowship, counsel, support, and love from both families into yours. This connection also calls forth from you depths of understanding, sacrifice, and forgiveness on a most personal level to them. This is an ongoing opportunity for you to practice Christian love and an edifying influence toward in-laws and extended families. Even when friction occurs, love demands that you continually seek to support and share life with these individuals who are part of your spouse's history, DNA, and heartbeat.

✎✎ THIS WEEK'S DARE ✎✎

Find a family project that needs attention and work on it together. Do whatever you can to operate as a team from beginning to completion. Purpose to encourage each other along the way.

DAY 18
Love inspires purity

*Because of immoralities, each man is to have his own wife,
and each woman is to have her own husband.*

1 Corinthians 7:2 NASB

God designed marriage to keep us sexually pure. The One who conceived the beauty of sexuality also ordained marriage as His perfect way for us to enjoy His gift to the fullest. God desires for us to have the rich blessings of His best. He created a context for sexuality that always promotes love, honors purity, guards safety, and rewards lifelong commitment. Sex is God's holy wedding gift to seal and bless the covenant a husband and wife have made. Those who seek to satisfy their sexual desires outside of His design fall into the poisonous trap of sinning against their own body, their spouse, and God.

If cultures honored God's holy design, sexually transmitted diseases and unwed pregnancies would cease. Marriage is God's ideal solution to sexual immorality. As you fully meet your spouse's needs, you're helping them walk in purity. But purity is much more than just avoiding affairs. It extends to keeping your eyes, viewing habits, and emotional attachments honoring to God. This brings a joyful peace to your marriage that only purity can offer.

⤙⤙⤙ PRAYER ⤙⤙⤙

"Father God, keep us faithful and pure in our marriage. Help us to guard against anything that threatens our intimacy, and bless the bond we have in our sexual relationship. In Jesus' name, amen."

Day 19

Love is fun

Enjoy life with the wife you love all the days of your fleeting life.

Ecclesiastes 9:9

Marriage was designed to bring delight. The Bible says a man should rejoice in his wife and be "exhilarated always with her love" (Proverbs 5:19 NASB). It says he should seek "how he may please his wife," and she should seek "how she may please her husband" (1 Corinthians 7:33–34). God intends marriage to be pleasurable for both of you in countless ways.

So while marital love goes much deeper than emotions, God created it to be rich with feeling. He made sexual interaction not merely a fruitful experience but a pleasurable one. Even though marriage is a oneness that requires hard work, we must not let it lose its sense of joy. God wants the smile on your spouse's face to bring a smile to yours.

Being with the person you love the most was never meant to dissolve into mere duty and obligation. So take pleasure in what God has begun and continues to grow in you. You were not born to bicker, but to bask in joy together. It's one of God's key places where life united in Him becomes abundant.

THIS WEEK'S DARE

Find a family project needing attention and work on it together. Do whatever you can to operate as a team from beginning to completion. Purpose to encourage each other along the way.

Day 20
Love causes growth

Husbands, love your wives, just as also Christ loved the church and gave Himself for her, to make her holy.

Ephesians 5:25–26

Marriage was intended to help us mature. A wife can be God's instrument to help make a man out of the boy she married. A strong man will help mature and polish his wife by his positive influence and loving interaction with her. Good friends and mentors sharpen you when you are around them.

Part of marriage's purpose is to help us refine and strengthen each other. Your spouse is given a front row seat for viewing your rough edges that don't resemble Christ. When your spouse exposes a flaw or weakness in your character, your first reaction should be to listen and learn. You should receive it as heavenly sandpaper, buffing you into a more complete Christlike image.

Your mate stands before you like a mirror, reflecting and exposing who you are. He or she is positioned like no one else to reveal areas in your life where correction is warranted. Allow God to use this person to make you more like Jesus, even as He works through you to cause growth in their life as well. You and your spouse should both bloom into Christlikeness from being with each other.

⤠ GO DEEPER ⤟

Read Ephesians 5:25–26 and Romans 8:28–29. In what ways does Scripture say we can help our spouse to become more like Christ?

Day 21

Love glorifies God

*This mystery is profound,
but I am talking about Christ and the church.*

Ephesians 5:32

At its heart, marriage is more than a man and a woman falling in love and spending life together. God has many priceless purposes for marriage. He created it to eliminate loneliness through companionship, multiply our effectiveness through teamwork, and mature us into Christlikeness. He designed marriage to guard our purity through sexual fulfillment, grow families through procreation, and bring about the enjoyment of walking in love and oneness. But God's ultimate purpose for marriage is a hidden mystery that is greater than all of these combined.

God masterfully orchestrated marriage to reveal the beauty of His glory. In fact, each of His purposes for marriage reveals a characteristic of God in eternity. Our oneness and companionship reflect His union in the Trinity. Our purity honors His holiness. Our procreation reflects Him as Creator of life. Our love is founded in the truth that God is love. And our love provides a living portrait of the gospel—Christ's unconditional love for His people, His church, His bride (Revelation 21:9). Your marriage is a mystery revealing His majesty.

☙ PRAYER ❧

"Lord Jesus, mold our hearts to glorify You through our marriage. Do what You need to do to keep us in a right relationship with You."

Day 22

Love prepares us for heaven

*I also saw the Holy City, new Jerusalem, coming down
out of heaven from God, prepared like a bride adorned
for her husband.*

Revelation 21:2

There will come a time when love and its many remarkable attributes will no longer take an effort to maintain. Instead, love will flow so naturally from us, it will be the only thing we consider doing. It will be like Jesus' love—freely given and totally selfless.

Till then, marriage is one of our main instructors on how love is supposed to be given and received. It teaches us how to defer to another, giving ourselves completely without reservation. It teaches us how to love someone without basing our affections on how hard they're working to please us.

Day after day, we should learn more about our relationship with God by seeing it portrayed in our dealings with each other. Marriage is not just an analogy He came up with to try describing His love for us. The marriage of Christ with His bride, the church, is life's ultimate story. By participating in it here, we get glimpses of it there.

∼ THIS WEEK'S DARE ∼

Choose to demonstrate patience by saying nothing negative to your spouse. It is better to hold your tongue than to say something you'll regret.

DAY 23
Love is patient

Be completely humble and gentle; be patient,
bearing with one another in love.

Ephesians 4:2 NIV

No one likes the fact that life requires patience. But the more you learn to love, the greater your capacity will be to demonstrate patience toward others. In fact, patience is one of the attributes that best defines what love is.

When you choose to be patient, you respond in a positive way to a negative situation. You are slow to anger, choosing to have a long fuse instead of a quick temper. Rather than being restless and demanding, love helps you settle down and begin extending mercy to those around you.

Patience brings an internal calm during an external storm. It is the choice to control your emotions rather than allowing your emotions to control you, and it shows discretion instead of returning evil for evil. "Bearing with one another in love" should become a motto you carry into every day and every potential altercation with your mate.

⟶ GO DEEPER ⟵

So many problems in marriage would be avoided or quickly resolved if husbands and wives followed the counsel in James 1:19. Study this verse and consider how you might apply it in your marriage.

DAY 24
Love is slow to anger

*A patient person shows great understanding,
but a quick-tempered one promotes foolishness.*

Proverbs 14:29

If your spouse offends you, do you quickly retaliate or do you stay under control? Do you find that anger is your emotional default when treated unfairly? If so, you are spreading poison rather than medicine.

No one likes to be around an impatient person. Impatience causes you to overreact in angry, foolish, and regrettable ways. The irony of anger toward a wrongful action is that it spawns new wrongs of its own. Anger almost never makes things better. It usually generates additional problems.

But patience stops problems in their tracks. It allows you to take a breath and clear the air. It acts with wisdom and doesn't rush to judgment, choosing instead to listen to what the other person is saying. Patience stands in the doorway, where anger is clawing to burst in, and waits to see the whole picture before passing judgment.

✥ THIS WEEK'S DARE ✥

Choose to demonstrate patience by saying nothing negative to your spouse. It is better to hold your tongue than to say something you'll regret.

Love responds wisely

*A hot-tempered man stirs up conflict,
but a man slow to anger calms strife.*

Proverbs 15:18

Patience is where love meets wisdom. As sure as a lack of it will turn your home into a war zone, the practice of patience will foster peace and quiet. Responding with wisdom is something every marriage needs if you want your relationship to stay healthy.

Patience helps you give your spouse permission to be human. It understands that everyone fails. When a mistake is made, it chooses to give them more time than they deserve to correct it. Patience gives you the ability to hold on during the tough times in your relationship rather than bailing out under the pressure. It is the gift of another chance, the promise that you will wait this one out for as long as it takes.

It turns out that few people are as hard to live with as an impatient person. Can your spouse count on having a patient wife or husband to live with?

PRAYER

"Father, help us to become very patient with one another. Give us the wisdom to be quick to listen, slow to speak, and slow to anger. In Jesus' name, amen."

DAY 26
Love listens

Understand this: everyone must be quick to hear,
slow to speak, and slow to anger.

James 1:19

The way you communicate to your spouse will reflect
the condition of your heart. If you are angry because of
your unmet expectations or their hurtful words, you will
tend to respond harshly. But this is where love takes time to
patiently listen and to give the other person consideration,
even if it is undeserved. It takes true resolve, but that's where
love must become your motivation.

Few of us listen patiently, and none of us do it naturally.
But a wise man or woman will pursue it as an essential ingredient to their marriage relationship.

Patience is a good starting point to demonstrate true
love. It may be more of a process, but it is a resolution worth
adopting. Think of it as a marathon, not just a sprint. You can
set a new tone in your communication by committing to
patiently listen. Don't interrupt. Don't talk over them. Make
sure they've said everything they need to say before you
choose to respond. And when you do, let love lead.

∞∞ THIS WEEK'S DARE ∞∞

Choose to demonstrate patience by saying nothing
negative to your spouse. It is better to hold your
tongue than to say something you'll regret.

DAY 27
Love is forbearing

*"The Lord, the Lord God, compassionate and gracious,
slow to anger, and abounding in lovingkindness and truth."*

Exodus 34:6 NASB

God's people had always known Him as their Creator, their Provider, and the Ruler over all creation. But at a key moment in history—after God gave the law on Mount Sinai and after the golden calf incident that followed—God revealed to Moses another facet of His nature: His forbearing patience.

The scene in Exodus 34, as seen through the smoky mist of God's glory on the mountaintop, pictures just the two of them there. The Lord appeared in front of Moses, proclaiming this truth as He passed by. No, "He will not leave the guilty unpunished," but He is not a God who quickly flashes His anger, although it would still be righteous to do so. Our God is "slow to anger."

This is why patience is called for in your marriage—not just because your spouse benefits from it, but because it is God's nature to be "compassionate and gracious." When you are patient with your spouse, you are being like your heavenly Father.

❧ GO DEEPER ❧

Read 2 Peter 3:9 and study how the patience of God is being demonstrated today in our generation. Why is God demonstrating patience rather than wrath? What does this say about His heart for us?

DAY 28
Love can be called on

"Please pardon the wrongdoing of this people in keeping with the greatness of Your faithful love."

Numbers 14:19

In Numbers 13, Moses sent spies into Canaan. But instead of trusting God, they brought back a fearful report to the people. After days of rebellion, God was most displeased with the lack of faith these leaders revealed. They doubted His ability to give them the Promised Land.

But Moses interceded for these distrusting people. And when he did, he appealed to God's loving patience in his intercession. Moses depended on the Lord's being "slow to anger and rich in faithful love, forgiving wrongdoing and rebellion" (Numbers 14:18). This was the solid-rock basis of his prayer.

In much the same way, your patient love should be an attribute your mate is able to call on at any time from you, even when they have clearly been in the wrong and your anger is justified. How will you respond the next time they need your patience?

༺ QUESTIONS ༻

Are you known for being a patient person? Are people calm around you, or concerned about you overreacting? Are you only patient when it is a small issue, or can you also demonstrate patience in very intense situations?

Love is consistently patient

Return to the LORD your God. For He is gracious
and compassionate, slow to anger, rich in faithful love.

Joel 2:13

God's patience is a major theme of Scripture. God revealed it to Moses and then consistently displayed it to His people. Nehemiah recalled it during a confession of the nation's sin (Nehemiah 9:17). David sought it for himself in seeking rescue from his enemies (Psalm 86:15), as well as forgiveness for his failings (Psalm 103:8). The prophets Joel, Jonah, and Nahum all experienced it firsthand. The apostle Paul likely had this attribute of God in mind when he began his description of love by saying, "Love is patient; love is kind" (1 Corinthians 13:4).

God's brand of patience—the patience He calls us to embody—is not an occasional thing. It is an ongoing, repetitive response that we keep doing, again and again. There may come a time when patience must act in judgment (Numbers 14:22–23), but it's a lot further down the line than most of us typically wait for. To be like God is to be patient.

THIS WEEK'S DARE

Think of an area where you struggle to show patience toward your spouse. Demonstrate love toward them by giving them more time to grow in this area. Commit this specific matter to prayer.

DAY 30
Love is God's Word

Your word is a lamp for my feet and a light on my path.

Psalm 119:105

For some people, the Bible seems just too big to understand. It's like an impossible challenge. But as a Christian, you're not left alone to try grasping the major themes and deep meanings of the Bible. The Holy Spirit, who now lives in your heart by way of salvation, is an illuminator of truth. "For the Spirit searches everything, even the deep things of God" (1 Corinthians 2:10). And because of His internal lamp, the Scriptures are now yours to read, absorb, and live by.

If this is not already a habit of yours, now is the time to begin reading a portion of the Bible every day. Ideally, read it together as husband and wife—in the morning, perhaps, or before bed. Be like the writer of Psalm 119, who could say, "I have sought You with all my heart; don't let me wander from Your commands. I have treasured Your word in my heart so that I may not sin against You" (Psalm 119:10–11).

☜ GO DEEPER ☞

Read Psalm 119:9–16 and see the wonderful benefits of the Word of God. Notice the psalmist's delight in Scripture and his commitment to make it a part of his daily life. Turn to page 372 in the appendix for a long list of additional blessings to be found in God's Word.

Day 31
Love outlasts anger

His anger lasts only a moment, but His favor, a lifetime.
Weeping may spend the night, but there is joy in the morning.

Psalm 30:5

Anger, being a powerful emotion, sometimes flares up quicker than our better judgment can head it off. We feel it rising up within us, leaving only a few seconds for us to choose whether or not to act on it. But once we recognize its appearance and we realize it wants to take over the situation, the wise man or woman restrains it. Anger may feel like lashing out from within us, but love won't let it take a breath.

Even God's anger, though always holy and justified, is quickly put behind Him after serving its purpose. Our anger, too, though sometimes appropriate, must remain under love's control. Otherwise, it will always want to write the script for what happens next, rather than playing its rightful role under the direction, authority, and restraint of godly patience.

If our love is to be like God's love, it must be slow to anger, ready to release, and quick to forgive.

❧ THIS WEEK'S DARE ❧

Think of an area where you struggle to show patience toward your spouse. Demonstrate love toward them by giving them more time to grow in this area. Commit this specific matter to prayer.

DAY 32
Love has a righteous anger

*For God's wrath is revealed from heaven
against all godlessness and unrighteousness.*

Romans 1:18

God has reasons for getting angry. He can always be counted on to oppose those who rise up against Him and His people, as He did toward the Egyptian pharaoh who enslaved the Israelites and pursued them at the Red Sea (Exodus 15:6). He is angry against those who inflict pain and suffering on the helpless and unprotected (Exodus 22:21–24). His wrath will ultimately burn against all who remain stubborn and unrepentant in the face of His gracious gospel (Romans 2:5–8).

From this we learn that love should be angry at those things that anger the heart of God, even in our spouses. We should be brokenhearted when His honor is attacked and His people mistreated. Yes, the Scripture warns us about being angry without a cause. But at times our anger *does* have a cause. And while love leads us to be restrained in our reactions, it is powerful enough to use anger when important matters are at stake. Righteous anger speaks the truth in love and has the goal of restoration rather than destruction.

PRAYER

"Father, give me the discernment and wisdom to express an appropriately righteous anger when I should. Use it to bring about restoration rather than further wrongs. In Jesus' name, amen."

DAY 33

Love overcomes pride

When pride comes, then comes dishonor,
but with the humble is wisdom.

Proverbs 11:2 NASB

What does it take to set you off, to ignite your anger? Often the situation you get mad about is not the main issue. It just happens to be the place and time where the anger already inside you bubbles to the surface. The most likely causes of anger are usually hidden deep within, lurking, waiting for an opening.

One of the most common causes of anger is pride—the sense that you are somehow better, more capable, more correct about things than your spouse is. Do you consider your husband or wife to be somewhat inferior to you, whether in appearance, in intelligence, or in the ability to cope with stress? Do you think that if given his or her tasks to undertake, you could do a much better job of completing them? When these thoughts are given room to run freely in your mind, they will eventually turn into angry conversations with your mate. Proverbs 18:12 says, "Before destruction, the heart of man is haughty, but humility goes before honor" (NASB).

THIS WEEK'S DARE

Think of an area where you struggle to show patience toward your spouse. Demonstrate love toward them by giving them more time to grow in this area. Commit this specific matter to prayer.

Day 34
Love roots out foolishness

A fool gives full vent to his anger,
but a wise man holds it in check.

Proverbs 29:11

Foolishness takes hold in our hearts very easily. This fact is most commonly noticed whenever we're accused of something we might have said or done. The wise man or woman listens and considers what's being leveled against them. If the accusation is true, they admit it. They take full responsibility for it. Even if they don't agree, they receive the complaint with humility—without anger—knowing that God will bring the truth to light.

The fool's reaction is quite different. When their spouse points out something they're unhappy with, a foolish husband or wife will usually turn the tables. They'll counterattack with something the other person has done that either equals the alleged offense or justifies why they acted that way.

When we refuse to seek counsel, and ignore it when it's given, anger will never be far behind. Love motivates us to seek wisdom, and to apply it once we recognize it.

☞☜ GO DEEPER ☞☜

Read Proverbs 14:29 and Proverbs 15:5. What do these verses teach about how wisdom and foolishness respond differently to situations? What do they reveal about you?

DAY 35
Love refrains from lust

What is the source of the wars and the fights among you? Don't they come from the cravings [lusts] that are at war within you?

James 4:1

We usually think of lust in a sexual context—desiring another person's affection, wishing to gratify ourselves with thoughts of possessing them. This is certainly a rampant, fast-moving disease in the human heart that eats away at the purity of marriage. But lust is actually any kind of pleasure we crave in an unhealthy, unwholesome manner. And one thing is common of all lusts: the futility of pursuing them makes us easily provoked.

"You desire and do not have. You murder and covet and cannot obtain. You fight and war" (James 4:2). When you sense that you're being deprived of something you think you need for happiness, it will cause you to lash out in unsuspecting ways. Much of your anger could be silenced into patience if you would remove unholy lusts from your life. Unobtainable desires can do nothing but kill you. The inner fear of not obtaining them will always *interfere* in your marriage. Let go of lust and let love lead.

❧ QUESTIONS ❧

Is there something you are longing for that is fueling your anger against others? Are you tolerating unhealthy desires in your heart? Have you considered what good might come from releasing them?

Day 36
Love does not covet

*Sin, seizing an opportunity through the commandment,
produced in me coveting of every kind.*

Romans 7:8

Often our main reason for wanting something is because another person has it. The comparison between where we are, and where others are, can lead us toward dissatisfaction, even if we were fairly content before we realized what we were missing. Jealousy is a dangerous emotion to live with.

Cain murdered Abel because his brother had received God's favor and blessing. Saul endeavored to kill David, who seemed to be getting more glory in the people's eyes than the king himself. The Pharisees sought to do away with Jesus because He was dominating their religious landscape.

Perhaps you've become jealous over the attention your spouse is getting from others. Perhaps you resent the fact that they trot out the door each morning and leave you home with the kids. Perhaps they stay trim without trying, while you struggle to stay fit. Jealousy left untreated will stir itself into simmering anger. If jealousy is starting to spring up from within you, then it's time for a heart-check.

✐ THIS WEEK'S DARE ✐

Ask the Lord to reveal any areas of jealousy or resentment in your heart toward your spouse. Admit this to God and ask for forgiveness, then dare to ask your spouse for forgiveness as well.

DAY 37
Love lays down its rights

*"My judgment is righteous, because I do not seek My own will,
but the will of Him who sent Me."*

John 5:30

The older brother in Jesus' parable of the prodigal son is a vivid example of someone who felt he deserved what he wasn't getting. Seeing his younger brother wined and dined despite a long season of rebellion, this firstborn son "became angry and didn't want to go in" (Luke 15:28). If anyone should be treated with honor, it should be him. Years of slaving for his father had apparently gone unnoticed.

His is an anger born of unmet expectations and of unyielding rights. And when we place requirements like these on our mates, we are guaranteeing that their failure to meet our demands will be met with frustrated anger. How many marriages have fallen into ruin because one or both spouses said, "I deserve happiness," and enforced their ultimatum by walking out?

Love doesn't lay claim to such rights. It doesn't use its own satisfaction as a barometer for whether or not to remain loving.

❧ GO DEEPER ❧

Jesus had every right not to suffer and die for someone else's sins. He could have lashed out in anger against His heavenly Father's will. Read Matthew 26:36–42 and notice how He yielded His rights instead. Aren't you glad He did? What would happen if you prayed His same prayer?

Day 38
Love is not bitter

Husbands, love your wives and don't become bitter against them.

Colossians 3:19

Bitterness leads to constant anger. The poison of bitterness can arise from any set of circumstances. It can be ingrained in a person at an early age, or it can grow like a weed over time after a particular loss or event. But bitterness will invariably color much more than the one or two disappointments that caused it to spike. When unresolved anger begins to fester in a person's heart, the result is a consistent pattern of hardness and unforgiveness.

Ephesians 4:31 groups bitterness along with "anger and wrath, insult and slander," showing it to be one flavor in a very sour mixture of unpleasant, easily triggered emotions. But love, by refusing to let bitterness take root, is successful at keeping all the others away as well.

Give your spouse permission to point out the first hint of harshness or ill will in your behavior and attitudes. It will keep anger from infecting your relationship.

❧ THIS WEEK'S DARE ❧

Ask the Lord to reveal any areas of jealousy or resentment in your heart toward your spouse. Admit this to God and ask for forgiveness, then dare to ask your spouse for forgiveness as well.

DAY 39

Love lives in reality

*"You will have suffering in this world.
Be courageous! I have conquered the world."*

John 16:33

Unrealistic expectations lead to a life of disappointment and frustration. Few of us want to accept the fact that life can be hard. Though we see others struggling and hear them tell about their hardships, we think our life and marriage will be different. We hang on to idealistic assumptions about the way our spouse will treat us, the kind of house we'll live in, the good health we'll always have. We don't see much point in preparing for disappointment.

But Jesus was certainly up-front with His disciples when it came to letting them know what to expect in life. And if we want to avoid the anger that flows from being disillusioned and exasperated with things—and with people, including our spouse—we will not insist on perfection in them. We will not base our moods on how things are going. We will put our confidence in God, who never changes, and choose to be content with a life that can change from one moment to the next.

∽ GO DEEPER ∾

Read 1 Peter 4:12–16 and look at how Peter helped others to keep their expectations realistic and God-honoring, even in times of hardship. Notice how he prepared them and encouraged them at the same time.

DAY 40
Love confesses sin

I said, "I will confess my transgressions to the LORD,"
and You took away the guilt of my sin.

Psalm 32:5

The more you live in sin, the more anger you will have in your life. The harder you work to keep from being exposed or held accountable, the quicker your trigger will be when these concealed areas come under attack.

Deposits of sin in the human heart distort our sense of reality and balance. David revealed this when his sins of adultery and murder were uncovered. His heightened sensitivity, inflamed by the energy he had expended to keep from being found out, made him bristle at a prophet's rebuke. He acted indignant against anyone who would dare commit such acts. But "you are the man," the prophet Nathan proclaimed. Hidden sin had left David easily riled.

Stay diligent every day to keep yourself open and vulnerable before the Lord and before your spouse. Sin is always looking for a place to stay. Make sure it finds your heart an unwelcome home.

⤜❧ THIS WEEK'S DARE ❧⤛

Ask the Lord to reveal any areas of jealousy or resentment in your heart toward your spouse. Admit this to God and ask for forgiveness, then dare to ask your spouse for forgiveness as well.

DAY 41
Love seeks mentors

Encourage each other daily, while it is still called today,
so that none of you is hardened by sin's deception.

Hebrews 3:13

Good marriage mentors warn you before you make a bad decision. They encourage you when you are ready to give up, and they cheer you on as you reach new levels of intimacy in your marriage. They become a key component in the way God blesses and protects you.

Do you have an older couple or a friend of the same gender you can turn to for good advice, for prayer support, and for regular accountability check-ups? Do you have someone who shoots straight with you? You and your spouse need these types of friends and mentors on a consistent basis.

To find a good mentor, look for a person who already has the kind of marriage you want. You look for a person whose heart for Christ comes first before everything else. You look for someone who doesn't live by his or her opinions but by the unchanging Word of God. Start praying for God to send this kind of person or couple into your life, and be watching for how He will answer.

☙ PRAYER ❧

"Lord, send us godly marriage mentors who will encourage us and keep us accountable. Give us moldable hearts to learn from them and to apply what they teach us. In Jesus' name, amen."

DAY 42
Love delays anger

*A person's insight gives him patience,
and his virtue is to overlook an offense.*

Proverbs 19:11

One of the best tools for keeping anger at bay is to have premeditated responses in place to match any offense that could arise. What if your spouse were to forget your birthday or anniversary, for example—what would be the best way to handle that? You can choose ahead of time that if such a thing were to happen, you would not let it send you off the deep end of anger.

Psalm 78, in recalling God's dealings with His people, mentions that the ancient Israelites were deceptive, unfaithful, and persistent in their sinning. "Yet He was compassionate; He atoned for their guilt and did not destroy them. He often turned His anger aside and did not unleash all His wrath" (verse 38). He chose to delay His anger, coming down on the side of patience and compassion. We, too, can determine in advance that we will not let any slight on our spouse's part elicit an angry response. Prepare to be patient.

◆◆◆ QUESTIONS ◆◆◆

What would happen if you decided that you were always going to delay your anger before expressing it? What if you chose to seek out more information and conclude the wisest course of action before you allowed yourself to respond?

DAY 43
Love does its homework

*It is the glory of God to conceal a matter
and the glory of kings to investigate a matter.*

Proverbs 25:2

Here's another premeditated promise you can make to yourself and your spouse. When you feel yourself getting irritated by something the other has said or done, put your anger on hold until you can get all the facts. Proverbs 18:13 says, "The one who gives an answer before he listens—this is foolishness and disgrace for him."

Sometimes there's a reason for what happened. In fact, what they did may have been the best choice to make, given the circumstances. Other factors may also have colored the situation. Maybe getting mad at you for paying a bill late had more to do with the frustrated mood they were already in.

Before acting on your assumptions, ask a few questions. Investigate. Try sitting down with your spouse and getting to the heart of the matter. And even if your suspicions turn out to be true—even if their reasons still leave you irritated—give them the benefit of the doubt. Your anger probably won't keep it from happening again. But your loving patience might.

∼∽ THIS WEEK'S DARE ∼∽

Write out a list of five things your spouse has done to make you angry. Ask God for patience and wisdom, and to keep you from harboring any bitterness. Tear up the list and throw it away as an act of love.

43

DAY 44
Love examines the heart

Search me, God, and know my heart;
test me and know my concerns.

Psalm 139:23

An angry response is often a warning light revealing that there is something wrong within our own hearts. Anger can rise up the back of our neck for so many reasons. We are wise, then, to ask questions of others before letting our anger fill in all the blanks and have its own way. But this should also give us a cue to ask ourselves some questions as well.

Is my anger flowing out of selfishness on my part? Would Jesus be angry in this situation? Is this current flare-up making me angry about something from the past that I'd already promised to forgive? Am I confronting my wife or husband's sins without really dealing with my own? How would I want my spouse to respond if I had done the same thing to them?

Decide in advance to make angry feelings an automatic trigger to begin probing your heart for answers. You might find in digging deeply that you're letting yourself get steamed up for all the wrong reasons.

ᕲᕳ GO DEEPER ᕲᕳ

Read Lamentations 3:39–40 and consider the reason that is given why we should stop complaining and start a self-examination instead.

Day 45
Love trusts God's purposes

We know that all things work together for the good of those who love God: those who are called according to His purpose.

Romans 8:28

Wise people don't grade life by the way they feel on any given day. They don't judge God's performance by how quickly and accurately He's answering their prayers or by the level of peace He's bringing into their homes. Even when there are things to be upset about and a spouse who's not cooperating, the loving wife or husband knows they're only seeing part of the picture.

God can take anything and use it for your good and His glory. He can turn a tense disagreement between you and your spouse into something that proves His power to heal. He can be deferred to as the avenger of wrongs (Romans 12:19), relieving you from the duties of judge and jury. And even when nothing seems to be going right, you can be utterly assured that "He does not withhold the good from those who live with integrity" (Psalm 84:11). Your anger may reveal you are not trusting the sovereignty of God. Don't let your anger spoil what God is up to in your life.

⌘ THIS WEEK'S DARE ⌘

Write out a list of five things your spouse has done to make you angry. Ask God for patience and wisdom, and to keep you from harboring any bitterness. Tear up the list and throw it away as an act of love.

DAY 46
Love dies to self

*"If anyone wants to come with Me, he must deny himself,
take up his cross daily, and follow Me."*

Luke 9:23

If any one thing stands out above all others in owning the
blame for our anger, it's this: our selfish desires. We wake
up thinking about ourselves. And if we don't intentionally
do something to thwart it, we will spend the rest of the
day—and the rest of our lives—catering to the self-centered
demands of our fleshly wants. It's our fallen nature. It's how
anger gets its fuel supply.

So accept the hard work of keeping your individual
tastes and preferences from dominating your marriage. And
expect this to be full-time employment. Die to your selfish
desires and let love live within. Enter any situation with
your spouse—especially one where a potential argument is
beginning to brew—with an up-front resolution to remove
all your wants and rights from the available firewood. When
you die to self, anger doesn't have what it takes to keep itself
going.

❧ GO DEEPER ❧

Look up Luke 9:23–27 and study the challenging call
to personal sacrifice that Jesus gives in this passage.
Consider the long-term consequences He mentions
of not dying to yourself.

Day 47
Love refuses to sin

*Be angry and do not sin. Don't let the sun
go down on your anger.*

Ephesians 4:26

Love does not sin in its anger. Seen in a spiritual vacuum, anger is neither right nor wrong. But obviously, it finds many more ways to behave in an ungodly fashion than it does to accomplish God's holy purposes. What causes anger to become sin are the objects of its rage and the actions that spin off from it. Even justifiable anger can lead us to sin if we are not careful.

Anger in marriage presents a widespread threat. Imagine your home with perhaps no fewer problems, but without the presence of anger to keep it stirred up and agitated. Imagine your relationship with the same history and issues, but without anger always reminding you of your past and eroding your hopes for the future.

When you promise never to mix anger with sin, your marriage becomes home to joy, peace, freedom, and renewed commitment. You'll be thankful for the day you stopped letting the sun set on your anger, ever again.

❧ THIS WEEK'S DARE ☙

Write out a list of five things your spouse has done to make you angry. Ask God for patience and wisdom, and to keep you from harboring any bitterness. Tear up the list and throw it away as an act of love.

DAY 48
Love is kind

Be kind to one another, tender-hearted, forgiving each other, just as God in Christ also has forgiven you.

Ephesians 4:32 NASB

Kindness is love in action. If patience is how love *reacts* in order to minimize a negative circumstance, then kindness is how love *acts* to maximize a positive circumstance. Patience avoids a problem; kindness creates a blessing. One is preventive, the other proactive. These two sides of love are the cornerstones on which many of the other attributes are built.

Love makes you kind. Kindness makes you likable. When you're kind, people want to be around you. They see you as being good *to* them and good *for* them.

It's also contagious. When someone demonstrates genuine kindness to you, it makes you want to do the same thing in return. But a person who is loving and mature won't always wait to respond in kindness. They'd rather be the first to show it. Are you that kind of person in your home with your spouse?

❧ QUESTIONS ❧

What would happen in your marriage if the Ephesians 4:32 passage mentioned above became your standard operating procedure? Consider how your vertical relationship with God should directly guide and impact your horizontal relationships with others.

DAY 49
Love finds favor

Do not let kindness and truth leave you; bind them around your neck, write them on the tablet of your heart. So you will find favor and good repute in the sight of God and man.

Proverbs 3:3–4 NASB

Kind people simply find favor wherever they go—even at home. Kindness is attractive because it gives value to the other person and honors them with gentleness and respect. When you're operating from kindness, you're careful how you treat your spouse, never being harsh. You're sensitive. Tender. Even if you need to say hard things, you'll bend over backwards to make your rebuke or challenge as easy as possible for them to hear.

It's the act of speaking the truth in love, which few of us tend to do naturally. We feel that if our words are true, the tone of communication should also be accepted. But love finds favor by speaking with gentleness, removing the heat from the discussion. This allows the focus to be on the truth in your statement, not on the manner in which it was delivered. A spoonful of kindness indeed helps the truth go down.

❧ PRAYER ❧

"Heavenly Father, help me to walk in kindness and truth. Give me the foresight to hold my tongue until I can filter my words through the standards of honesty and love. In Jesus' name, amen."

DAY 50
Love is helpful

A kind man benefits himself,
but a cruel man brings disaster on himself.

Proverbs 11:17

Being kind means you meet the needs of the moment. You become more helpful. If it's housework, you get busy. A listening ear? You give it. Kindness graces a wife with the ability to serve her husband without worrying about her rights. Kindness makes a husband curious to discover what his wife needs, then motivates him to be the one who steps up and ensures those needs are met—even if his are put on hold.

Wasn't kindness one of the key things that drew you and your spouse together in the first place? When you married, weren't you expecting to enjoy his or her kindness for the rest of your life? Didn't your mate feel the same way about you, thinking they could always count on your wanting to be helpful? Even though the years can take the edge off that desire, your enjoyment in marriage is still linked to the daily level of kindness expressed.

☙ THIS WEEK'S DARE ❧

Find ways to demonstrate unexpected gestures of kindness to your spouse during the week.

DAY 51
Love keeps an open mind

Instruct them to do good, to be rich in good works,
to be generous, willing to share.

1 Timothy 6:18

Kindness inspires you to be agreeable. Instead of being obstinate, reluctant, or stubborn, you choose to cooperate and be flexible. Rather than complaining and making excuses, you look for reasons to compromise and accommodate. A kind husband ends thousands of potential arguments by his willingness to listen first rather than demand his way. A wise wife shows respect for her husband's final decision, even when she has a different view. Kindness makes you willing to stop, think, and evaluate, not to immediately dismiss the other's opinion.

When we are willing to listen, to share, and to consider others before ourselves, we open up the avenues of peace, love, and blessing. Yes, it takes wisdom and maturity to always take the high road, but it's a path that leads to benefits we all want for ourselves. These rewards await those who are resolved and willing, who don't close off their hearts to their spouse.

⌘ GO DEEPER ⌘

Read the account of King Rehoboam in 2 Chronicles 10 (especially verses 6–11 and 18–19) and how his lack of kindness completely divided his kingdom. How should this influence the way you treat those who are around you?

Love takes the initiative

*Therefore, God's chosen ones, holy and loved, put on heartfelt
compassion, kindness, humility, gentleness, and patience.*

Colossians 3:12

Kindness thinks ahead, then takes the first step. It doesn't
sit around waiting to be prompted or coerced before getting
off the couch. The kind husband or wife will be the one who
greets first, smiles first, serves first, and forgives first. They
don't require the other to get his or her act together before
showing love.

Jesus described the kindness of love in His parable of the
Good Samaritan, found in Luke 10. A Jewish man attacked
by robbers is left for dead on a remote road. Two religious
leaders, respected among their people, walk by without
choosing to stop. But a common man of another race stops
to help the man. Bandaging his wounds, he carries him to
safety and pays all his medical expenses. Taking the initiative, he demonstrated true kindness in every way. When
acting from kindness, you see the need, then make your
move. First.

THIS WEEK'S DARE

Find ways to demonstrate unexpected gestures of
kindness to your spouse during the week.

DAY 53
Love reveals the kindness of God

Do you think lightly of the riches of His kindness . . .
not knowing that the kindness of God leads you to repentance?

Romans 2:4 NASB

It's the reason our eyes can behold breathtaking sunsets, our ears enjoy beautiful melodies, and our arms feel a warm embrace. Life could be endless misery. But instead, God allows us to enjoy it . . . because of His lovingkindness.

When you discover how amazingly kind God is, countless questions are easily answered. For example, Why does God not strike us dead when we sin? Why does He hold back judgment and give us time to repent? It's His kindness (Romans 2:3–6). Why does He offer salvation and forgiveness as a gift? Why can undeserving sinners receive it through faith in His Son? Why would heaven not be earned by our good behavior? God's not unjust or unholy. So why?

Salvation is freely given, the Bible says, to show how surpassingly great God's kindness is toward us (Ephesians 2:1–9)—His pure lovingkindness. Therefore, no one has to hesitate to receive His free gift of salvation by grace alone. Because when we receive it through faith, we reveal and honor the gracious kindness of our wonderful God.

⟶ GO DEEPER ⟵

Salvation is a free gift, but comes at a great cost to the Giver. Read Ephesians 2:1–9 and learn why God would offer so much, so freely. Focus on verse 7.

DAY 54
Love is demonstrated by Jesus

When the kindness of God our Savior
and His love for mankind appeared, He saved us.

Titus 3:4–5 NASB

The life of Jesus was a model of kindness. It was not soft, distant, or out of touch with real life. His kindness drove Him to dirty His hands, weary His body, and bloody a cruel cross. From His compassion to the isolated leper to His willingness to feed the hungry masses, kindness was embodied in Christ.

This same kindness reaches us today. He finds us soaked in sin. He meets us at our worst. And yet He still loves us. That's the definition of kindness.

You may have many complaints against your wife or husband, from the way they clean house to the way they handle money. And while they may be resisting God's authority over their lives in any number of areas, love calls you to extend kindness toward them—sacrificial, servant-hearted, and tender. If your kindness is to be like Christ's, it must be "gracious to the ungrateful" (Luke 6:35). It must remain merciful even in the face of hard evidence to the contrary. As He watches your life, does He see Himself reflected in your kindness?

THIS WEEK'S DARE

Find ways to demonstrate unexpected gestures of kindness to your spouse during the week.

DAY 55
Love is proven by action

Little children, we must not love
in word or speech, but in deed and truth.

1 John 3:18

When the Bible declares, "God is love" (1 John 4:8), that's all we should need to hear to believe it. And yet God has chosen to put His words into action. He "proves His own love for us in that while we were still sinners, Christ died for us!" (Romans 5:8). He "sent His One and Only Son into the world so that we might live through Him" (1 John 4:9). He proved it. He gave His love an understandable definition by turning it from a noun into a verb.

If God Himself knows that our human minds and hearts need to see love to believe it, then your spouse is not being unreasonable to expect your love to show itself in observable actions. Love may always be somewhat hard to measure and define, but the closest we come to understanding it is by recognizing the actions it creates. Love that doesn't identify itself through expression is meaningless to your spouse. "Better is open rebuke than hidden love" (Proverbs 27:5 NIV). Make your love obvious. Get busy!

✌ PRAYER ✍

"Heavenly Father, I pray that You would help my love to go beyond thoughts, feelings, and words, and be translated into daily actions. In Jesus' name, amen."

DAY 56
Love is not selfish

Be devoted to one another in brotherly love;
give preference to one another in honor.

Romans 12:10 NASB

Love is never satisfied except in the welfare of others. You can't be acting out of real love and selfishness at the same time. Choosing to love your mate will cause you to say "no" to what you want so you can say "yes" to what they need. That's putting the happiness of your partner before your own. It does not mean, of course, that you can never experience happiness, but you don't negate the happiness of your spouse so you can enjoy it yourself.

When a husband puts his own interests in front of his wife, that's a sign of selfishness. When a wife complains about what it takes to meet the genuine needs of her husband, that too is a sign of selfishness. But loving couples who are enjoying the full purpose of marriage are bent on taking good care of the other flawed human they get to share life with. That's because true love always looks for ways to say "yes."

⟪⟫ QUESTIONS ⟪⟫

What habit of yours could be considered very selfish by those in your family? How would it improve your home to back off from continuing this?

Day 57
Love is others-centered

Do nothing out of selfish ambition or vain conceit,
but in humility consider others better than yourselves.

Philippians 2:3 NIV

We live in a world that is enamored with *self*. The culture around us teaches us to focus on our appearance, feelings, and personal desires as the top priority. The goal, it seems, is to chase the highest level of happiness possible. However, the danger from this kind of thinking becomes painfully apparent once inside a marriage relationship.

If there were ever a word that basically means the opposite of love, it's selfishness. In fact, almost every sinful action ever committed can be traced back to a selfish motive. It is a trait we hate in other people, though we easily justify it in ourselves.

Yet you can't point out the many ways your spouse is selfish without admitting that you can be selfish too. Remember, your partner also has the challenge of loving a selfish person. So determine to be the first to demonstrate real love to them, with your eyes wide open.

THIS WEEK'S DARE

Sometime this week, buy something for your spouse that says, "I was thinking of you."

DAY 58
Love is the standard

Turn my heart toward your statutes and not toward selfish gain.

Psalm 119:36 NIV

Why do we have such low standards for ourselves, yet we have such high expectations for our mate? The answer is a painful pill to swallow. We are all selfish.

One ironic aspect of selfishness is that even generous actions can be selfish if the motive is to gain bragging rights or receive a reward. If you do something seemingly good to deceitfully manipulate your husband or wife, you are still being selfish. The bottom line is you either make decisions out of love for others or out of love for yourself.

No one knows you as well as your spouse, which means you cannot fool them for long if your motives are impure. But it also means no one will be quicker to recognize a change when you deliberately start sacrificing your wants and wishes to make sure his or her needs are met. When love becomes the standard by which you operate, you've found the target for which God intends us all to aim.

❧ GO DEEPER ❧

Study the challenge given in Philippians 2:3–4 by the apostle Paul. Notice what he calls you away from and what focus he encourages in its place. How would this improve your marriage if you and your spouse obeyed this one passage?

Day 59
Love sets priorities

*The one who pursues righteousness and faithful love
will find life, righteousness, and honor.*

Proverbs 21:21

Love leads to inner joy. When you prioritize the well-being of your mate, there is a fulfillment that cannot be duplicated by selfish actions. It is a benefit that God created and reserves for those who genuinely demonstrate love. The truth is, when you relinquish your rights for the sake of your mate, you get a chance to lose yourself to the greater purpose of marriage.

A good test to check your own priorities in marriage is to ask yourself these questions. Do I truly want what's best for my husband or wife? Do I want them to feel loved by me? Do they believe I have their best interests in mind? Do they see me as looking out for myself first, or them first?

As you honestly answer these questions, ask God to guide your heart as you consider how to prioritize your mate with your time, energy, and finances. Then let your spouse be joyfully surprised with the selflessness of your love.

❧ THIS WEEK'S DARE ❧

Sometime this week, buy something for your spouse that says, "I was thinking of you."

DAY 60

Love is thoughtful

How precious also are Your thoughts to me. . . .
If I should count them, they would outnumber the sand.

Psalm 139:17–18 NASB

For most couples, things begin to change after marriage. The wife finally has secured her man; the husband has won his trophy. The hunt is over and the pursuing done. Sparks of romance slowly burn into gray embers, and the motivation for thoughtfulness cools. We drift into focusing on our job, our friends, our problems, and our personal desires. After a while, we unintentionally begin to ignore the needs of our mate.

But the fact that marriage has added another person to our life does not change. Therefore, if our thinking doesn't mature enough to include this person, we catch ourselves being surprised rather than being thoughtful. That's where love learns to think, to plan, to consider in advance. It's not a mindless feeling that rides on waves of emotion and falls asleep mentally. It keeps busy, knowing that loving thoughts precede loving actions.

✎ GO DEEPER ✎

Read 2 Samuel 9:1–13 and recognize the amazing impact a few minutes of thoughtfulness had on a young lame boy. What is something thoughtful you can do in the next few days for your mate?

DAY 61
Love matures

What a man desires is unfailing love.

Proverbs 19:22 NIV

When you first fell in love, being thoughtful came quite naturally. You spent hours dreaming of what your loved one looked like, wondering what he or she was doing, rehearsing impressive things to say, then enjoying sweet memories of the time you spent together. You honestly confessed, "I can't stop thinking about you." But once life removes the freshness of your feelings, thoughtful actions often get left by the wayside.

Thoughtlessness is a silent enemy to a loving relationship. If you don't learn to be thoughtful, you will end up regretting many missed opportunities to demonstrate love. And though young love is certainly new and exciting, it's your continued acts of thoughtfulness that mean the most over time. That's because love has to mature. And maturity puts others before yourself, both in thought and in deed. When you choose to be thoughtful for no other reason than to value your mate, that's a sign of maturing love. By your actions, you will say to your spouse, "My love was thinking of you."

THIS WEEK'S DARE

Sometime this week, buy something for your spouse that says, "I was thinking of you."

Love is understanding

Discretion will watch over you,
and understanding will guard you.

Proverbs 2:11

Let's be honest. The differences between men and women create opportunities for misunderstanding. Men, for example, tend to think in headlines and say exactly what they mean. Not much is needed to understand the message. Their words are more literal and shouldn't be overanalyzed. But women often think and speak between the lines. They tend to hint. A man often has to listen for what is implied if he wants to get the full message.

If a couple doesn't understand this about one another, the fallout can result in endless disagreements. He's frustrated wondering why she speaks in riddles and doesn't just come out and say things. She's frustrated wondering why he's so inconsiderate and can't add two and two together and just figure it out.

Love requires understanding—on both sides—the kind of love that builds bridges through the constructive combination of patience, kindness, and selflessness. Love teaches us how to meet in the middle, to respect and appreciate how our spouse uniquely thinks.

⋙ PRAYER ⋘

"Heavenly Father, give me discernment and understanding in how my spouse uniquely thinks and speaks. Give us a breakthrough in our communication that results in us better honoring one another and You. In Jesus' name, amen."

DAY 63
Love is discerning

Everyone should look out not only for his own interests,
but also for the interests of others.

Philippians 2:4

A woman deeply longs for her husband to be thoughtful. It is a key to helping her feel loved. Few things validate her worth like knowing her thoughts are given merit. When she speaks, a wise man will listen like a detective to discover the unspoken needs and desires her words imply. In like manner, a considerate wife will learn to communicate truthfully and not say one thing while meaning another.

When communication breaks down, we often become angry and speak harshly to one another, then determine later if we should have said it. But the discerning nature of love teaches us to engage our minds before engaging our lips. Love thinks before speaking. It filters words through a grid of truth and kindness.

When was the last time you spent a few minutes thinking about how you could better understand and demonstrate love to your spouse? Remember, great marriages come from great thinking.

❧ QUESTIONS ❧

Would your spouse say that you are a thoughtful person? Do you take time to think through upcoming special events, birthdays, or anniversaries when you could "wow" your spouse with your calculated kindness?

Day 64
Love is not rude

If one blesses his neighbor with a loud voice early in the morning, it will be counted as a curse to him.

Proverbs 27:14

Nothing irritates others as quickly as being rude. Rudeness means unnecessarily saying or doing things that are unpleasant for another person. To be rude is to act in an unbecoming, embarrassing, or irritating manner. In marriage, this could include things like a foul mouth, poor table manners, or a habit of making sarcastic quips.

However you look at it, no one enjoys being around a rude person. Rude behavior may seem insignificant to the person who is doing it, but it is unpleasant to those on the receiving end.

Love has something to say about this. When a man is driven by love, he intentionally behaves in a way that's more pleasant for his wife to be around, more conducive to putting her at ease. If a woman desires to love her husband, she purposefully avoids things that frustrate him or cause him discomfort.

❧ THIS WEEK'S DARE ❧

During this week, contact your spouse and ask how they're doing. Have no other agenda but to encourage and value them. Should they have a need, do what you can to meet it.

DAY 65
Love is polite

All of you should be like-minded and sympathetic,
should love believers, and be compassionate and humble.

1 Peter 3:8

People who practice good etiquette tend to raise the respect level of the environment around them. If we were being honest, however, most of us would have to admit that the etiquette we tend to use at home is much different than the one we employ with friends, coworkers, or even with total strangers. But if we dare to love, we'll also want to give our best to our own. If we don't let love motivate us to make needed changes in our behavior, the quality of our marriage relationship will suffer for it.

The practice of politeness is one way to express to your wife or husband, "I value you enough to exercise self-control around you. I want to be a person who's a pleasure to be with." When you allow love to change your behavior, you create an atmosphere of honor in your relationship.

❦ GO DEEPER ❦

Read Leviticus 19:32 and observe the honor that God desires to be communicated to those around us. What are some practical things you could do for your spouse that could communicate this kind of honor rather than rudeness?

Day 66
Love is gracious

It is well with the man who is gracious.

Psalm 112:5 NASB

Genuine love minds its manners. This is not an insignificant matter where marriage is concerned. Rather, it puts an outward face on our inward desire to love.

There are two main reasons why people are rude: *ignorance* and *selfishness*. Neither, of course, is a good thing. A child is born ignorant of etiquette, needing lots of help and training. As adults, we display our ignorance at another level. We know the rules, but we can be blind to how we break them, or be too self-centered to care. In fact, we may not realize how unpleasant we can be to live with.

Women tend to be much better at certain types of manners than men, though they can be rude in other ways. But men especially need to learn this important lesson. A man of discretion will find out what is appropriate, then adjust his behavior accordingly. This sensitivity is a gentle way of demonstrating value and love for others, especially in your home.

❧ THIS WEEK'S DARE ❧

During this week, contact your spouse and ask how they're doing. Have no other agenda but to encourage and value them. Should they have a need, do what you can to meet it.

DAY 67
Love is considerate

*No one should seek his own good,
but the good of the other person.*

1 Corinthians 10:24

How does your spouse feel about the way you speak and act around them? How does your behavior affect your mate's sense of worth? Would your husband or wife say you're a blessing, or that you're condescending and embarrassing? Remember, love is not rude. Quite the opposite, love lifts us to a higher standard.

Do you wish your spouse would quit doing the things that bother you? Then it's time to stop doing the things that bother them as well. Will you be thoughtful and loving enough to discover the likes and dislikes of your spouse? And if you are able to avoid any behavior that causes life to be unpleasant for them, will you make whatever adjustments are required to accommodate their sensitivities?

When you treat your mate the way you want to be treated, you demonstrate love through your consideration of them. So guard the Golden Rule, and dare to be delightful!

PRAYER

"Heavenly Father, reveal to me any ways where I have been insensitive and rude around my spouse. Show me my blind spots, and give me the wisdom and desire to add grace to my behavior. In Jesus' name, amen."

DAY 68
Love thinks of others

"Therefore, whatever you want others
to do for you, do also the same for them."

Matthew 7:12

In many ways, love can be reduced to very simple terms. Perhaps one of its simplest is Jesus' teaching known as the Golden Rule. The remedy for rudeness around your house is as basic as this: a deliberate decision to treat your mate the way you'd most like them to treat you.

Those who were part of the first-century church in Corinth were known as a particularly gifted people. And yet a pervasive sense of rudeness played a big part in their poor reputation. They talked over each other in worship, turned the Lord's Supper into a church potluck, and put their friends in awkward positions by flaunting their sins in front of each other.

Love, by contrast, always treats others with Golden Rule respect. If you are wondering if something is rude or not, the Golden Rule will tell you. If you need counsel on how to handle a sensitive issue, ask yourself what you would desire that others do to you? The Golden Rule gives us a standard to live by without us ever having to open our mouths or learn painful lessons the hard way.

THIS WEEK'S DARE

During this week, contact your spouse and ask how they're doing. Have no other agenda but to encourage and value them. Should they have a need, do what you can to meet it.

DAY 69
Love avoids an argument

*An endless dripping on a rainy day and
a nagging wife are alike.*

Proverbs 27:15

One of the sweetest sounds in marriage is the silence that could have been a nagging comment. This is not the same as saying that there is no room for improvement in your wife or husband's behavior. It may be they are truly acting in ways that are inconsiderate of your time and feelings. But it does mean you are giving up the role of being his or her rule enforcer.

Not every plate that goes unreturned to the kitchen sink is worthy of lecture. Just because you can't agree on who was responsible for a certain task or phone call is not an automatic reason for telling your spouse you can never count on them. In a loving home, the need to complain, nag, and pass blame are replaced by a desire to edify and encourage. Pointing out fault may feel like a basic right. Words of accusation may come quickly to your lips. But love gets in the habit of swallowing them down before they add insult to injury.

QUESTIONS

What words of correction have you tended to repeat to your spouse? How effective has it been in helping them correct a certain behavior? Is your method encouraging, or discouraging? If you had the same weakness, how would you want your spouse to approach you regarding the subject?

DAY 70
Love doesn't gossip

A gossip goes around revealing a secret,
but the trustworthy keeps a confidence.

Proverbs 11:13

Gossip is sharing dishonoring information with someone who is not a part of the problem or the solution. The allure of gossip is that it helps us find justification for our feelings about a certain person. When sharing our whispered thoughts behind their back, our complaints are reinforced by others we hope will agree with us. Their sympathies make it easier for us to feel sorry for ourselves. "A gossip's words are like choice food that goes down to one's innermost being" (Proverbs 26:22).

While gossip is always to be avoided in any instance or relationship, it is especially important to assure your spouse that any complaint or unhappiness in marriage will never become part of your outside conversations. They need to know that when you are visiting with friends or talking to a parent on the phone, the words you use to describe them will always be positive and honoring. There may be counseling settings where honesty and health demands that you speak candidly about unappealing matters. But avoid every temptation to run your spouse down when speaking with others.

☙ GO DEEPER ❧

When we discover negative information about someone, we can respond in either a loving or unloving way. Study Proverbs 17:9 and consider two consequences of our choice.

Day 71
Love doesn't embarrass

For if any Macedonians should come with me and find you unprepared, we, not to mention you, would be embarrassed.

2 Corinthians 9:4

Love covers shame. It has a knack for putting others in a position where they can succeed and are kept from situations that cause them unease or embarrassment. If you know your wife or husband is uncomfortable in a certain situation, do your actions amplify their awkwardness, or do you work to ease their minds? A drop of thoughtlessness on your part can bring an unnecessary storm of dishonor to them.

Every husband and wife knows things about the other that they could use to humiliate them. Through the years, you will be given many opportunities to parade your spouse's problems in front of your friends and relatives. But love calls you to protect their reputation. A morsel of gossip or a moment of laughter is not worth the unnecessary pain of humiliation and damage it can bring to your trust. Unless your spouse is injuring themselves or others, you need to guard their secrets and their honor.

❧ THIS WEEK'S DARE ❧

Ask your spouse to tell you three things that cause him or her irritation. Do so without attacking them or justifying your behavior. This is from their perspective only.

Day 72
Love minds its manners

*Whatever is needed . . . let it be given to them
every day without fail.*

Ezra 6:9

When we are hosting guests in our home or are responsible in some way for another person, we bend over backwards to make sure they have what they need. We double check their accommodations and take care to ensure their maximum comfort. But often when it comes to marriage, our familiarity causes us to overlook the cues that tell us what our spouse needs. We leave them to fend for themselves, thereby forfeiting the blessing of serving them.

But love doesn't save all its manners for just guests. Love causes a man to notice when a pillow or a foot rub would help his wife relax and unwind. Love causes a woman to recognize when her husband's day would start better with a home-cooked breakfast rather than the usual coffee and cereal. When your spouse describes what it means to feel at home, it should include the ongoing joy of being served and cared for by you.

GO DEEPER

Jesus challenged His disciples to embrace the mentality of going the extra mile and serving others who were mistreating them. Read Matthew 5:38–42 and look for the verse that would make the most difference in your marriage. How can you apply it this week?

DAY 73
Love honors requests

"Give to the one who asks you, and don't turn away from the one who wants to borrow from you."

Matthew 5:42

Love is often a matter of careful study and thoughtfulness, of looking ahead to see a need in your spouse, then resolving to meet it. But many times your wife or husband will be very up-front about what they want from you. They may also have requested that you stop doing something that irritates or dishonors them. That's when love is as simple as complying to an obvious request.

And yet our human natures often respond negatively to such appeals. We may go along but let them know it's a real effort, something we expect to be reciprocated.

The above teaching of Jesus, however, was spoken in the context of dealing with our enemies. He instructed us to honor the requests even of those who persecute and mistreat us. How much more should we always be ready to answer our spouse's call for help, understanding, or a listening ear—than that of an enemy? When love is called to action, it goes without hesitation or agenda.

ᨀ THIS WEEK'S DARE ᨀ

Ask your spouse to tell you three things that cause him or her irritation. Do so without attacking them or justifying your behavior. This is from their perspective only.

DAY 74
Love is not irritable

*Patience is better than power, and controlling one's temper,
than capturing a city.*

Proverbs 16:32

Love is hard to offend and quick to forgive. It doesn't immediately chafe at being confronted or called to account for something said or done. It doesn't stomp off in a rage, parade its anger, nor does it retreat into moodiness and shut others out.

How easily do you get irritated and offended? Some people have the motto, "Never pass up an opportunity to get upset with your spouse." When something goes wrong, they quickly take full advantage of it by expressing how hurt or frustrated they are. This, however, is the opposite reaction of love. To be *irritable* means to be near the point of a knife. Not far from being poked. People who are irritable are locked, loaded, and ready to overreact.

If you are walking under the influence of love, you will be a joy, not a jerk. Ask yourself, "Am I a calming breeze, or a storm waiting to happen?"

━━ PRAYER ━━

"Heavenly Father, help me to be someone who is so mature and secure that I am hard to offend and quick to forgive. Bring my emotions and moods under Your loving control. In Jesus' name, amen."

DAY 75
Love shows restraint

The intelligent person restrains his words,
and one who keeps a cool head is a man of understanding.

Proverbs 17:27

Love doesn't turn sour under pressure. Minor problems don't yield major reactions. The truth is, love does not get angry or hurt unless there is a legitimate and just reason in the sight of God.

A loving husband will remain calm and patient, showing mercy and restraining his temper. Rage and violence are out of the question—always. A loving wife is not overly sensitive or cranky, but exercises emotional self-control. She chooses to be a flower among the thorns and responds in a pleasant manner during prickly situations.

Love lowers your stress and helps you release the venom that can build up inside. By making calmness and patience its default settings, love neutralizes the explosiveness that can ramp up before reason has had a chance to kick in. It then sets up your heart to respond to your spouse with patience and encouragement rather than anger and exasperation.

☙ THIS WEEK'S DARE ❧

Ask your spouse to tell you three things that cause him or her irritation. Do so without attacking them or justifying your behavior. This is from their perspective only.

DAY 76
Love lowers stress

Refrain from anger and give up your rage;
do not be agitated—it can only bring harm.

Psalm 37:8

One of the key reasons for acting irritable is stress. Stress weighs you down, drains your energy, and weakens your health. There are *relational* causes for stress: arguing, division, and bitterness. There are *excessive* causes for it: overworking, overplaying, and overspending. And there are even *deficiencies* that bring it on: lack of rest, nutrition, or exercise. Oftentimes we inflict these daggers on ourselves. This sets us up to be irritable before anyone else is involved at all.

Life is a marathon, not a sprint. This means we must balance, prioritize, and pace ourselves. Too often we throw caution to the wind and run full steam ahead, then find ourselves gasping for air, wound up in knots, and ready to snap. But love reminds us to remove the pressures that interfere with what matters most, and to protect our time and relationship with God, as well as with our spouse.

⁓ GO DEEPER ⁓

If we let the world determine our path and standards, we will foolishly weigh ourselves down with many sorrows. Read Matthew 11:28–30 and consider what Jesus does to reduce the stress of those who trust themselves to Him.

Love cultivates kindness

The mouth speaks from the overflow of the heart.

Matthew 12:34

When it comes to being irritable, the heart of the problem is primarily a problem in the heart. Some people are like lemons—when life squeezes them, they pour out a sour response. Some are more like peaches—even when the pressure is on, the result is still sweet.

Love will lead you to forgive instead of holding a grudge. To be grateful instead of greedy. To be content rather than rushing into more debt. Love encourages you to be happy when someone else succeeds rather than lying awake at night in envy. Love says "share the inheritance" rather than "fight with your relatives." It reminds you to prioritize your family rather than sacrifice them for a promotion at work.

Brave choices like these are not the result of following your heart. Your feelings during moments of high stress will tend to be more dangerous than discerning. If you ever expect to make loving decisions on a daily basis, you will have to lead your heart to do it.

∽ QUESTIONS ∾

Jesus said that your words reveal what is in your heart. What are some of the other things that reveal what is going on inside your heart? How do your attitudes, actions, and longings reveal where you are?

DAY 78
Love finds contentment

Godliness with contentment is a great gain.

1 Timothy 6:6

If you are easily angered, it's an indicator that a hidden area of selfishness or insecurity is present where love is supposed to rule. And selfishness wears many masks.

Lust, for example, is the result of being ungrateful for what we have and choosing to covet or burn with passion for something that is forbidden. When a person's heart is lustful, it will also become easily frustrated and angered (James 4:1–3). Lust is never satisfied and will produce a lifetime of frustration if it is not repented of and released from your life.

Greed is another indicator of inner selfishness. Wanting more money and possessions will frustrate us with unfulfilled desires (1 Timothy 6:9–10). Strong desires coupled with dissatisfaction lead you to lash out at anyone who stands in your way.

Love will lead you to be grateful instead of greedy, and to be content rather than chasing unhealthy desires. When you allow God's love to rule your heart, it will result in true satisfaction. When love becomes your greatest motive, it lights a pathway to contentment.

⟜ THIS WEEK'S DARE ⟜

Choose to take a weekly day of rest and worship, starting this week. Make a list of areas where you need to add margin to your schedule, then resolve to release anything not adding true value.

DAY 79
Love holds no grudge

*All bitterness, anger and wrath, insult and slander
must be removed from you, along with all wickedness.*

Ephesians 4:31

You can't be truly loving and bitter with your mate at
the same time. When you harbor silent resentment, it will
hinder the free flow of openness and tenderness in your
relationship.

Bitterness takes root any time we refuse to work through
our anger. We bottle it up, causing it to grow into a grudge,
yet it does more damage to ourselves than to anyone else.
Then when provoked, all this unresolved animosity leaks
out. It's been said that bitterness is like drinking a cup of
poison, expecting the other person to get sick.

But when love enters our heart, it calms us down and
inspires us to quit focusing on ourselves. It loosens our grasp,
helping us to let go of unnecessary things. Love leads us to
forgive instead of holding a grudge. It helps us heal from
past hurts. Love is the best medicine for the heart, a gift that
God offers to everyone willing to receive it.

❧ GO DEEPER ❧

Read Hebrews 12:14–15. Who are you to be at peace
with, according to this passage? How diligently
should you be looking to identify if any bitterness is
in your life? If you are bitter, who do these verses say
will be defiled by it?

DAY 80
Love forgives

. . . accepting one another and forgiving one another
if anyone has a complaint against another.

Colossians 3:13

How many of your disagreements could be avoided altogether simply by keeping past issues from being brought back up? When old hurts are given permission to keep wounding, they will always fester and further contaminate your relationships. Even when a spat erupts about something current, yesterday's problems can quickly take over, further inflaming the moment. Past hurts muddy the waters and amplify present tension. Reactions then become overreactions and cause your mate to second-guess your logic and sense of fairness.

Love doesn't dwell on the past. It keeps short accounts. It has a great memory for certain things, but not for issues that have already taken their turn at dividing you.

Clarity of judgment is much more likely when you single out issues and deal with them one at a time. Some words and disputes, of course, can probably never be forgotten. But love turns every thought of them into a reminder that forgiveness is a choice.

❧ THIS WEEK'S DARE ☙

Choose to take a weekly day of rest and worship, starting this week. Make a list of areas where you need to add margin to your schedule, then resolve to release anything not adding true value.

DAY 81
Love adds margin

"You will certainly wear out both yourself and these people who are with you, because the task is too heavy for you."

Exodus 18:18

You can't do everything. And love understands the wisdom of living inside this reality.

If your marriage is to become what God intended, you will not be able to succeed in your role by giving your spouse the leftovers of your time and energy. Your heart may desperately want to meet all the expectations of everyone else in your life. But you cannot be your best for your spouse when you constantly push yourself to the limits, filling every waking hour with activity—even good, productive activity.

Like an engine needs oil to keep it from overheating, like precious cargo needs cushioning to keep it from breaking in transit, your life needs built-in margin to keep it from splitting apart. So make plans for some quietness. Set aside some funds for emergencies. Say no to less important opportunities so you can put needed space in your agenda. Force your schedule to accommodate time together, just to talk and pray. Ask yourself what needs to be eliminated so your marriage can breathe more deeply and freely.

❧ PRAYER ❧

"Lord, help me to balance out my time to include quality time with You and with my spouse. Teach me to become a wise steward of the time You have given me."

DAY 82
Love requires rest

You are to labor six days and do all your work,
but the seventh day is a Sabbath to the Lord your God.

Exodus 20:9–10

The notion of a Sabbath rest is not an arbitrary concept. God has created into mankind a rhythm that cycles around the seven-day week. Therefore, a day set aside for worship and rest is not merely a good principle of life. It is essential. You cannot live well without it. It allows you to clear your head and recharge your batteries.

The cost of resisting proper rest for yourself and your family is a recipe for burnout. When problems arise—and they will—you are not able to handle them from a position of strength and clear-headed perspective. You're not prepared to listen fully. This often causes you to overreact, or perhaps not to engage at all.

Making yourself obedient to God in the matter of resting will return to you in many ways. Your home will more easily maintain an atmosphere of kindness. Your priorities will be simpler to keep in place. Getting adequate rest is one of the ways love works hard at savoring your relationship.

✎ THIS WEEK'S DARE ✎

Choose to take a weekly day of rest and worship, starting this week. Make a list of areas where you need to add margin to your schedule, then resolve to release anything not adding true value.

Love refuses to worry

*The worries of this age, the seduction of wealth,
and the desires for other things enter in and
choke the word, and it becomes unfruitful.*

Mark 4:19

Some people believe that worry is impossible to escape. To not worry, they think, is not to care, or not to live in reality. But worry is always a distraction from what God wants our thoughts to be focused on. *Worry* literally means "to divide the mind." It keeps us from loving, serving, and obeying the Lord with full devotion. It is a sin against God.

As people bound for heaven by the saving work of Jesus Christ, we are free to live without fear of the future, and therefore free to live without fear in the present. Bad things that might happen are swallowed up by the assurance that "the Lord is for me; I will not be afraid" (Psalm 118:6).

So even though our fickle emotions will always be susceptible to worrying, we can spare each other untold hours of turmoil by committing to keep worry out of our hearts. Because it is built on the prideful assumption that God is not in control of our lives—and that *we are*—worry is a waste of valuable time.

GO DEEPER

Read Luke 10:38–42 and observe how worry destroyed this woman's ability to delight in the Lord and enjoy His presence. How did worry affect her priorities and the way she treated others?

Love rejoices in the Lord

Rejoice in the Lord always. I will say it again: Rejoice!

Philippians 4:4

There is reason for joy on even the most distressing day. When you choose to focus on God's blessings, you fill the spaces in your heart that would rather fret and complain. You buff away the friction points where worry likes to attach itself.

God is so confident in the abundance of joy available to you that He has actually made rejoicing a command. More than that, the Greek word for *rejoice* in this verse carries a present, active tense. It is an activity of mind and heart to be done *right now*—and to continue being done from this moment forward. Maintaining a joyfulness of spirit is simply too important to ignore. The key here is rejoicing "in the Lord," who holds time and circumstance in His hand. Regardless of what's wrong around you, you can always rejoice in God's love, the gift of salvation, and the hope of heaven.

No matter how challenging your life has become, you can inject a welcome, needed element into your home and marriage by seeking things to be joyful about. Worry cannot remain when it's being constantly overshadowed by rejoicing.

❧ QUESTIONS ❧

What is the track record of worry in your life? How often have the things you have worried about failed to happen? Compare this to God's track record of faithfulness. Who should you trust in the future?

Day 85

Love prays through anxiety

*Don't worry about anything, but in everything,
through prayer and petition with thanksgiving,
let your requests be made known to God.*

Philippians 4:6

Just as anger is a trigger that something is amiss in our hearts, worry is a trigger that we've given up on prayer. We've deemed worry to be more effective, more reliable than God. When we pray, we don't always feel like He is listening. When we worry, we feel more in control.

But the Scripture uses the extremes of "anything" and "everything" to express how completely our lives should be bathed in prayer. The practice of communicating with God freely and continually throughout the day can encompass any issue of concern to you. We are invited by God to lay out our personal requests before Him. In fact, the Lord's Prayer contains as many as six petitions in the space of its few words (Matthew 6:9–13).

Knowing that God is powerful and loving, a wise man and woman turn all their worries into prayers. When one or both of you is showing signs of fearfulness and doubt, make prayer your established refuge where you can always go.

THIS WEEK'S DARE

Pray to God and commit to give Him whatever issues you are worried about. Admit that you have no control over these issues, and ask God to forgive you for not trusting Him. Resolve to turn any future worries into prayers.

Day 86
Love is thankful

*. . . rooted and built up in Him and established in the faith,
just as you were taught, and overflowing with thankfulness.*

Colossians 2:7

An objective look at the facts would likely confirm that
ninety-five percent of the things we worry about never come
to pass. This makes the track record of worry extremely low
on reliability. Worry takes and makes demands, but for no
good reason. Nearly all of the energy it requires is wasted on
itself. It becomes nothing more than a worry-go-round.

But trading worry for thankfulness allows us to observe
God's track record instead. And what we see is in stark
contrast. Even in suffering we find His reliability flawless and unfailing. Thanksgiving helps us look to the past
with appreciation, filling our hearts with awe at what He's
done in our lives, even when worry was convincing us He
wasn't. Gratitude keeps us attuned to the positives of what
He's doing in our present circumstances, rather than feeling defeated or being sidetracked into believing the worst.
Thankfulness is not a trick to ignore the pain in reality. It
keeps worry from interpreting life through a faulty lens.

❧ GO DEEPER ❧

Read 1 Thessalonians 5:15–19. What does verse 15
say we should do instead of repaying evil for evil?
According to these verses, what is God's will for
your life? What would happen to your worry if you
applied verses 16–18 "always . . . without ceasing . . .
and in everything"?

Love thinks of God

I will reflect on all You have done and meditate on Your actions.

Psalm 77:12

Worry denies that God cares for us. It questions that His very nature is to love, protect, and defend His children. And when worry infiltrates our marriages, whether in regard to each other or in trying to deal with life's general uncertainties, it blinds us to the help our God provides. It makes His powerful, eternal attributes somehow less secure in our minds.

We can never spend too much time meditating on the character of God. Troubles and hardships can color our view of ultimate reality. But when we recall how God describes Himself in His Word and how He's proven Himself in our lives, we can trust the picture He paints. He is unchanging and in control. He is faithful and true. "The Lord is righteous in all His ways and gracious in all His acts" (Psalm 145:17).

Do not let worry have the last word on who God is and how He operates in your life. "You will keep him in perfect peace, whose mind is stayed on You, because he trusts in You" (Isaiah 26:3 NKJV).

⤜⤳ THIS WEEK'S DARE ⤜⤳

Pray to God and commit to give Him whatever issues you are worried about. Admit that you have no control over these issues and ask God for forgiveness for not trusting Him. Resolve to turn any future worries into prayers.

DAY 88
Love trusts God's promises

And my God will supply all your needs
according to His riches in glory in Christ Jesus.

Philippians 4:19

God has promised that you can cast "all your care upon Him, because He cares about you" (1 Peter 5:7). He has said, "I will never leave you or forsake you" (Hebrews 13:5). He has boldly declared that you are "able to do all things through Him" who strengthens you (Philippians 4:13). And as the verse above states, He possesses more than enough resources to meet "all your needs" (Philippians 4:19).

Worry is how our heart questions every one of these promises. It causes us to think that God doesn't care what we're going through. Our life feels too big for us to handle. We see things falling apart and jump to wrong conclusions about His ability and concern. But God is not going to ruin His reputation on your problems. He is telling you to trust Him.

When we join together to eliminate worry from our marriages, we lay claim to another of God's promises—the enjoyment of peace that "surpasses every thought" and can "guard our hearts and minds in Christ Jesus" (Philippians 4:7). Peace can only exist in the absence of worry. That's a promise.

❧ PRAYER ❧

"Lord Jesus, forgive me for not trusting You with my needs. Help me to be wise with what You have given me, and to keep my faith in You for the future."

DAY 89
Love believes the best

. . . bears all things, believes all things,
hopes all things, endures all things.

1 Corinthians 13:7

Deep in your heart is a room. It's called the *Appreciation Room*. It's where positive and encouraging thoughts about your spouse are kept. Every so often, you enjoy visiting this special place. Inside are wonderful things you've discovered about your mate that cause your appreciation for them to increase.

Down another corridor of your heart lies the *Depreciation Room*, and unfortunately you visit there as well. Inside are things that bother and irritate you about your spouse, placed there out of frustration and disappointment. But know this: the more time you spend in this place, the more your heart devalues your spouse. In fact, divorces are plotted here. Spending time in the *Depreciation Room* kills marriages.

Love knows about the *Depreciation Room*, but chooses not to live there. Love chooses to believe the best about people. And when our worst hopes are proven to be true, love makes every effort to deal with them and move forward. As much as possible, love focuses on the positive.

THIS WEEK'S DARE

Pray to God and commit to give Him whatever issues you are worried about. Admit that you have no control over these issues and ask God for forgiveness for not trusting Him. Resolve to turn any future worries into prayers.

Day 90
Love thinks positively

*If there is any excellence and if anything
worthy of praise, dwell on these things.*

Philippians 4:8 NASB

Love gives people the benefit of the doubt. It refuses to fill in the unknowns with negative assumptions. It's time to let love lead your thoughts, to focus on the things you love most in your spouse—"whatever is true, whatever is honorable, whatever is just, whatever is pure, whatever is lovely, whatever is commendable" (Philippians 4:8). It's time to meditate on the positives.

Your spouse is a living, breathing, endless book to be read. Dreams and hopes have yet to be realized. Talents and abilities are still waiting to be discovered like hidden treasure. Depths of character and strength are still being crafted. But the choice to explore them starts with a decision made by you.

You must develop the habit of reining in your negative thoughts and focusing on the positive attributes of your mate. This is a crucial step as you learn to lead your heart to truly love your spouse. It is a decision that you make, whether they deserve it or not.

QUESTIONS

What would happen to your feelings toward your spouse if you focused primarily on their strengths and positive attributes? How would it affect your marriage if their value tripled in your mind and heart?

Day 91
Love resists the devil

"Get behind Me, Satan! You are an offense to Me."
Matthew 16:23

Jesus not only explained that the person of Satan is a reality, but He modeled how to resist him using the Scripture (Matthew 4:1–11). Satan, meaning *accuser*, will combine truth, lies, and negative assumptions in your mind about your spouse (Revelation 12:10). He is very divisive, using your pride, fear, or anger to get you to betray one another (John 13:1–3).

In Genesis 3, Eve was deceived when Satan claimed God was withholding good from her and made her question whether God could be trusted. Satan also falsely argued that Job would curse God if Job's blessings and possessions were taken away (Job 1:9–11).

In marriage, Satan manipulates us into mistrusting our mate's motives. He'll feed any bitterness or pride in us by claiming, "Your spouse doesn't understand or care about you. You're unappreciated and deserve better." Sound familiar?

Love, however, believes the best about others and gives them the benefit of the doubt. You must humbly resist Satan, forgive your spouse, and shine the light of honest, loving conversation on the dark lies of his accusations.

GO DEEPER

Study James 4:6–12 and 1 Peter 5:6–11 to learn how to humble yourself and resist the schemes of the devil. Also study Ephesians 6:10–19.

Love expresses gratitude

I thank my God in all my remembrance of you.

Philippians 1:3 NASB

Heaven is filled with thanksgiving toward God. Therefore, teaching us to be thankful on Earth is a priority of God's will for us. His Word commands us to give thanks continually in all circumstances. He saves our souls, answers our prayers, and extends His grace so that we will overflow with thanksgiving.

Ungratefulness is a sin that breeds dissatisfaction and causes depression. It also robs others from receiving our appreciation when they bless us. But our expression of thanks gives honor to God and brings joy to those who receive it.

Your happiness in life is directly related to the depth of your gratitude. A grateful person can find contentment regardless of his or her circumstances. A thankful husband praises his wife by acknowledging the specific ways she helps him. The gratitude a wife expresses to her husband is often more attractive to him than her outward beauty. You won't fully enjoy your marriage until you begin expressing sincere appreciation to one another. God has given you a priceless gift in a life partner. Be grateful!

THIS WEEK'S DARE

Make a list of positive attributes about your spouse, then choose one each day and thank your spouse for having this characteristic.

DAY 93
Love does not complain

Do everything without complaining or arguing.

Philippians 2:14 NIV

Gripes grow and ferment in the *whinery* of an ungrateful heart. The Scriptures say we should give "thanks to God the Father for everything" (Ephesians 5:20 NIV). But there are still those who seem to find every reason to complain. No problem is too small for them to gripe about.

Grumbling, groaning, and murmuring are like poison in the atmosphere of marriage. It discourages everyone who hears it and provides a poor example to our children. It also demonstrates a lack of patience toward others and a lack of faith in God. Either we trust in His power and goodness, or we don't.

When we complain, the Bible says our grumbling is actually against God, because He is in control and allows each circumstance in our lives. Our complaints go directly into His ears so that He hears every word (Numbers 14:27–28).

Day by day and moment by moment, we have a choice to make. We can focus on the negative and continually complain about it, or we can fix our eyes on Jesus and "rejoice evermore. Pray without ceasing. In everything give thanks" (1 Thessalonians 5:16–18 KJV).

⟾ GO DEEPER ⟾

Read James 5:7–11 and study the powerful reasons mentioned why we should never complain.

DAY 94

Love grows in gratefulness

. . . always giving thanks for all things.

Ephesians 5:20 NASB

An attitude of gratitude should describe the profile of our lifestyle. This process begins when we realize we have sinned against a holy God and deserve judgment and separation from Him. Yet through His love, God sent Jesus to die for our sins so that we can be forgiven and have eternal life. In response to Him, your deepest gratefulness is born.

Gratefulness grows when we daily recognize the countless ways we've been blessed. It grows when we realize that we have so much more than we deserve. It grows when we remember that every good thing is actually a gift from a loving God.

However, feeling grateful without communicating it is like clouds that refuse to rain. Gratefulness shines when we start openly expressing to God and others our sincere appreciation. We should go beyond the words "thank you" and get very specific as to how we've been blessed. There is no substitute for expressing appreciation. It is one of the most fulfilling and rewarding ways to package love.

❦ THIS WEEK'S DARE ❦

Make a list of positive attributes about your spouse, then choose one each day and thank your spouse for having this characteristic.

DAY 95
Love fuels hope

Jesus looked at them and said, "With men this is impossible, but with God all things are possible."

Matthew 19:26

God is in the business of resurrecting dead things. Throughout Scripture, He continually brought life back to situations where death seemed to rule. He brought rain to a land in drought and allowed crops to flourish. He restored Job's wealth after he had lost everything. And of course, He raised Christ from the grave, giving us a hope and a future.

God can also resurrect marriages that seem to be dead. When a couple has experienced the pain and suffering of a failing relationship, He sometimes allows them to get to the point of desperation. It's when they cry out to Him and place their faith in Him that He steps in and begins to rekindle the fire that was once extinguished. He reminds us that marriage is worth fighting for, and worth the time, focus, and sacrifice.

When God is part of the marriage, there is never a time to quit. And there is always a place for hope. Even resurrection.

❧ PRAYER ❧

"Father God, please continue to work in our marriage. Stir our hearts to yearn for more of You in our lives. Build in us a love for You and for each other. In Jesus' name, amen."

DAY 96
Love casts a vision

[Love] always protects, always trusts,
always hopes, always perseveres.

1 Corinthians 13:7 NIV

What do you think your marriage will look like several years down the road? The images that appear in your mind will reveal what you expect from your relationship in the future. For many, these images may not look very bright. For others, they may include joyful days and greater intimacy. The truth is, many couples accept failure because they don't have a vision of success in the coming years.

Have you ever thought of asking God to give you a vision of what your marriage could be like? Can you imagine walking with your spouse through good times and bad, all the while remaining devoted to each other and to God? Can you visualize God taking you to greater depths of love and understanding?

One powerful aspect of love is that it hopes. It aims for what's best. And no matter where you are today, your marriage can achieve wonderful growth if you center it on God.

What's stopping you from getting on your knees now and begging Him for His vision for your future? Be ready to put this vision into words and action as God gives it to you in answer to your prayer. That's a vision worth pursuing.

THIS WEEK'S DARE

Make a list of positive attributes about your spouse, then choose one each day and thank your spouse for having this characteristic.

Love is not envious

Jealousy . . . burns like blazing fire, like a mighty flame.

Song of Solomon 8:6 NIV

The word *jealousy* comes from the root word for *zeal* and means to burn with an intense fire. There are actually two forms: a *legitimate* jealousy based upon love, and an *illegitimate* jealousy based upon envy. Legitimate jealousy sparks when someone you love, who belongs to you, turns his or her heart away and replaces you with someone else. The Bible describes God as having this kind of righteous jealousy *for* His people.

The illegitimate kind of jealousy is rooted in selfishness. It's to be jealous *of* someone or "moved with envy." When you were married, you were given the role of becoming your spouse's biggest cheerleader. Both of you became one and were to share in the enjoyment of the other. But if selfishness enters the picture, any good thing happening to only one of you can be a catalyst for envy rather than congratulations. Love is not jealous of the other's success but is the first to celebrate it.

⌒∾ GO DEEPER ∾⌒

Instead of celebrating God's blessings on another person, envy causes you to mistreat them, although they may have done nothing wrong to you. Study Proverbs 3:29–33 and consider how you might apply this in your marriage and relationships. What kind of person does God bless according to this passage?

Love tolerates no rivals

I, *the* LORD *your God,* am a jealous God.

Exodus 20:5

Of all the ways we are capable of sinning against God, it's interesting that He chose the first two of His ten commandments to establish that He is a "jealous God," not to be replaced by substitutes. The entire story of the Bible is in many ways the ongoing account of this jealousy—how He actively pursued His children's affection and devotion, sometimes by dealing with their internal rebellion, sometimes by dealing with other nations who were leading them astray.

He knew, of course, that their idols were cheap imitations that lured them away from fellowship with Him. He mocked the artisans whose handmade creations had to be fastened "with nails" so they would not "fall over" (Isaiah 41:7). His is a holy and righteous jealousy. It stirs Him to fiery wrath. It causes Him to be "a consuming fire" (Hebrews 12:29).

But this is the fire of His love, forged in the knowledge that He is the only One worthy of our worship, our "first love" (Revelation 2:4 NASB). The reason He tolerates no rivals is because nothing can rival the One True God. He knows we can only be satisfied in Him.

❧ PRAYER ❧

"Heavenly Father, help me not to trust in any substitute—no temporary pleasure, no long-held habit—that would replace what I can only find in You. In Jesus' name, amen."

DAY 99
Love is jealous for God

For I am jealous over you with a godly jealousy.

2 Corinthians 11:2

The legitimate, loving form of jealousy—God's jealousy—is tied to the idea of replacement. It is jealous over anything that takes us or our loved ones away from wholeheartedly following the Lord. Phinehas was honored for rising up in angry judgment against his Hebrew countrymen who were mocking God to His face by sleeping with idolatrous foreign women. In passionate defense of God, he was given honor for being "jealous with My jealousy among them" (Numbers 25:11 NASB).

After Jesus drove the moneychangers from the temple, His disciples understood it as fulfillment of this prophecy: "Zeal for Your house will consume Me" (John 2:17).

Godly jealousy makes us long for our spouses and children to put God first in their lives. It is why we grieve over them whenever they replace first-love affection for Him with other alternatives. If we weren't jealous on behalf of God, we might not become so upset. But our zeal for Him to be given His rightful place of honor and gratitude causes us to act, to pray, and to speak up in His defense.

❧ THIS WEEK'S DARE ❧

Determine to become your spouse's biggest fan and to reject any thoughts of ungodly jealousy. Share with your spouse how glad you are about a success he or she recently enjoyed.

Day 100
Love defuses jealousy

Fury is cruel, and anger is a flood,
but who can withstand jealousy?

Proverbs 27:4

Do you struggle with being jealous of others? Your friend is more popular and you feel hatred toward her. Your coworker gets the promotion, so you can't sleep that night. He may have done nothing wrong, but you became bitter because of his success. It has been said that people are fine with you succeeding, just as long as it is not more than them.

Jealousy is a common struggle. It is sparked when someone else upstages us and gets something we want. Instead of congratulating them, we fume in anger and think ill of them. If we're not careful, jealousy can slither like a viper into our hearts and strike our motivations and relationships, even our marriage.

The Bible says that envy leads to fighting, quarreling, and every evil thing. If we don't defuse our anger by learning to love, we may eventually begin plotting against others. We may even wish ill on our mates because of a success they enjoy. Don't let the poison of jealousy prevent you from living the life of love that God intended.

❧ GO DEEPER ❧

Read 1 Samuel 18:1–9 and consider the difference between Jonathan's response and Saul's response to David's great success in battle. Look at the amazing impact that love made in affecting their responses.

Day 101
Love celebrates success

Let us walk with decency, as in the daylight . . .
not in quarreling and jealousy.

Romans 13:13

There is a string of jealousy seen throughout Scripture. It caused the first murder when Cain despised God's acceptance of his brother's offering. Sarah sent away her handmaiden because Hagar could bear children while Sarah could not. Joseph's brothers saw he was their father's favorite, so they threw him into a pit and sold him as a slave. The chief priests envied Jesus and plotted His betrayal and crucifixion.

If you are not careful, jealousy can also infect your marriage. But love leads us to celebrate the successes of our spouse rather than resenting them. A loving husband doesn't mind his wife being better at something. He sees her as completing him, not competing with him. A loving wife will cheer for her man when he wins. She does not compare her weaknesses to his strengths. She throws a celebration, not a pity party.

It is time to let humility and gratefulness destroy any jealousy and then draw you closer together through unselfish love. "Rejoice with those who rejoice" (Romans 12:15).

◈ THIS WEEK'S DARE ◈

Determine to become your spouse's biggest fan and to reject any thoughts of ungodly jealousy. Share with your spouse how glad you are about a success he or she recently enjoyed.

Day 102
Love doesn't wish ill

Love does no wrong to a neighbor.
Love, therefore, is the fulfillment of the law.

Romans 13:10

Love leads you to deal with any kind of envy or covetousness that creeps into your heart. Not only does love cause you to question your own motives for wanting attention or advancement, it prevents you from taking any kind of delight in another person's failure or misfortune.

To achieve this freedom of mind and conscience, resist any temptation to compare yourself with others. "Each person should examine his own work, and then he will have reason for boasting in himself alone, and not in respect to someone else" (Galatians 6:4). Count the blessings you have received from the Lord without referencing how they stack up against those of others. Do not think evil of anyone or "plan any harm against your neighbor" (Proverbs 3:29). Rather, rejoice in the success of others, delighting in the fact that they are experiencing God's favor. Having tasted that the Lord is good, it's time to rid yourself of "all wickedness, all deceit, hypocrisy, envy, and slander" (1 Peter 2:1).

❧ PRAYER ❧

"Lord, expose any ungodly motive in our hearts. Teach us to walk in purity so Your hand will rest in favor on our lives. Forgive us of sinful thinking, and renew our focus on You."

DAY 103
Love makes good impressions

Greet one another with a kiss of love.

1 Peter 5:14

You can tell a lot about the state of a couple's relationship from the way they greet one another. You can see it in their expression and countenance, as well as how they speak to each other. It is even more obvious by their physical contact, by the tender yet respectful way they touch.

The Bible has more to say about greetings than you might expect. The apostle Paul took time to encourage his readers to greet one another warmly when they met. Jesus said that part of being godly includes being humble and gracious enough to address even our enemies with kindness.

Think of the opportunities you have to greet your spouse on a regular basis. When coming through the door. When meeting for lunch. When talking on the phone. It doesn't have to be bold and dramatic every time. But adding warmth and enthusiasm to your greeting gives you the chance to touch your mate's heart in subtle, even unspoken ways.

❧ THIS WEEK'S DARE ❧

Determine to become your spouse's biggest fan and to reject any thoughts of ungodly jealousy. Share with your spouse how glad you are about a success he or she recently enjoyed.

Day 104
Love greets with value

I hope to see you soon, and we will talk face to face. . . .
The friends send you greetings. Greet the friends by name.

3 John 14

How do you greet your friends, coworkers, and neighbors? How about acquaintances and those you meet in public? You may even acknowledge someone you don't necessarily like, out of courtesy. So if you're this nice and polite to other people, doesn't your spouse deserve the same? Times ten?

When someone communicates they're glad to see you, your personal sense of self-worth increases. That's because a good greeting sets the stage for positive and healthy interaction. Like love, it puts wind in your sails.

Think about your greeting. Does it make your spouse feel honored and appreciated? Do they feel loved? Even when you're not getting along too well, you can lessen the tension and give them value by the way you greet them. Put some thought into what you want to say and how you want to say it. Remember, love is a choice. So choose to change your greeting.

∽ GO DEEPER ∾

Read Matthew 5:43–48 and note that Jesus includes greeting as a way to demonstrate love. The test of our love is not how we treat our friends. If your spouse has become like an enemy to you, how would Jesus' words affect how loving you should still behave around them?

DAY 105
Love blesses with greetings

While the son was still a long way off,
his father saw him and was filled with compassion.
He ran, threw his arms around his neck, and kissed him.

Luke 15:20

Look up the story of the prodigal son that Jesus told in Luke 15. This young, rebellious man wasted his inheritance money on a foolish lifestyle. Soon his bad choices caught up with him, and he found himself eating scraps in a pigpen. Humbled and ashamed, he went home to face his father. But the cold greeting he was expecting was not the one he received.

How do you think it made him feel to receive his father's embrace and hear his thankful tone? He no doubt felt loved and treasured once again. He knew in an instant, before a single word was spoken, that he was fully accepted and pleasing to his father.

What kind of greeting would make your mate feel like that? How could you excite his or her various senses with a simple word, a touch, a tone of voice? A loving greeting blesses people through what they see, hear, and feel.

☙ QUESTIONS ❧

How did you greet your spouse when you were first married? How has it changed over the years? Is it better or worse? What are some simple changes you can make to take it to the next level of kindness?

Day 106
Love blesses all the senses

They were thrilled at the light of my countenance.

Job 29:24

The opportunity for blessing your mate with kind, thoughtful greetings is enhanced even more if you try to captivate each of their senses in the process. The sound of your voice, greeting them by your own pet name for them, used by no one else but you. The touch of your hand on their shoulder, or your bodies drawn close in a loving embrace. The smell of your perfume or aftershave, left to linger after the taste of a romantic kiss. And perhaps sweetest of all, a smile they can see that reminds them how dearly they are loved, always wished for, and genuinely adored.

Some have rightly claimed that a frowning, fallen countenance on the face of a Christian is a poor testimony of the joy God extends to all His people. It could be just as accurately stated that a sour, disinterested expression on your face is a silent insult to your wife or husband. Think of what they see when they look at you. Make sure it's a look that says love, even without saying a word.

❧ THIS WEEK'S DARE ❧

Think of a specific way you'd like to greet your spouse this week. Do it with a smile and with enthusiasm. Allow your greeting to reflect your love for them.

Love is unconditional

God proves His own love for us in that
while we were still sinners Christ died for us!

Romans 5:8

If someone were to ask you, "Why do you love your spouse?"—what would you say? Most men would mention their wife's beauty, her sense of humor, her kindness, or what a good mother she is. Women would probably say something about their husband's good looks, his personality, or how hard he works.

But what if your wife or husband stopped being all these things? What if through a sudden decline in health or a stressful life situation, your mate lost all the attractive aspects that made them who they are? Would you still love them? If your reasons for loving your spouse only have to do with his or her qualities—and then those qualities gradually disappear—your basis for love is over.

The only way love can last a lifetime is if it's unconditional. And unconditional love is not based on how deserving the other person is, but rather on a choice to love them, no matter the circumstances.

GO DEEPER

One of the greatest explanations of God's love is found in Romans 5:6–10. Read this passage and consider how unlovable we were to God. Yet note how wholeheartedly His love is demonstrated at that point.

DAY 108
Love is a choice

We love because He first loved us.

1 John 4:19

The reality is this: true love is not determined by the one *being* loved, but rather by the one *choosing* to love. The Bible refers to this kind of love by using the Greek word *agape*. It differs from other types of love, which are—*phileo* (friendship) and *eros* (sexual). Both of these aspects have their place in marriage, but if your togetherness totally depends on having common interests or enjoying a healthy sex life, then the foundation for your relationship is unstable.

Phileo and *eros* are more responsive in nature and can fluctuate based on feelings. *Agape* love is unconditional. It needs no other reason than itself to continue loving. And unless this forms the bedrock of your marriage, the wear and tear of time will destroy what you have built. *Agape* love is "in sickness and health" love, "for richer or poorer" love, "for better or worse" love. It is the only kind of love that is *true* love.

❧❧ THIS WEEK'S DARE ❧❧

Think of a specific way you'd like to greet your spouse this week. Do it with a smile and with enthusiasm. Allow your greeting to reflect your love for them.

DAY 109
Love is the foundation

Love consists in this: not that we loved God, but that He loved us and sent His Son to be the propitiation for our sins.

1 John 4:10

God doesn't love us because we are lovable, but because He is so loving. If He insisted that we prove ourselves worthy of His love, we would fail miserably. Each day would provide Him ample justification for rejecting us, for being done with us. But God's love is a choice He makes completely because of who He is. It's something we receive from Him and then share with others.

If a man says to his wife, "I don't love you anymore," he is actually saying, "I never loved you unconditionally to begin with." His love was based on feelings or circumstances rather than commitment. That's a marriage built on *phileo* or *eros* love—a marriage built on sand instead of rock.

There must be a stronger foundation than mere friendship or sexual attraction. Unconditional love, or *agape* love, will not be swayed by time or circumstance. It will last forever because it is God's kind of love.

⮞ PRAYER ⮜

"Lord, we thank You for Your compassionate love. Teach us to love one another as You love us, and forgive us when we cling to our selfishness. Renew in us a clean heart for Your glory. In Jesus' name, amen."

DAY 110
Love is divinely inspired

*Whoever keeps His word, truly in him
the love of God is perfected.*

1 John 2:5

When you build your marriage with *agape* love as the foundation, then the friendship and romantic aspects of your love become more endearing than ever before. When your enjoyment of each other as best friends and lovers is based on unwavering commitment, you will experience an intimacy that cannot be achieved any other way.

But you will struggle and fail to attain this kind of marriage unless you allow God to begin growing His love within you. *Agape* love does not come from within. It can only come from God. But thankfully—by your choice—it can become your kind of love as well when you receive it and share it. And don't be surprised when your spouse becomes even more lovable to you than you remember. No longer will you say, "I love you because . . ." Now you will say, "I love you, period."

THIS WEEK'S DARE

Think of a specific way you'd like to greet your spouse this week. Do it with a smile and with enthusiasm. Allow your greeting to reflect your love for them.

Love never ends

*For I am persuaded that neither death nor life . . .
nor any other created thing will have the power
to separate us from the love of God.*

Romans 8:38–39

The unconditional nature of God's love is greater than any challenge our sin could bring against it. That's why the apostle Paul describes God's love with a series of powerful extremes. It's a poetic way to say that nothing—absolutely nothing—is able to "separate us from the love of God."

"Neither death nor life." (Everything is either dead or alive.) "Nor things present, nor things to come." (Everything either is, has been, or will be.) "Nor height, nor depth." (Nothing can outreach or overextend His unconditional love for us.) "Nor any other created thing." (This fills every imaginable loophole you could think of.) Absolutely nothing separates us from His love.

And neither should anything separate your love for your husband or wife. The love you've promised the other in marriage cannot include escape clauses and negotiated terms. You simply must not look at it this way. It either *is* true love, or it's not. But if you want it to be God's kind of love, it must be ready and willing to go all the way.

QUESTIONS

If God's love is unconditional, then is there anything that anyone has done or will do that will separate you from His love? What would happen to your heart if you truly believed and received God's unchanging love for you?

Day 112
Love has a symbol

"This is the sign of the covenant that I have confirmed."

Genesis 9:17

The rings you exchanged at the wedding altar do more than just confirm your marital status. Like the rainbow in Noah's day, like the bread and wine of our Communion table, the ring represents a promise. It is a visible sign of the vows you took on your wedding day.

This means every time the glint of its gold or silver catches your eye, you can take it as a reminder of the unconditional love you committed to each other. In the same way, your wife or husband carries around your promise to them on their ring finger everywhere they go. It's more than a gem or precious metal. It never stops whispering the vows you shared "for as long as we both shall live."

God has always used signs to give His covenants a tangible form. He knows that life tends to make us forget what He said, as well as to forget what we ourselves have agreed to in our dealings with others. Let your wedding ring serve as an ongoing prompter to remember your promise.

GO DEEPER

Read Genesis 9:8–17 and observe the characteristics of God's covenant with Noah after the flood. How does God communicate that He will never look back while also keeping His everlasting covenant? How are the rainbow and your wedding rings similar in purpose?

DAY 113
Love is for better, for worse

*Though the fig tree does not bud and there is no fruit
on the vines . . . yet I will triumph in the LORD.*

Habakkuk 3:17–18

Does your love have a place it will not go beyond? Even
though you willingly promised to love your spouse forever
in the soft glow of your wedding ceremony, were you just
repeating the script? Were you like many who, though promising for better or for worse, really only meant "for better"?

You may look from the outside in at other people's marriages and suppose that many, if not most, have a much
easier time than you do. You may determine that your spouse
has brought challenges into your marriage you can no longer tolerate—things you didn't know or foresee, or perhaps
overlooked.

Do not give up on having true love for your spouse. Even
if much of the feeling and desire has been replaced by
resentment and distrust, God is able to grow in you a love
that will last. Unconditional love will give you the ability to
rise up from the ashes of life's worst, and be thankful for how
the heat of battle has melded your hearts into one.

⟐ THIS WEEK'S DARE ⟐

Do something out of the ordinary for your spouse—
something that proves (to you and to them) that your
love is based on your choice and nothing else.

Love is for richer, for poorer

During a severe testing by affliction, their abundance of joy and their deep poverty overflowed into the wealth of their generosity.

2 Corinthians 8:2

Each of us comes into marriage with an idea of what we hope it eventually looks like. We may have a picture of our dream house in mind. We may imagine a certain number of children. We may see ourselves free to explore our pleasures and hobbies on the weekend.

But what happens if your husband doesn't make enough money to suit you? What happens if your wife insists on being a stay-at-home mom? What happens if your closest friends always seem able to afford the lifestyle you crave, or if the pressure of debt is weighing you down? Is there still an "abundance of joy" in your love for each other, despite your financial lack? Have you cushioned your marriage from needing wealth in order to thrive?

When wants disguise themselves as needs, the love between you often becomes conditional. Your communication is tainted with words and glances of disappointment. Assure your mate that your love does not have a monetary price tag—that you have counted the cost, and deemed them worth any sacrifice.

GO DEEPER

Read Proverbs 19:22. What does it say is more important than wealth? Are your wedding promises more important to you than your financial status?

Love is in sickness, in health

Though my physical condition was a trial for you,
you did not despise or reject me.

Galatians 4:14

One of the greatest proofs of true love is found in the anguish of disease, injury, and limitation. You have little way of knowing that your wife or husband will be stricken with illness or become lost to you for long, lonely seasons in the dense fog of depression. The tender ways they once expressed their love to you may be impossible for them to summon up any more. The scales of servanthood may tip heavily in your direction, now and for the rest of your life.

If you and your spouse are in good physical and emotional health, promise each other—ahead of any such issues—that no need or request on their part will ever be too great for your love. And if love is already demanding that you honor your mate by serving them through sickness, do so with generous joy and gratitude. You are living proof that God's love is alive and well, having redeemed your life from sin's decay, and inspiring the same sacrificial love in your heart for your mate.

❧ THIS WEEK'S DARE ❧

Do something out of the ordinary for your spouse—something that proves (to you and to them) that your love is based on your choice and nothing else.

DAY 116
Love is for life

"May the LORD do this to me, and even more,
if anything but death separates you and me."

Ruth 1:17

The call of Jesus on our lives is for "our all"—all we have, all we are. He tested the heart of the prideful and rich young ruler by commanding him to "sell all you have and give to the poor" (Mark 10:21). He challenged His disciples and others to love God "with all your heart, with all your understanding, and with all your strength" (Mark 12:33). Jesus then proved that He Himself was willing to do the same, giving His all to die in the place of sinners—people like us, who were not just unworthy but who actively resisted Him.

It is no surprise, then, that the love He grows and develops within us calls for the greatest promise we can offer—our life. All of it. Every day that's left. When we promised the same to our bride or groom, we could offer no more. We affirmed that our love was so deep and all-encompassing, it would require every breath we have to expend, all the way to the final one we take on Earth. True love can be no less.

❧ PRAYER ❧

"Father God, brand our hearts with a love for our mate. Protect us from any interference that might sway our focus, and keep us bound together with You until death. Thank You, Father. In Jesus' name, amen."

DAY 117
Love cherishes

Husbands should love their wives as their own bodies.

Ephesians 5:28

There is a significant bond between a husband and a wife that is unlike anything else. The truth is, you are *part* of one another. Whatever touches the other, touches you. For example, you would never cut off your own hand if it was injured, but would pay whatever you could afford for the best medical treatment possible. That's because your hand is priceless to you. It is part of who you are.

And so is your mate.

Marriage is a beautiful mystery created by God. It is a relationship that joins two lives together as one. This not only happens physically, but also spiritually and emotionally. You start off sharing the same house, the same bed, and the same last name. When your spouse goes through a tragedy, both of you feel it. When you find success at your job, both of you rejoice. Let your identity as individuals be joined into one, inseparable, worthy of the same care you give your own body.

❧ THIS WEEK'S DARE ❧

Do something out of the ordinary for your spouse—something that proves (to you and to them) that your love is based on your choice and nothing else.

DAY 118
Love nourishes

He who loves his own wife loves himself; for no one ever hated his own flesh, but nourishes and cherishes it.

Ephesians 5:28–29 NASB

At some point in your marriage, you will experience a profound disappointment: the sobering reality that you married an imperfect person, like yourself.

This, however, does not change the fact that your spouse is still a part of you. Both of you are considered to be the same flesh. You must treat him or her with the same nurture and care that you treat yourself.

But there is a flip side to this coin. When you *mistreat* your mate, you are also mistreating yourself. Think about it: your lives are now interwoven together. Your spouse cannot experience joy or pain, blessing or cursing, without it also affecting you. So when you attack your mate, it's like attacking your own body. When you show love to your spouse, you are showing love to yourself as well. God has united you in such a way that you must think of the other as if he or she were you.

❧ GO DEEPER ❧

Read Ephesians 5:28–31 in context. Paul argued from multiple angles why a man should nourish and cherish his wife like his own body. How do you treat your eyes, ears, or hands? How did Christ love His bride? How could this affect the gentle love you show toward your spouse?

Love stays content

The sleep of the worker is sweet, whether he eats little or much;
but the abundance of the rich permits him no sleep.

Ecclesiastes 5:12

How would you like to be happy regardless of your circumstances? That's the attainable promise of contentment. When your satisfaction is already predetermined, your pleasure threshold can become whatever you tell it to be. If you don't have as much as others around you, then that's fine with you. If you can't afford much for Christmas this year, it will still be just as worshipful and enjoyable. In fact, you'll be giving yourself one of life's greatest gifts—the freedom of unconditional joy.

Contentment allows you to wait on making a purchase rather than wrestling with whether or not you're overextending yourself. It helps you raise children who can create more fun with a cardboard box than with a boxful of video games. And it even contributes to getting a good night's sleep. With food, clothing, and the strength of Christ we can learn to be completely content. Happy people are not born; they're made. And the happiest people on Earth are those who need no more than they already have to satisfy them.

❧ QUESTIONS ❧

What are some of the first indications that you're struggling with a contentment issue? How do you navigate the fine line between being satisfied and being lazy?

DAY 120
Love adds worth

Let your fountain be blessed, and take pleasure in the wife
of your youth. . . . Be lost in her love forever.

Proverbs 5:18–19

Don't let the culture around you determine the worth of your marriage. To compare it with something that could be discarded or replaced is to dishonor God's purpose for it. That would be like amputating a limb. Instead, your marriage should be a picture of love between two imperfect people who choose to love each other regardless.

Whenever a husband looks into the eyes of his wife, he should remember that "he who loves his wife loves himself" (Ephesians 5:28), and a wife should remember that when she loves him, she is also giving love and honor to herself. Always be watching for ways to esteem and protect what God has given you in each other, never being shy about letting the other hear you say how richly you value them.

When you look at your mate, you're looking at a part of you. So treat her well. Speak of him highly. Nourish and cherish the love of your life.

❧❧ THIS WEEK'S DARE ❧❧

Look for a need in your spouse that you could meet this week. Choose a gesture that says, "I cherish you," and do it for them with a smile.

Love presents itself well

How much more pleasing is your love than wine,
and the fragrance of your perfume than any spice!

Song of Solomon 4:10 NIV

The implications of being one in body with your spouse can carry over into areas that may seem minor by comparison, yet they open up special ways to bless and honor your mate. When you were dating, for example, you paid a great deal of attention to your personal appearance before meeting each other. You thought ahead to please them with the way your hair and outfit looked, the way your perfume or cologne smelled.

The familiarity of marriage, however, can lower your incentive for making yourself attractive to your mate. You may spend a lot of time on yourself before going to work or church, but usually not just to spend time with your wife or husband. What if, instead, you revived the practice of making yourself look good for your mate, even at home—dressing up, fixing your hair, accentuating the little things they've always loved about you? When you don't consider your body to be yours alone, you're able to put your best foot forward again for your spouse.

⤜✺ GO DEEPER ✺⤛

Read Song of Solomon 4:9–11 and consider how Solomon's bride prepared herself to please her husband with her face, clothes, and perfume. What could you do to lovingly make yourself more attractive to your spouse?

Love lets others win

I have no one else like-minded
who will genuinely care about your interests.

Philippians 2:20

Unfortunately, stubbornness comes as a standard feature on both husband and wife models. Defending your rights and opinions is a foundational part of the human make-up. It's detrimental, though, inside a marriage relationship, and it steals away time and productivity from your relationship. It can also cause great frustration for both of you. Granted, being stubborn is not always bad. Some things are worth standing up for and protecting. Our priorities, morals, and obedience to God should be guarded with great effort.

There's only one way to get beyond stalemates, and that's by being "willing." It's an attitude and spirit of cooperation that should permeate our conversations. It's like a palm tree by the ocean that endures the greatest winds because it is able to gracefully bend. It's time to ground yourself in truth, yet be willing to lean toward the preference of your husband or wife whenever possible, just to demonstrate love.

☙ THIS WEEK'S DARE ❧

Look for a need in your spouse that you could meet this week. Choose a gesture that says, "I cherish you," and do it for them with a smile.

Love is willing

Have this attitude in yourselves which was also in Christ Jesus.

Philippians 2:5 NASB

Jesus had every right to refuse becoming a man, but He yielded to the Father's plan and did it—because He was willing. He had the right to be served by all mankind, but came to serve us instead. He had the right to live in peace and safety, yet willingly laid down His life for our sins. He was even willing to endure the grueling torture of the cross. He loved, cooperated, and chose to do His Father's will instead of His own.

Love means laying down what you have the right to claim—for the good of others.

In order for any of your marital arguments to continue, you and your spouse have to stay entrenched and unbending. But the moment one of you says, "I'm willing to go your way on this one," the argument is over. And though the follow-through may cost you some pride and discomfort, you have made a loving, lasting investment in your marriage.

❧ PRAYER ❧

"God, please remind us that we don't deserve Your love, so we should not expect our spouse to deserve ours. Help us to love willingly, and to choose others over ourselves. In Jesus' name, amen."

DAY 124
Love yields its position

*The wisdom that is from above is first pure,
then peaceable, gentle, willing to yield.*

James 3:17 NKJV

Whenever you and your spouse have a disagreement, the wise and loving thing to do is to start with a willingness to yield your rights. That's not to say your mate is necessarily correct or being wise about a matter, but that you are choosing to give strong consideration to their preference as a way of valuing them.

Instead of treating your spouse like an enemy, start by treating them as your closest, most honored friend. Give their words full weight. No, you won't always see eye-to-eye. Two people who always share the same perspectives won't have any balance or flavor to enhance their relationship. Rather, your differences are for listening to and learning from.

If it doesn't matter in the long run, and especially in eternity, then give up your rights and choose to honor the one you love. It will be good for you—and good for your marriage.

✎ THIS WEEK'S DARE ✎

Look for a need in your spouse that you could meet this week. Choose a gesture that says, "I cherish you," and do it for them with a smile.

DAY 125
Love fights fair

"If a house is divided against itself, that house cannot stand."

Mark 3:25

Like it or not, conflict in marriage is simply inevitable. The storms of life will test you and reveal what you're really made of. Work demands, health issues, in-law arguments, and financial needs will flare up in varying degrees, adding pressure and heat to your relationship. This sets the stage for disagreements. You argue and fight. You experience conflict. But you are not alone. Every couple goes through it, though not every couple survives it.

When love steps in, it changes things. Love reminds you that your marriage is too valuable to allow it to self-destruct, and that your love for your spouse is more important than whatever you're fighting about. Love reminds you that conflict can actually be turned around for good. Married couples who learn to work through conflict tend to be closer, more trusting, more intimate, and more deeply connected afterwards.

GO DEEPER

Read Colossians 3:12–14. If you were an actor and put on the clothes of your character, it would help you step into that role. Paul is challenging believers to put on the character traits of Christ. He is not asking them to be fake, but to start acting like who they are in Christ. What if these traits guided you during conflict? How would you act differently?

Love stays in bounds

A gentle answer turns away anger,
but a harsh word stirs up wrath.

Proverbs 15:1

When you tied the knot as bride and groom, you joined not only your hopes and dreams but also your imperfections and emotional baggage. From the moment you returned from your honeymoon, you began the process of discovering how sinful and selfish each of you could be.

The deepest, most heartbreaking damage you'll ever do to your marriage will most likely occur in the thick of conflict. That's because this is when your pride is strongest. Your anger is hottest. Your words contain the most venom and you make the worst decisions.

If you don't have guidelines for how you'll approach hot topics, you won't stay in bounds when the action heats up. The wisest way is to learn to fight clean by establishing healthy rules of engagement. Conflict in marriage is par for the course, but it can be dealt with in such a way that you come out healthier on the other side.

QUESTIONS

How do wisdom and discernment affect your behavior during conflict? Proverbs 19:11 says our discretion helps us to be slow to anger and to overlook the transgressions of others. How does carefully considering the consequences of our actions guide us to be more considerate?

DAY 127

Love maintains its dignity

The Lord is my portion; I have promised to keep Your words.

Psalm 119:57

There are two types of boundaries for dealing with conflict. "We" boundaries are rules you both agree on beforehand that apply during an altercation. These could include: 1) We will never fight in public or in front of our children. 2) We will not bring up old, unrelated items from the past. 3) We will never touch one another in a harmful way. 4) We will never go to bed angry with one another. 5) Divorce is not an option. Whatever it takes, we will work this out.

"Me" boundaries are rules you personally practice on your own, promises you make to yourself before any hostilities arise. Examples are: 1) I will listen first before speaking. 2) I will deal with my own issues first. 3) I will speak gently and keep my voice down.

Fighting fair means changing your weapons. Disagreeing with dignity. It should result in building a bridge instead of burning it down.

THIS WEEK'S DARE

Demonstrate love by willingly choosing to give in to an area of disagreement between you and your spouse. Tell them that you are putting his or her preference first.

DAY 128
Love doesn't start fights

To start a conflict is to release a flood;
stop the dispute before it breaks out.

Proverbs 17:14

Sometimes the fight comes looking for *you*. And love can only react, doing all it can to soften the situation. But how many of the arguments in your home are ones you instigate? How many of your disagreements are the result of unkind, accusatory thoughts you've allowed yourself to dwell on until they have no place to go but out?

The wise man or woman understands that when complaints are given permission to stew, they will almost always simmer into a boil over time. That's why love works to flush these kinds of thoughts from its system, refusing to spark an altercation. It knows that the beginning of strife is like water being poured out, never to go back into the glass again. Soak any anger or frustration of yours in the cool water of forgiveness and in the seeking of peace. Arguments can flare up and rage out of control, so extinguish the single match before it lights a fire.

⤜❧ GO DEEPER ❧⤛

Read 1 Peter 3:8–12 and consider the many strong standards Peter challenges believers to live by in their interactions with others. These are not to be ignored or discarded during a fight, but rather more closely held to.

DAY 129
Love controls its words

When there are many words, sin is unavoidable,
but the one who controls his lips is wise.

Proverbs 10:19

The Bible says that "life and death are in the power of the tongue" (Proverbs 18:21). Few things can go wrong or get worse by waiting and listening. This is not the same as inaction. It does not mean trying your best to ignore your spouse while they rant and rave. Listening, done well, is a real effort. Keeping your thoughts from transforming themselves into spoken words can often take heroic restraint.

But love makes you willing to sit and patiently wait, knowing that reactionary words tossed into a situation like this only escalate the turmoil. Love won't even allow you to form comeback comments in your head, choosing instead to let the process of listening totally occupy your mind. You keep yourself clean of poisons that seek to do further harm to both your own heart and your marriage.

Your spouse may be completely in the wrong by speaking to you this way. Yet love still maintains the power to do the right thing and—even if it doesn't feel like it yet—to carry the day when your spouse is getting carried away.

❧ THIS WEEK'S DARE ❧

Demonstrate love by willingly choosing to give in to an area of disagreement between you and your spouse. Tell them that you are putting his or her preference first.

DAY 130
Love deals with self first

"Why do you look at the speck in your brother's eye
but don't notice the log in your own eye?"

Matthew 7:3

Dealing with your own issues first is always the right thing to do. The human tendency toward blaming others often puts the cart before the horse. Being focused on another person's faults is how insecure people cope with their own inadequacies. Rather than recognizing and admitting their own errors, they turn the searchlight on someone else, and use it to justify what they themselves have done wrong.

Although quite universal, this faultfinding mentality will always keep your marriage on edge by highlighting problems while downplaying personal responsibility. The truth is, just as the church must be the first to take blame for the sorry state of the culture around it (1 Peter 4:17), a loving spouse dissatisfied with their marriage must look first to their own heart to see where the trouble lies. Jesus noted, in fact, that we see more clearly when we have repented of our own faults first. No one makes a mess of their marriage all by themselves, but if healing is to occur, it should always start with "me."

PRAYER

"Jesus, help us to stay clean individually before You, and to worry about our own sin before judging our mate. Give us a sensitive heart to Your voice, and the strength to obey it."

Love controls the volume

For calmness puts great offenses to rest.

Ecclesiastes 10:4

We've all been in public places where a sudden burst of high volume, whether from a cry for help or an argument breaking out, stuns everyone within earshot. But noise and violence in a personal disagreement, though strong enough to get an immediate response, are actually signs of weakness. When an angry wife or husband resorts to raising their voice, they're revealing that what they have to say is too weak to stand on its own. Shouting is a very artificial form of power.

With five hundred wives to manage, Solomon wisely noted that "a gentle answer turns away anger, but a harsh word stirs up wrath" (Proverbs 15:1).

It's possible, however, that your natural personality leans toward being loud, not just when you're upset but even when you're enjoying yourself. Still, the dynamics of marital disputes call for a calm head and a sensible tone of voice. If your opinion or position demands the support of high volume, you are wise to wait until the intensity level of your emotions can come back down to a resting pulse rate. Love doesn't need thunder. Gentle rain does the job.

THIS WEEK'S DARE

Demonstrate love by willingly choosing to give in to an area of disagreement between you and your spouse. Tell them that you are putting his or her preference first.

DAY 132

Love is brave enough to ask

*"Until now you have asked for nothing in My name.
Ask and you will receive, that your joy may be complete."*

John 16:24

No matter how well you plan ahead or strategically save and invest, life is able to throw you some pitches you can't hit. Job loss, medical bills, and other unexpected expenses can weaken you enough financially until you don't see any way to stay afloat. Or perhaps your deficit is not caused by a setback at all, but rather by a bold new vision God has given you for ministry or a new business, and you're needing money in order to get it off the ground.

It is not a contradiction of contentment for you to go to God in prayer, boldly asking in His name for what you lack. He knows your need but will often wait for you to exercise your faith in Him before choosing to supply. He knows the main thing you need to be growing each day is not your financial reserves but your willingness to depend on Him for everything. He promises that when you ask in His name and for His greater purposes, He will supply all you need for each day—whatever is required for you to do His will in your life.

❧ GO DEEPER ❧

Jesus said in Matthew 6:8 that God knows your needs before you ask. If you need money, then follow the prayer guide of Matthew 7:7–11.

DAY 133
Love leads

Above all else, guard your heart, for it is the wellspring of life.

Proverbs 4:23 NIV

One of the most important things you should learn on your Love Dare journey is that you should not just *follow* your heart, you should *lead* it. You don't let your feelings and emotions do the driving. You put them in the back seat and tell them where you're going.

A newlywed takes delight in the one they now call their spouse. Their love is fresh and young, and the hopes for a romantic future linger in their hearts. However, there is something equally as powerful as fresh, new love. It comes from the *decision* to delight in your spouse and to love him or her no matter how long you've been married. In other words, love that *chooses* to love is just as powerful as love that *feels* like loving. In many ways, it's a truer love because it has its eyes wide open.

Love that tries to follow its feelings will inevitably stray from the path. Only when love is leading can you be assured that you're going in the right direction.

∾ QUESTIONS ∾

How might people use the phrase "I need to follow my heart" to justify sin? Does God want us to follow our hearts if it means going against His Word? Proverbs 23:19 (NASB) says to "direct your heart." How would this bring about better decisions?

DAY 134
Love treasures

"Where your treasure is, there your heart will be also."
Matthew 6:21

You get to choose what you treasure. It's not like you're born with certain pre-sets and preferences you're destined to operate from. If you're irritable, it's because you choose to be. If you pick at your mate more than you praise them, it's because you've led your heart into criticism.

So now it's time to lead your heart back out. Learn to delight in your spouse again, then watch your heart actually start enjoying who they are. Discover what many have found out before you—the secret to loving your mate is not in changing them but simply in loving them.

It's a real and radical change of heart. For some, delight may only be a small step away. For others, it may require a giant leap. But if you've been delighted before, you can be delighted again, even if a lot has happened to change your perceptions. The responsibility is yours to relearn what you love about this one you've promised your life to.

THIS WEEK'S DARE

Purposefully neglect an activity you would normally do so you can spend quality time with your spouse. Do something he or she would love to do or a project they'd really like to work on. Just be together.

Love takes pleasure

*He brought me to the banquet hall,
and he looked on me with love.*

Song of Solomon 2:4

It may surprise you to know that the Bible contains many romantic love stories, none more blatant than the Song of Solomon. Listen to the way these two lovers take pleasure in one another—

The woman: "Like an apricot tree among the trees of the forest, so is my love among the young men. I delight to sit in his shade, and his fruit is sweet to my taste" (Song of Solomon 2:3).

The man: "Arise, my darling. Come away, my beautiful one. My dove, in the clefts of the rock, in the crevices of the cliff, let me see your face, let me hear your voice; for your voice is sweet, and your face is lovely" (Song of Solomon 2:13–14).

Too sappy? Not for those who lead their heart to delight in their beloved—even when the new wears off. It's time to remember why you once fell in love. To laugh again, to flirt again, to dream again. Delightfully.

⚜ GO DEEPER ⚜

Read the full account of Song of Solomon 2:1–14 in context. Consider the passionate delight that both lovers allow themselves to feel and express for one another. Could God make your marriage passionate and joyful? Is anything too difficult for Him?

DAY 136
Love delights in diversity

You observe my travels and my rest;
You are aware of all my ways.

Psalm 139:3

Your spouse's personality was one of the chief things that drew you to notice them at first. But in marriage, you've found that some aspects aren't always easy to live with. Sometimes you don't want them to be so quiet and introspective, or so busy and social. By focusing on the negative, you can lose an appreciation for your wife or husband as a uniquely created person.

But love helps you realize that your spouse has been created by God with a distinct temperament. From fingerprints given in the womb to the influence of family and friends, God has formed your mate into one of a kind. They are a trophy of His endless creativity. They have had experiences in life that cause them to react a particular way to challenges. Rather than making it your job to change them until their every move, action, and attitude meets with your approval, love opens the door for you to prize their existing personality. Learn to look for the upside even in those aspects of your spouse that sometimes frustrate you. Be a fan of who they really are.

⋙ THIS WEEK'S DARE ⋘

Purposefully neglect an activity you would normally do so you can spend quality time with your spouse. Do something he or she would love to do or a project they'd really like to work on. Just be together.

DAY 137
Love is appreciative

Esteem them very highly in love because of their work.

1 Thessalonians 5:13

One of the missing ingredients in too many homes and marriages is the simple compliment. But it could make a surprise return if you began spending time noticing all the blessings that are yours because of your mate. Perhaps she's especially good about keeping the finances in order. Perhaps he brings a creativity to your relationship that would make life boring without him. Maybe your spouse often hears from others what a hard worker they are, or what a great singer, or what a tremendously caring friend. But how often do they enjoy knowing that you've noticed it too?

This is not something that needs to be forced or manufactured. When you take real delight in the accomplishments and capabilities of your mate, it will be impossible to keep your appreciation from coming out. More than that, it will enlarge your gratitude to God for giving you this one unique person to love and continually get to know. Revel in the joy of the person your spouse is becoming.

❧ PRAYER ❧

"Lord Jesus, help me value and appreciate my spouse, even during times of frustration. Remind me of the privilege to have a life partner, and to count my blessings. In Your name I pray, amen."

Day 138
Love overlooks flaws

Do not stare at me because I am dark,
for the sun has gazed on me.

Song of Solomon 1:6

We know the Song of Solomon primarily by the descriptive way the two lovers describe their mate's appearance. The man in the poem is obviously taken by her attractiveness. He sees her as beautiful—the "most beautiful of women" (Song of Solomon 1:8). And yet she admits that she has been forced to work hard in the fields, that her skin is dark and weatherworn. It's obviously a sensitive area to her, one she can physically feel when people notice her.

Even the most self-confident among us are attuned to the flaws and blemishes in our bodies. We don't and can't measure up to the image our culture declares most attractive. But love makes us look at our spouse—flaws and all—and see the ideal we most delight in. Whatever their body shape or muscle tone, we choose to declare that this person who is uniquely ours is the perfect shape and size for us. We take whatever sensitivities they have, and we lavish them in true love. We don't just overlook. We delight!

∽ THIS WEEK'S DARE ∼

Purposefully neglect an activity you would normally do so you can spend quality time with your spouse. Do something he or she would love to do or a project they'd really like to work on. Just be together.

DAY 139

Love is our new identity

Be imitators of God, as beloved children;
and walk in love, just as Christ also loved you.

Ephesians 5:1–2 NASB

We are each born with a need to be loved. We may not always admit it or be able to articulate it, but our Creator God certainly knows this to be true. We long to be cared for and thought highly of. We are incapable of surviving on self-confidence alone.

This is why God, knowing how unworthy we are to deserve anything but His banishment and wrath, has chosen through Christ to call us and treat us as "beloved children."

You may or may not have a hard time believing or receiving this fact, this gift. But if you have been rescued from the punishment of your sins by faith in the Lord Jesus, then "look at how great a love the Father has given us" (1 John 3:1)—the same heartfelt fondness that caused Him to say over His One and Only, "You are My beloved Son. I take delight in You!" (Luke 3:22). "Beloved" is not just a name God calls us; it is our new identity in eternity. Even now, we are unconditionally loved by God. That's who we are. Having been loved so lavishly by Him, how can we dare love our mates any less?

⟨⟨ GO DEEPER ⟩⟩

Read Romans 9:21–26 and consider the mercy God has shown us. Those who repent of their sins and place their faith in Jesus become God's "Beloved."

DAY 140
Love is your gift to give

"*I am my beloved's and my beloved is mine.*"
Song of Solomon 6:3 NASB

Obviously, being identified as God's beloved is a choice on His part, not ours. If not for His redemptive plan to seek out lost and straying sinners, we would have no access to His throne of grace, no hope of being loved in an ultimate, eternal way. But our identity in Him has been changed from Enemy to Friend, from Lost to Saved, from Sinner to Beloved.

What an honor, then, to be empowered by God through His gift of marriage to experience at least a taste of what it's like to define our mate's identity. This person is now totally and unconditionally accepted by you and carries a new identity: "my beloved."

This is the high privilege placed upon you by God, the source of all love. It's what makes your spouse so much more than your partner and friend, your companion and helper. You are in the exclusive position of redefining who they are and loving this one in the most complete way love can be expressed on Earth. May he or she never know a day when they don't feel and know themselves to be dearly beloved.

❧ QUESTIONS ❧

Knowing the incredible value God places on your spouse, how much do you think you truly value them in your heart? Would they say you give them high value? Would they say you cherish them?

DAY 141
Love is honorable

I will honor them, and they will not be insignificant.

Jeremiah 30:19

There are several words in our language that have powerful meanings. Whenever these words are used, there is an air of respect associated with them. These words never lose their timeless quality, class, and dignity. One of these is the word *honor*.

To honor someone means to give them respect and high esteem, to treat them as being special and of great worth. When you speak to them, you keep your language clean and understandable. You are courteous and polite. When they speak to you, you take them seriously, giving their words weight and significance. When they ask you to do something, you accommodate them if at all possible, simply out of respect for who they are. It is a call to acknowledge the position or value of someone else.

This is especially true in marriage, where honor is not to be seen as too lofty a goal or too stuffy a concept, but rather a theme for the way you desire to treat your beloved. Always.

⤚ THIS WEEK'S DARE ⤙

Choose a way to show honor and respect to your spouse that is above and beyond your normal routine. Show your mate that he or she is highly esteemed in your eyes.

Day 142
Love esteems others

Pay your obligations to everyone: . . . respect to those you owe respect, and honor to those you owe honor.

Romans 13:7

Would your mate say you honor and respect them? Are they set apart and highly valued in your eyes? Do you regard it as part of your promise to esteem them with dignity and kindness?

Perhaps you don't think they feel such an obligation toward you. And perhaps you're right—they really don't. But that's not the issue with love. Love honors even when it's rejected. Love treats its beloved as special and sacred even when an ungrateful attitude is all you get in return.

Honoring your mate means giving him or her your full attention, not talking to them from behind a newspaper or with one eye on the television. When decisions are being made that affect both of you or your whole family, you give your mate's voice and opinion equal influence in your mind. You honor what they have to say. They matter. And because of the way you treat them, they should know it.

GO DEEPER

Read 1 Peter 2:17 and consider the ramifications of living this out. Who does this passage say that we should honor? Does this also include your spouse? If your spouse knows Christ, then they are also a member of the "brotherhood."

Day 143
Love is holy

*Marriage must be respected by all,
and the marriage bed kept undefiled.*

Hebrews 13:4

When two people marry, each spouse becomes "holy" to the other by way of "holy matrimony." This means no other person is supposed to enjoy this level of commitment and endearment other than you. You share physical intimacy, establish a home, and bear your children with this person. Your heart, your possessions, and your life become bonded with this one individual.

The word *holy* actually forms the basis for honor—the very reason why we give respect and high regard to our husband or wife. To say your mate should be holy to you doesn't mean that he or she is perfect. Holiness means they are set apart for a higher purpose—no longer common or everyday, but special and unique. A person who has become holy to you has a place no one can rival in your heart. He or she is sacred to you, a person to be honored, praised, and defended. That should be a fitting description of your beloved.

THIS WEEK'S DARE

Choose a way to show honor and respect to your spouse that is above and beyond your normal routine. Show your mate that he or she is highly esteemed in your eyes.

Day 144
Love chooses to honor

I will most gladly spend and be spent for you.
If I love you more, am I to be loved less?

2 Corinthians 12:15

It's marvelous when a husband and wife are joined in the purpose of honoring one another, when they're following the biblical command to be "devoted to one another" in love (Romans 12:10 NASB), recognizing their marriage as holy before the Lord. Few experiences in life are more rejuvenating than finding unity together around the higher purposes of God.

But when your attempts at honor go unreciprocated, you are to give honor just the same. That's what love dares to do—to say, "Of all the relationships I have, I will value ours the most. Of all the things I'm willing to sacrifice, I will sacrifice the most for you. With all your failures, sins, mistakes, and faults—past and present—I still choose to love and honor you."

That's how you create an atmosphere for love to be rekindled. That's how you lead your heart to truly love your mate again. That's the beauty of honor.

❧ PRAYER ❧

"Lord, help us to honor one another instead of demeaning or criticizing. May our words be filled with encouragement and grace. Remind us that loving one another pleases You. In Jesus' name, amen."

Day 145
Love meets in the middle

See how the farmer waits for the precious fruit of the earth and is patient with it until it receives the early and the late rains.

James 5:7

It should not surprise you at all to realize that one of you is much more interested in sexual activity than the other. Where one of you could go weeks without even thinking about it, the other could be ready at almost any time. This is one of those balancing acts that grows character within a marriage, but only for those wise enough not to let it divide them completely.

God writes many lessons in patience on our homework pages. He wants us to learn what it means to yield our rights, to wait our turn, to give preference to the other in love. The right course for handling this discrepancy in desire is for one of you to ease off your demands for frequent activity, while the other commits to satisfying you sexually more often than he or she might desire it. Your goal should always be to honor God as well as each other, both of you making the kind of sacrifices that work to tie your hearts even closer together.

THIS WEEK'S DARE

Choose a way to show honor and respect to your spouse that is above and beyond your normal routine. Show your mate that he or she is highly esteemed in your eyes.

DAY 146
Love honors God's holiness

*Holy, holy, holy, Lord God, the Almighty,
who was, who is, and who is coming.*

Revelation 4:8

The reason marriage is holy is because the One who created it sets it apart as holy. It bears the marks of His design. When we are the most dedicated to treating our relationship with the honor it warrants, our interactions as husband and wife share some of the same characteristics of the God we serve.

He is holy, for example, in His truthfulness, never deceiving or operating from motives that are underhanded or less than honest. He is holy in His love, never wavering or threatening to withhold Himself from us, willing to sacrifice greatly in order to make His love known and experienced. He is holy in His power and wisdom, always acting rightly and fairly in His judgments.

Within His gift of marriage, we get to see up close what happens when something is touched by Almighty God. He takes two very sinful and selfish people and unites them in a sacred union. We see Him making our relationship a major part of how we testify to His holy presence among us.

❧ GO DEEPER ☙

Study 1 Peter 1:13–16. Why should our lives be holy according to this passage? How much of our behavior should be impacted? If holiness means to be set apart unto God as pure and special, how might this impact a marriage?

DAY 147

Love is willing to submit

*Submit yourselves for the Lord's sake
to every human institution.*

1 Peter 2:13 NASB

The Bible teaches that God intends for there to be an orderliness to all our relationships. Jesus is seen in Scripture submitting to earthly rulers as well as to His Father, committing Himself "to the One who judges justly" (1 Peter 2:23).

Christians are therefore called to be masters of submission, treating those in authority over us with honor. This guards God's name from being spoken against (1 Timothy 6:1–2).

This teaching also applies to marriage. While both husband and wife are individually accountable to God, He has established an order in families that is intended to bring us into greater unity. The children are to submit to their parents (Ephesians 6:1–3), the wife to her husband (1 Peter 3:1), the husband to Christ (1 Corinthians 11:3), even as Christ submitted to His heavenly Father. When we place ourselves in respectful submission to those over us, it empowers us to lead those under our care with humility and service. Love obeys this command "as to the Lord" (Ephesians 5:22), and He blesses us according to His unchanging Word.

⟶ QUESTIONS ⟵

Do you honor those in authority over you? What are you saying to your spouse and children by the way you respond to authority? What kind of example do you set for those under your supervision?

Love excels in its role

Wives, in the same way be submissive to your husbands so that, if any of them do not believe the word, they may be won over without words by the behavior of their wives.

1 Peter 3:1 NIV

There are two types of power—the power of position and the power of influence. Those who stand in places of position or authority have great responsibility for the ones under their care. They also have greater pressure to perform their duties well, greater consequences for failure, and greater account-ability before God.

In many ways, however, it is the one under authority, with the power of influence, who has a greater impact on decision-making. Like Joseph before Pharaoh (Genesis 41:37–40), like Esther before the king (Esther 4:13–17), like Nehemiah rebuilding the walls (Nehemiah 2:1–5), those who honored another's authority were able to change the course of history.

In a marriage governed by biblical standards, the husband bears the responsibility to lead. But when his wife demonstrates love and respect in submitting to him, she wins the right to influence him and their family more than any other.

❧ THIS WEEK'S DARE ❧

Talk with your spouse about establishing healthy rules of engagement. If they are not ready to do this, then write out your own personal rules to "fight" by. Resolve to abide by them when the next disagreement occurs.

DAY 149
Love endures pressure

Obey your leaders and submit to them, for they keep watch over your souls as those who will give an account.

Hebrews 13:17

The pressure on those in authority is greater than on those who serve under them. Coaches are the first to lose their jobs when their teams aren't playing well. Leaders and supervisors are the ones called into meetings with upper management to report on performance. They are held accountable not only for themselves but also for those under their watch.

The husband, as spiritual leader in the home, feels the pressure of standing before God on behalf of his marriage and family. He understands that others are looking to him for leadership, needing him to take a stand or to cast a vision. It's an uncomfortable, responsible place to be. That's why when important decisions are needing to be made, he is often hesitant to commit to a course of action. Doubts and fears can lead to indecision. The wise wife knows this and prayerfully supports her husband in his role, allowing him to lead "with joy and not with grief, for that would be unprofitable for you" (Hebrews 13:17). Love works together for the benefit of all.

❧ GO DEEPER ❧

Read Hebrews 13:17 in context. Consider the pressure of accountability that leaders must bear before God. Why does this passage exhort us to submit to our leadership? How might God honor you if you honor this passage?

Love seeks counsel

Does a wise man answer with empty counsel or
fill himself with the hot east wind?

Job 15:2

Although the thought of submission in marriage feels unfair to many women, the biblical marriage is not a one-sided dictatorship. Rather, the Bible instructs husbands to seek their wife's counsel, living with them "in an understanding way" (1 Peter 3:7). A husband should know that God has given him his wife to be his "helper" (Genesis 2:18), to offer unique insights he would never think of, to share with him out of the wisdom God has given her.

Often the Lord will speak more clearly to the woman than to the man, or at least she will be the one who's listening more carefully to what He has to say. When Pilate was deliberating on what to do with Jesus, who had been brought before him for judgment, God spoke to Pilate's wife. She said to her husband, "Have nothing to do with that righteous man" (Matthew 27:19). She had the better discernment of the situation.

Husbands are not lords over their castle. A wise husband will know how desperately he needs his wife's input and counsel in order to function and lead.

❧ THIS WEEK'S DARE ❧

Talk with your spouse about establishing healthy rules of engagement. If they are not ready to do this, then write out your own personal rules to "fight" by. Resolve to abide by them when the next disagreement occurs.

DAY 151
Love prays for wisdom

*"Please, Lord, let Your ear be attentive to the prayer
of Your servant and to that of Your servants who
delight to revere Your name."*

Nehemiah 1:11

When a woman shares her opinion with her husband
about a family decision, and he believes her to be right, they
should unite around this shared conclusion. But if after
spending time in prayer, he is convinced the Lord is leading
him to choose an alternate plan, he should follow God's leading, even if unpopular at home.

But this is not the end of the matter, for husbands are certainly capable of getting their spiritual signals crossed and
launching out on misinformation. This is when a godly wife,
rather than berating her man to his face or behind his back,
takes up his case in prayer. She knows that a man's heart "is
like channels of water in the hand of the Lord; He turns it
wherever He wishes" (Proverbs 21:1 NASB). And even if her
husband persists in going against what he should do, the
Lord will use this—even though it's potentially costly in the
short term—to bring about His larger purpose in your family's life. Prayer can do what badgering never can.

PRAYER

*"Lord, give us the wisdom to communicate in a way
that prioritizes love above all else. Help us to value
each other and to bring out the best in one another.
In Jesus' name we pray, amen."*

Day 152

Love respectfully appeals

"My Father! If it is possible, let this cup pass from Me.
Yet not as I will, but as You will."

Matthew 26:39

Contrary to popular opinion, the Bible does not relegate women to a shy, inactive role with no recourse for making their voice heard in marriage. Great figures in biblical history were not afraid to appeal their cause when they felt they were being led astray or given too much weight to carry. Daniel appealed to the Babylonian officials about their forced nutritional program (Daniel 1:8). Esther appealed to the king for the protection of the Jews (Esther 7:3–4). Even Jesus appealed to His Father for another way to bring about His people's salvation.

The same holds true in marriage. Wives who are frustrated with the direction their husbands are taking them are sanctioned by Scripture with the privilege of asking, seeking, and knocking. But this is best done with honor and respect, knowing that at some point the matter must be laid down and entrusted into the hands of God. This is the strength of submission, the power to put Him first in all things, confident that He will not give snakes and stones to those who ask for fish and bread (Matthew 7:7–12).

⟣ THIS WEEK'S DARE ⟢

Talk with your spouse about establishing healthy rules of engagement. If they are not ready to do this, then write out your own personal rules to "fight" by. Resolve to abide by them when the next disagreement occurs.

DAY 153
Love works and waits

Neither the one who plants nor the one who waters is anything, but only God who gives the growth.

1 Corinthians 3:7

You cannot change your spouse. As much as you may want to, you cannot play God, reach into their heart, and mold them into what you want them to be. But that's what many couples spend a large part of their time trying to do. In fact, insanity has been described as doing the same thing over and over and expecting different results.

But here's what you *can* do. You can become a "wise farmer." A farmer cannot make a seed grow into a fruitful crop. He cannot argue, manipulate, or demand it to bear fruit. But he can plant the seed into fertile soil, give it water and nutrients, protect it from weeds, and then turn it over to God. Millions of farmers have made a livelihood from this process over the centuries. They know that not every seed sprouts. But most will grow when planted in proper soil and given what they need. In like manner, a wise husband or wife will create an environment of love for their spouse to grow in, and then daily entrust them to God.

～ GO DEEPER ～

Look at the types of environments that 1 Peter 3:1–9 commands us to create for our mates in marriage. What might God do in our marriages if we obeyed His Word this way?

DAY 154
Love relies on God

"Keep asking, and it will be given to you.
Keep searching, and you will find. Keep knocking,
and the door will be opened to you."

Matthew 7:7

There is no guarantee that anything in this book will change your spouse. That's not what this book is about. It's about you learning and daring to live a life of love.

Like all marriages, yours certainly contains some weeds that need to be pulled, both in yourself and in your spouse. You are tasked with nurturing the soil of your mate's heart, and then depending on God for the results. But you won't be able to do this alone. You will need something more powerful than anything else you have available to you. And that "something more powerful" is—effective prayer.

Begin to pray for exactly what your mate needs. Pray for his heart. Pray for her attitude. Pray for truth to replace lies and forgiveness to replace bitterness. Pray for a genuine breakthrough in your marriage. Pray for love and honor to become the norm. For romance and intimacy to go to a deeper level.

One of the most loving things you can ever do for your spouse is to pray for them.

❧ QUESTIONS ❧

How often do you pray for your spouse? Do you lift them up in prayer regularly? If not, what is standing in your way? For keys on making your prayer life more effective, see pages 368–371 in the appendix.

Love intercedes

*Beloved, I pray that in all respects you may prosper
and be in good health, just as your soul prospers.*

3 John 2 NASB

Prayer really does work. It's a spiritual phenomenon created by an unlimited, powerful God. And because of His willingness to respond to us, prayer yields amazing results.

Do you feel like giving up on your marriage? Jesus said to pray instead of quitting, "to pray always and not become discouraged" (Luke 18:1). Are you stressed out and worried? Prayer can bring peace to your storms, guarding "your hearts and your minds in Christ Jesus" (Philippians 4:7). Do you need a major breakthrough? Prayer can make the difference, just as it did for the apostle Peter in prison (Acts 12:1–17).

God is sovereign. He does things His way. He's not a genie in a lamp that submits to our every wish. But He does love us and desires an intimate relationship with us. This doesn't happen apart from prayer.

There are some key elements that must be in place for prayer to be effective. But suffice it to say that prayer is most effective when coming from a humble heart that is in a right relationship with God and others.

THIS WEEK'S DARE

Begin praying for your spouse's heart. Pray for three specific areas where you desire for God to work in your spouse's life and in your marriage.

Day 156

Love prays strategically

Therefore, confess your sins to one another,
and pray for one another. . . . The effective prayer
of a righteous man can accomplish much.

James 5:16 NASB

You may frequently find yourself upset with each other, unhappy about the way your wife or husband does certain things. But have you ever wondered if there's a more important reason why God gives you such overwhelming insight into your spouse's hidden faults? Do you really think it's for endless nagging? No. It's for effective kneeling.

No one knows better how to pray for your mate than you do. Has your scolding or nagging been working? The answer is no, because that's not what changes a heart. It's time to try talking to God in your prayer closet instead. A husband will find that God can "fix" his wife a lot better than *he* can. A wife will accomplish more through strategic prayer than from all her persuasive efforts.

Turn your complaints into prayers and watch the Master work while you keep your hands clean. If your spouse doesn't have any type of relationship with God, then it's clear what you need to start praying for.

❧ GO DEEPER ❧

The power of prayer is emphasized in James 5:16–20. Read this passage and think about how it might benefit your marriage. Verse 16 explains that if we are right with God and pray diligently, much can be accomplished.

Love prays continually

"*I vow that I will not sin against the* Lord
by ceasing to pray for you."

1 Samuel 12:23

If you know you need to be praying for your spouse, but you're not sure exactly how to do it, let the Bible be your teacher. The apostle Paul, in his New Testament letters, frequently prayed for the people in the early churches. He didn't pray in general terms, mentioning only surface needs. He prayed for their hearts, praying that their love would "keep on growing" (Philippians 1:9). He thanked God for them, praising Him for the privilege of having these individuals in his life.

Follow this example yourself in your marriage. Pray through Matthew 5:3–12, asking that your spouse be "pure in heart," eager to "hunger and thirst for righteousness." Pray that they would have an "undivided" mind and heart to live in perfect freedom before God (Psalm 86:11). Ask that He would give them a "new heart" and a "new spirit," removing their "heart of stone" and giving them one that is ever available to His use (Ezekiel 36:26). Pray for contentment. Pray for rest from worry. Pray for their ability to trust God's goodness in spite of fearful conditions. Never bypass the slightest inclination to be praying for your mate.

❧ THIS WEEK'S DARE ❧

Begin praying for your spouse's heart. Pray for three specific areas where you desire for God to work in your spouse's life and in your marriage.

Day 158
Love prays with abandon

Now to Him who is able to do
above and beyond all that we ask or think . . .

Ephesians 3:20

Jesus has come to give you life "in abundance" (John 10:10) because He is a God who is not limited by earthly boundaries. He can multiply loaves and fishes until there are full baskets left over. There is no limit to what He can do to fulfill His purposes in your life.

So pray with boldness for the success of your marriage. *Ask big!* Be confident that He hears "anything according to His will" (1 John 5:14) and that nothing prevents Him from doing whatever He desires, no matter how impossible it seems to us.

It is God's will that you and your spouse be totally united in mind and purpose, that you grow together in Him, and that you are enabled to serve Him with freedom and generosity. If you know of something God could do to turn these into realities, don't be afraid to ask. Leave it to Him to decide what is best, but never be left to wonder if "you do not have because you do not ask" (James 4:2).

❧ PRAYER ❧

"Jesus, help us to build our faith in You, and to believe in Your provision for every need. We also ask You to give us a vision of what You want to do in our lives for Your glory. In Your name, amen."

Love promotes intimacy

You are my hiding place; You protect me from trouble.

Psalm 32:7

Each of us comes into life with an inborn hunger to be known, loved, and accepted. We want people to know our name, to recognize us when they see us, and to value who we are. The prospect of sharing our home with another person who knows us down to the most intimate detail is part of the deep pleasure of marriage.

Yet this great blessing is also the site of its greatest danger. Someone who knows us this intimately can either love us at depths we never imagined, or can wound us in ways we may never fully recover from. It's both the fire and the fear of marriage.

Are the secrets your spouse knows about you reasons for shame, or are they reasons for drawing you closer? If your spouse were to answer this same question, would they say you make them feel *safe* or *scared*? Marriage is designed by God to be a haven of protection where two people who know each other best, love each other the most. This is the beauty of true intimacy.

✎ THIS WEEK'S DARE ✎

Begin praying for your spouse's heart. Pray for three specific areas where you desire for God to work in your spouse's life and in your marriage.

DAY 160
Love casts out fear

There is no fear in love; instead, perfect love drives out fear.

1 John 4:18

If your home is not considered a place of safety, you will both be tempted to seek it somewhere else. Perhaps you might feel tempted to look to another person, initiating a relationship that either flirts with adultery or actually enters in. You may look for comfort in work or in outside hobbies, something that keeps you around people who respect and accept you more than your spouse seems to.

Be sure you are not putting your *mate* in this position by anything you're doing or saying. They should not feel pressured to be perfect in order to receive your approval. They should not walk on eggshells in the very place where they ought to feel the most comfortable in their bare feet. The atmosphere in your marriage should be one of freedom. Like Adam and Eve in the garden, your closeness should only intensify your intimacy. Being "naked" and "not ashamed" should be able to exist in the same sentence, right in your home (Genesis 2:25).

∾ GO DEEPER ∾

How would your spouse feel around you if you applied Romans 12:10–15 to your marriage? Read this passage and imagine the overwhelming love your mate would feel if you gave them preference, honor, and blessing, if you rejoiced and wept with them.

DAY 161
Love provides safety

*Those parts of the body that we think to be less honorable,
we clothe these with greater honor.*

1 Corinthians 12:23

Marriage has unloaded another person's baggage into your life, and yours into theirs. But this is your opportunity to wrap all this private information in the protective embrace of your love, and promise to be the one who can best help him or her deal with it. Rather than becoming blackmail material to pull out in defense of your anger, these matters should always be treated with sensitivity and gentleness.

Some of these secrets may need correcting. Therefore, you can be an agent of healing and repair—by listening in love and offering support. Some of these secrets just need to be accepted. They are part of this person's make-up and history. In either case, you and you alone wield the power either to reject your spouse because of this, or to welcome them in—warts and all. They will either know they're in a place of safety, or they will recoil into themselves and be lost to you. Loving them well should be your life's work.

QUESTIONS

Does your spouse feel safe with you? If not, what do you need to do to give them a sense of healthy protection? What can you do to build their confidence in your desire to make them feel secure?

DAY 162
Love builds trust

"Even the very hairs of your head are all numbered.
So don't be afraid."

Matthew 10:30–31 NIV

No one knows you better than God does, the One who made you. And yet God, who knows thousands of secrets about every one of us, still loves us at a depth we cannot begin to fathom. How much more should we—as imperfect people—reach out to our spouses with understanding, accepting them for who they are?

This may be an area where you've failed in the past. You may have been very insensitive about some of the touchy areas in your mate's life, not being careful at all about handling their fears and insecurities with compassionate love. If so, don't expect your mate to give you wide-open access to their heart. You must begin to rebuild trust. Jesus Himself is described as One who doesn't barge into people's lives but who stands at the door and knocks (Revelation 3:20).

The reality of intimacy always takes time to develop, especially after being compromised. But your commitment to re-establishing it can happen today—for anyone willing to take the dare.

‿❧ THIS WEEK'S DARE ❧‿

Determine to guard your mate's secrets (unless they are dangerous to them or you) and to pray for them. Talk with your spouse, and resolve to demonstrate love in spite of these issues. Make them feel safe.

Day 163
Love understands

*Happy is a man who finds wisdom
and who acquires understanding.*

Proverbs 3:13

How much do you know about your mate?

When a man is trying to win the heart of a woman, he studies her. He learns her likes, dislikes, habits, and hobbies. But after he wins her heart and marries her, he often stops making the investment to learn about her. This is also true in many cases for women, who start off admiring and building respect for the man they desire to be with. But after marriage, those feelings begin to fade as reality reveals that her "prince" is a flawed and imperfect man.

Although you may love each other very much, there are still many hidden things to discover about your spouse—things that require time, observation, and keen discernment to listen for. And every new piece of understanding you gather about this unique person will help draw you closer together. It can even give you favor in their eyes. "Good understanding produces favor" (Proverbs 13:15 NASB). It leads to a more fulfilling marriage.

❧ GO DEEPER ❧

Read Proverbs 20:5. What deep things might be going on in the heart of your mate? A person who is understanding can draw it out of them. Will you be that person? For a guide on how to glean new insight into your spouse's heart, see page 374 in the appendix.

DAY 164
Love studies

A house is built by wisdom, and it is established
by understanding; by knowledge the rooms are
filled with every precious and beautiful treasure.

Proverbs 24:3–4

Consider the following perspective when it comes to learning all you can about the person you married. If the amount you studied your spouse before marriage was equal to a high school diploma, then you should continue to learn about your mate until you gain a "college degree," then a "master's degree," and ultimately a "doctorate degree." Think of it as a lifelong journey that draws your heart ever closer to your mate.

Do you know his or her greatest hopes and dreams? Do you fully understand how they prefer to give and receive love? Do you know your spouse's greatest fears and why they struggle with them? Do you have a feel for what they plan to accomplish within this calendar year? Could you name one or two things you could do in the next month that would absolutely delight them?

Desire to know this person even better than you do now. Make him or her your chosen field of study, and you will fill your home with the kind of riches only love can provide.

∞ THIS WEEK'S DARE ∞

Determine to guard your mate's secrets (unless they are dangerous to them or you) and to pray for them. Talk with your spouse, and resolve to demonstrate love in spite of these issues. Make them feel safe.

Day 165
Love seeks knowledge

The mind of the discerning acquires knowledge,
and the ear of the wise seeks it.

Proverbs 18:15

Some of the problems you have in relating to your spouse are simply because you don't understand them. These differences—even the ones that seem insignificant—can be the cause of many fights and conflicts in your marriage. That's because, as the Bible says, we tend to revile those things we don't understand (Jude 10).

There are reasons for his or her tastes and preferences. Each nuance in your spouse's character has a back story. Each element of who they are, how they think, and what they're like is couched in a set of guiding principles, which often make sense only to the person who holds them. But it's worth the time it will take to study why they are the way they are.

There is a depth of beauty and meaning inside your wife or husband that will amaze you as you discover more of it. Some of it was woven in the womb by the hands of God, and some of it was forged by time and circumstance. Enter the mystery of your mate with expectation and enthusiasm.

PRAYER

"Lord, help us value one another as You have made us, and to appreciate and love one another as unto You. Work on our hearts, that we would seek to glorify You above all else. In Jesus' name, amen."

DAY 166

Love is insightful

Counsel in a man's heart is deep water;
but a man of understanding draws it up.

Proverbs 20:5

If you miss the level of intimacy you once shared with your spouse, one of the best ways to unlock their heart again is by making a commitment to know them. Study them.

Ask questions. Love initiates conversations. In order to get your mate to open up, they need to know that your desire for understanding them is real and genuine. As they feel safe, you will be given permission to go deeper into their heart.

Listen. The goal of understanding your mate is to hear them, not to tell them what you think. Even if your spouse is not very talkative, love calls you to draw out the "deep water" that dwells within them.

Ask God for discernment. Things like gender differences, family backgrounds, and varied life experiences can cloud your ability to know your mate's heart and motivations. But God is a giver of wisdom. "From His mouth come knowledge and understanding" (Proverbs 2:6). The Lord will show you what you need to know to love your spouse better.

✥ THIS WEEK'S DARE ✥

Determine to guard your mate's secrets (unless they are dangerous to them or you) and to pray for them. Talk with your spouse, and resolve to demonstrate love in spite of these issues. Make them feel safe.

DAY 167
Love recognizes gifting

According to the grace given to us, we have different gifts.

Romans 12:6

God is much too creative to stop at merely saving us, and too generous to keep us from enjoying Him to the greatest extent possible. Therefore, He blesses each of His people with certain gifts that enable us to serve Him, to serve our fellowman, and to complement the work of others in His body, the church.

This means if your spouse is a believer in Christ, he or she has been blessed with distinct abilities in the areas of discernment, service, teaching, exhorting, or any of a range of gifts described in Romans 12. Perhaps your mate is especially gifted at leading and organizing, or at giving or showing mercy. As their spouse, it can be your privilege to help them discover and utilize these strengths. You can play a key role in encouraging them not to let these go to waste but to employ them in their everyday life.

Watch for and affirm what God is doing in your wife or husband's life. First Peter 4:10 says, "As each one has received a special gift, employ it in serving one another as good stewards of the manifold grace of God" (NASB).

GO DEEPER

Read Romans 12:4–8 to see the seven different motivational gifts that God gives to His people. Ask God to help you understand your and your spouse's gifts.

Day 168
Love expresses itself well

I also try to please all people in all things,
not seeking my own profit.

1 Corinthians 10:33

People communicate and receive love in different ways. The more we study our spouse, the more we learn how to love in a way that means the most to them. Just because you feel the most loved by one expression doesn't mean your spouse will. That's because we all recognize love differently.

There are several "languages of love" that speak to each of us in personal and unique ways. And more interesting, they also track quite closely with some of the spiritual gifts.

A husband may feel the most loved when he hears you praise him and thank him verbally. A wife with a spirit of generosity may be impacted by receiving a gift that you purchased for her. Your mate may feel the most loved when you serve their needs around the house, or physically hold and caress their body, or sit and talk for an hour. You can discover how your spouse needs love by observing what they tend to do for you and by listening to what's important to them. As you glean insight into your spouse's gifts, you may also uncover the most loving ways to their heart.

❧ QUESTIONS ❧

How does your spouse feel loved the most? In what ways do they like to demonstrate their love to you? What can you learn from this?

DAY 169
Love understands differences

*You husbands . . . live with your wives in an understanding
way, as with someone weaker, since she is a woman;
and show her honor as a fellow heir of the grace of life.*

1 Peter 3:7 NASB

Men and women have clearly been created by God with
many differences, not just biological. We think and reason
differently. We react and respond differently. We're *supposed*
to be different. But it still adds to the challenge of marriage.

This reality calls for more than being tolerant of each
other. It calls us to thank God for His wisdom in providing
us a counterbalance to our own natural tendencies. Your
husband's adventurous side, for example, has been placed
there partly to help you move beyond your fears and into
new, uncharted experiences. Your wife's delicate side should
soften some of your coarse edges, helping you exercise self-
control and learn the value of gentleness.

Before expecting your mate to see things the same way
you do, realize that God has a purpose in adding this variety
into marriage. Everything it requires of your patience, it
gives back in making you a more whole person.

✐ THIS WEEK'S DARE ✐

Prepare a special dinner at home, just for the two of
you. Focus this time on getting to know your spouse
better, perhaps in areas you've rarely talked about.
Determine to make it an enjoyable evening for you
and your mate.

DAY 170
Love learns from the past

For I am mindful of the sincere faith within you, which first dwelt in your grandmother Lois and your mother Eunice.

2 Timothy 1:5 NASB

No matter how similarly the two of you were raised, you can find many enlightening clues into your spouse's heart by seeking to understand their upbringing and family situation. You do well, if possible, to get to know their parents and siblings, loving them in the Lord but also seeking to discern the dynamics of their relationship.

As you talk with each other about what growing up was like, you may discover why your husband shuts down when you ask even mildly about something he said or did. You may learn why she so quickly bristles whenever anyone seems to be controlling or trying to dominate her. Many of these themes were born amid their upbringing. But loving your spouse for life will mean noticing and being patient with the fact that their past will strongly color their perceptions of you and others.

Love is willing to dig deep to understand everything there is to know about this person, in order to love them better.

❧ GO DEEPER ❧

Read how deception (Genesis 12:13; 26:6–7; 27:19; 29:25) and favoritism (Genesis 22:2; 25:28; 29:30; 37:2–3; 43:34) were two issues repeatedly passed down to each generation from Abraham, to Isaac, to Jacob, and to Joseph. What are your family's tendencies?

DAY 171
Love admires

*How can we thank God for you in return for all
the joy we experience because of you before our God?*

1 Thessalonians 3:9

Whether from raw, natural ability or from hard work and training, your spouse is an expert at something, probably several things. They may be good at building projects, or at handling people, or at calming a tense situation with their peaceful spirit. They may have a knack for organizing work teams, handling finances, or graciously hosting a dinner party. And because you may have known this about them for a long time, it's been easy letting them fill these roles in your marriage without truly noticing how good they are at them. People also tend to have one or more subjects they are very knowledgeable about.

But love never ceases to be amazed at what your spouse can do. It doesn't save its admiration only for those at work, at church, or outside the home who can accomplish noteworthy things. This person you married is exceptional in ways you may have overlooked. Don't just utilize them for what they are able to do. Value it. Honor it. Appreciate it. Admire them for it.

⤜⤙ THIS WEEK'S DARE ⤜⤙

Prepare a special dinner at home, just for the two of you. Focus this time on getting to know your spouse better, perhaps in areas you've rarely talked about. Determine to make it an enjoyable evening for you and your mate.

DAY 172
Love seeks to heal

The Lord is near the brokenhearted;
He saves those crushed in spirit.

Psalm 34:18

Do you know your spouse's greatest pains and fears? Are you aware of the places where their hearts are the most tender and sensitive to the touch? Have you truly stopped to listen lately or to ask what they still experience from a certain loss or betrayal they've undergone? Are there sins from the past they cannot seem to move beyond, cannot seem to receive God's forgiveness in ways that truly release them from feeling guilty and ashamed?

You may at times grow impatient with how long it's taking them to deal with some painful matter of the heart. But your job is not to be the timekeeper. In fact, there may be ways God can use you to speed up their healing process, to encourage them to keep this from stripping away their ability to enjoy life and embrace new opportunities. But your main role as their loving spouse is to be there, tenderly listening to what they say and how they say it. Loving unconditionally means loving even the parts that are messy and complicated. Jesus came to reach out and bring healing to what seemed worthless and lost. As His followers, we can join Him as His agents of redemption.

❧ PRAYER ❧

"Jesus, help us to be Your hands, ears, and voice for one another, and also to be an agent of healing for our spouse. Remind us of our role as spouse and friend, and bless us as we seek to honor You."

Love longs to fulfill

*"If only You would bless me, extend my border,
let Your hand be with me, and keep me from harm,
so that I will not cause any pain."*

1 Chronicles 4:10

Not every dream and desire in your spouse's heart is one they really need to pursue. Nor are you wise to let their wants and wishes be your complete guiding principles, outranking your devotion to God and His will. But whenever love is able to say yes—even if it comes at a great sacrifice or through intensely dedicated work—fulfilling another's dreams is one of the greatest joys of marriage.

Could you name a few of your wife or husband's dreams? What have they wished for since they were a little boy or girl? Where do they hope to take a trip one day? What would make them know that their work had been worthwhile and effective? What do the two of you sometimes imagine when you're sitting around sharing "what ifs"?

Don't become so busy following your own hopes and dreams that you tunnel yourself off from what your spouse longs to see in their life and in your life together. Make their desires as important to you as they are to them.

❧ THIS WEEK'S DARE ❧

Prepare a special dinner at home, just for the two of you. Focus this time on getting to know your spouse better, perhaps in areas you've rarely talked about. Determine to make it an enjoyable evening for you and your mate.

Love communicates

"I am telling you the truth. It is for your benefit that I go away, because if I don't go away the Counselor will not come to you."

John 16:7

Jesus' disciples did not understand all He was saying when He told them of His upcoming death, nor of His resurrection and the coming of the Holy Spirit. But the New Testament shines with examples of how, looking back, they could see what He meant. Imagine how different the early church would have been if Jesus hadn't prepared them for what was coming. He loved them too much to leave them uninformed.

Communication breakdowns occur in marriage for different reasons. But love shoulders the responsibility for sharing important information. It doesn't change lanes on your spouse without turning on its blinker. When changes are coming, when an observation has been made that requires some sort of action, love takes the time to talk it out. It should be a regular practice in your marriage to sit down and talk through what's coming up in the next weeks and months.

Surprise may have its rightful place in marriage, but in the best relationships, plans and opinions are freely discussed.

☙ GO DEEPER ❧

Read Matthew 16:21–22 and see how Jesus began sharing His plans with His disciples. He gave them the information they needed to prepare them for the tragedies that awaited Him in Jerusalem.

Day 175
Love lives with understanding

Good understanding gains favor.

Proverbs 13:15 NKJV

Understanding is powerful. Many communication problems in marriage come from not talking enough, from assuming we've made ourselves clear when we haven't. But often, the reason we don't understand each other well comes from not *listening* enough, not really wanting to hear what the other is saying. Sometimes we hear what we *want* to hear, even if it's not what's being said.

But love is so tuned in to understanding our spouse's heart, it makes us willing to hold back our own thoughts until we can fully grasp theirs. One of the best ways to do this is by the art of reflective listening, repeating back to them the words and feelings they've just shared to make sure we heard them well. This values your spouse while clarifying and uncovering deeper meaning. When your mate hears you say back what they have communicated, they will feel understood, they'll relax, they'll begin trusting you with more of their heart, and then desire to hear more from you. Be careful not to enter any serious conversation with your spouse without first seeking to understand them. Listen for the truth, and reflect it back in love.

❧ QUESTIONS ❧

Would your spouse say you listen to them? Do they feel like you truly value what they say? How could you increase their self-worth in future conversations?

Love is impossible without God

I have loved you with an everlasting love; therefore,
I have continued to extend faithful love to you.

Jeremiah 31:3

You have probably already discovered that you cannot manufacture unconditional love (*agape* love) out of your own heart. It's impossible. It's beyond your capabilities.

You may have demonstrated kindness and unselfishness in some form, and you may have learned to be more thoughtful and considerate than you used to be. But sincerely loving someone unselfishly and unconditionally is another matter altogether.

Like it or not, *agape* love isn't something you can do. It's something only God can do. But because of His great love for you—and His love for your spouse—He chooses to express His love *through* you.

"Love is from God" (1 John 4:7). And only those who have allowed Him into their heart through faith in His Son, Jesus—only those who have received the Spirit of Christ through belief in His death and resurrection—are able to tap into love's real power.

⌒⌒ THIS WEEK'S DARE ⌒⌒

Have you realized your need for God to change your heart and to give you the ability to love? Ask Him to show you where you stand with Him, and for the strength and grace to settle your eternal destination.

Love finds its source in God

For all have sinned and fall short of the glory of God.

Romans 3:23

You may be convinced that with enough hard work and commitment, you can muster up unconditional, long-term, sacrificial love from your own heart. But how many times has your love failed to keep you from lying, lusting, overreacting, thinking evil of this person you've vowed before God to love for the rest of your life? How many times has your love proven incapable of motivating you to forgive, or of bringing about a peaceable end to an ongoing argument?

It's this failure that exposes mankind's sinful condition. It tells us something about ourselves we may not like to hear, but it's true just the same. We have all sinned and fallen short of God's commands and His standard of holiness. We've all demonstrated selfishness, hatred, and pride. And unless something is done to cleanse us of these ungodly attributes, we will stand before God guilty as charged. That's why if you're not right with God, you can't truly love your spouse, because He is the source of true love.

∽∾ GO DEEPER ∽∾

Read the sobering reality of our sinfulness described in Romans 3:10–20. This New Testament passage reflects the Old Testament passages of Psalms 14:1–3 and 53:1–3. It also reflects the way people are today.

DAY 178
Love abides in Christ

*"If you remain in Me and My words remain in you,
ask whatever you want and it will be done for you."*

John 15:7

You can't give what you don't have. You can't call up inner reserves and resources that aren't there to be summoned. You cannot pay out love in greater measure than you own. You can try, but you will fail.

So the hard news is this: love that is able to withstand every pressure is out of your reach, as long as you're only looking within yourself to find it. Love that is able to keep loving when all its reasons and desires have been stripped away is not something we humans are capable of. That's why you need someone who can give you that kind of love.

"Apart from me," Jesus said, "you can do nothing" (John 15:5 NASB). Through a relationship with Him, God has promised to dwell in your heart through faith so that you can "know the love of Christ which surpasses knowledge" (Ephesians 3:19 NASB). When you surrender yourself to Christ, His power can work in you and through you.

✐ THIS WEEK'S DARE ✐

Have you realized your need for God to change your heart and to give you the ability to love? Ask Him to show you where you stand with Him, and for the strength and grace to settle your eternal destination.

Love comes through Christ

I am able to do all things through Him who strengthens me.

Philippians 4:13

Even at our very best, we are not able to live up to God's standards. But He "is able to do far more abundantly beyond all that we ask or think, according to the power that works within us" (Ephesians 3:20 NASB). That's how you are able to love your spouse.

So this unsettling secret—as defeating as it may feel— has a happy ending for those who will stop resisting and receive the love God has for them. We are not failures for being unable to love our spouses as perfectly as we intend to. Weakness is not something to feel embarrassed or ashamed of, but rather something to boast about because it enables Christ's power to reside within us (2 Corinthians 12:9). The love He has "poured out in our hearts through the Holy Spirit" (Romans 5:5) is always available, every time we choose to turn to Him. One thing is for sure: you won't be able to love like Him without Him.

⟶ PRAYER ⟵

"Lord Jesus, give us the faith to depend on You for our needs, for guidance, for comfort, and forgiveness. We praise You for loving and providing for us, and we ask You to keep us safe."

Love is waiting for you

For everyone who calls on the name of the Lord will be saved.

Romans 10:13

Perhaps you've never given your heart to Christ, but you sense Him drawing you. You may be realizing for the first time that you, too, are guilty of breaking God's commands, and your sin will keep you from knowing Him. But Scripture says if you repent by turning away from your sin and turning to God, He is willing to forgive you because of the sacrifice His Son made on the cross. He can free you so you can receive His love and forgiveness. Then you can share it with the one you've been called to love.

Perhaps you're already a believer, but you'd admit that you've walked away from fellowship with God. You're not in the Word or in prayer. You've not been an example of Christ to others like He desires. The truth is, you cannot *live* without Him, and you cannot *love* without Him. But there is no telling what He could do in your marriage if you surrender your heart and put your trust in Him.

∞∾ THIS WEEK'S DARE ∾∞

Have you realized your need for God to change your heart and to give you the ability to love? Ask Him to show you where you stand with Him, and for the strength and grace to settle your eternal destination.

Day 181
Love is the nature of God

The one who does not love does not know God,
because God is love.

1 John 4:8

If you described yourself in one word, what would you say? God, as vast and unsearchable as His many attributes are, describes Himself in this way: "God is love."

This is not an opinion for us to evaluate. Rather, this is a truth with which to navigate life. It is an established given, an unquestioned beginning point.

Love is in Him and pouring through Him at all times. From the beauty of His creation, the gift of His Son, the way He blesses our lives, to the way He's preparing a home for us in heaven, God is overwhelmingly loving toward us. Even when evil surrounds us, He can reveal His love in the midst of it. If we don't frame our thinking around this truth, we are believing a lie—one that will always lead us toward confusion, distrust, and disillusionment.

So don't let anyone deceive you. Put this among the things you absolutely rest in, revealed to you through His inspired Word. God is the ultimate expression of love. It's not just what He does; it's who He is. And He cannot be false to Himself.

⟞ GO DEEPER ⟝

Read 1 John 4:7–12 and 1 John 4:15–17. Consider how the standards and commands concerning our lives are directly tied to who God is. Examine how our character and behavior come from His.

DAY 182
Love is from God

Let us love one another, because love is from God,
and everyone who loves has been born of God and knows God.

1 John 4:7

The only reason love exists in our corrupted world is because God, our Creator, is love. Everything we know about love comes from Him. If He were not love, we would never have experienced it from Him and could never express it to others.

If love were a product, God would be its trademark and copyright. If love were a book, God would be its author. Love's origins are in God. It starts with Him. This is the only reason any of us know anything about love.

He was not forced to create us with the ability to give and receive love. Yet even with the fallen nature of man and our capability for evil, love continues to exist because God exists. He has created love into the fabric of our world so that we can know Him, and so that others can also know Him through the love we put on display. "We love because He first loved us" (1 John 4:19).

⤜⤛ QUESTIONS ⤜⤛

When was the last time you truly thanked God for His love for you? Does your life reflect your gratefulness to Him? Is there evidence by the way you love your spouse?

Love is given by the Spirit

God's love has been poured out in our hearts
through the Holy Spirit who was given to us.

Romans 5:5

The Holy Spirit is an often unknown and misunderstood member of the Trinity. When we surrender our lives to Jesus Christ, God gives us the gift of His Spirit in our hearts. He is an encourager, enabler, and revealer of truth to us. The Bible says that He is also our Source of love from God. If you have realized that God cares for you, this was the work of the Spirit.

He reveals love to us. He even goes so far as to pour it out in our hearts. Love is not something He rations out in small doses or guards closely to keep from running out. He rains it down in buckets, more than we can hold. He is wildly generous with His love.

If you feel as though God's love is insufficient for what you need, you either haven't been listening for Him or haven't been looking around at what He's already done to prove it. When the rain pours, we know it. We hear it. We feel it. The same goes for God's love. He has made it difficult to miss.

∾ THIS WEEK'S DARE ∾

Ask the Lord for a thirst to know Him more, and to make your heart a fertile place for His truth and love.

Love is revealed by the Spirit

*. . . to know the love of Christ which surpasses knowledge,
that you may be filled up to all the fullness of God.*

Ephesians 3:19 NASB

You may feel, based on past experiences or a troubled upbringing, that you have been cheated of knowing love the way it's supposed to be lived and expressed. You may feel incapable of loving, not having it modeled very well.

But the Bible declares that love is something we can know and experience. We have been enabled by the Holy Spirit "to know the love of Christ," a love that "surpasses knowledge." Something beyond our ability to comprehend has been brought within our reach. We can live in the love of God. The closer we walk with Him, the more our faith grows. Then His Spirit opens our eyes more and more to the length, width, height, and depth of God's love toward us.

Love is for all who daily receive it by faith and who desire to pour themselves and their hearts into their marriage. Love may be a mystery, but it is one whose riddles are revealed as we choose to live in the One who is love.

⤳⤳ GO DEEPER ⤳⤳

Read 1 John 4:16. The apostle John explained how he and Jesus' other disciples experienced God's love firsthand. Pray that God will open your eyes to His love and enable you by faith to believe in what He has done.

DAY 185
Love is a fruit of the Spirit

The fruit of the Spirit is love.

Galatians 5:22

We couldn't express love toward others if the Holy Spirit didn't produce it within us. God is the One who manufactures the love we feel and want to share. He is the Creator of every noble quality that comes out of our lives, as seen by the list of healthy "fruit" in Galatians 5:22–23. And at the front of the list, ranking first before all others, is the fruit of love.

This is good news. It means that instead of feeling restricted by our own limitations or ignorance—or even feeling *unloving*—all is not lost. The responsibility of loving is not yours to shoulder alone. You have the Source of all love teaching you and guiding you from within. So confess your sins to God, obey the commands of Christ, and walk in His Spirit. Then He will grow and produce the fresh fruit of His love in your thoughts, speech, attitudes, and actions.

The endless resources of God are being marshaled on your behalf to create love in your heart, the kind your spouse can be cared for and warmed by as you let God's love become yours.

⌘ THIS WEEK'S DARE ⌘

Ask the Lord for a thirst to know Him more, and to make your heart a fertile place for His truth and love.

Love is Jesus Christ

*For while we were still helpless, at the
appointed moment, Christ died for the ungodly.*

Romans 5:6

All the previous days lead to no other conclusion than this: you cannot love on your own. Love is found in Jesus Christ.

Jesus has come "to seek and to save" you (Luke 19:10). Everything you've failed at, every minute you've wasted trying to fix things your own way—all of it can be forgiven and made right by trusting the One who first gave life to you. Maybe you've never done this before. Then today is your day. "Now is the acceptable time; look, now is the day of salvation" (2 Corinthians 6:2).

Maybe you gave your life to Christ years ago, but you've gone back to trying to earn His favor through your good works and best efforts. Let this be the day you rest again in His unconditional love for you so you can truly love your spouse the same way. Or maybe you're saved but you've wandered far from your spiritual roots. Then "repent and turn back, that your sins may be wiped out so that seasons of refreshing may come from the presence of the Lord" (Acts 3:19). There is no greater joy than being at total peace with God.

❧ PRAYER ❧

"Lord, I admit I am a sinner, and I ask You to forgive me and to save me. I place my trust in You as my Lord and Savior, and I ask You to take my life and use it for Your glory. In Your name, amen."

Love points to salvation

He Himself bore our sins in His body on the cross,
so that we might die to sin and live to righteousness;
for by His wounds you were healed.

1 Peter 2:24 NASB

The Bible says we are born in a state of sin from the moment we arrive on Earth. "All of us have become like something unclean, and all our righteous acts are like a polluted garment" (Isaiah 64:6). God does not send innocent people to hell. We deserve it. We simply can't be good enough to live with a pure and holy God.

His great mercy is revealed, however, by making a way for *any* of us to receive redemption from our sins. "God has sent His only begotten Son into the world so that we might live through Him" (1 John 4:9 NASB). "He humbled Himself by becoming obedient to the point of death—even to death on a cross" (Philippians 2:8). By His death, He nullified the very idea that you are unloved. Our faith is not in an abstract theory or in mere, spoken promises. It is sealed in a real event that has forever shaped history. Just look at the cross. He proved His love for you there.

THIS WEEK'S DARE

Ask the Lord for a thirst to know Him more, and to make your heart a fertile place for His truth and love.

DAY 188
Love is a gift

*The wages of sin is death, but the free gift of God
is eternal life in Christ Jesus our Lord.*

Romans 6:23

God's sacrificial love cannot be fully understood. "But God proves His own love for us in that while we were still sinners Christ died for us" (Romans 5:8).

Nor can love like this be earned. "For by grace you are saved through faith, and this is not from yourselves; it is God's gift—not from works, so that no one can boast" (Ephesians 2:8–9).

But this love must be received. "If you confess with your mouth, 'Jesus is Lord,' and believe in your heart that God raised Him from the dead, you will be saved. With the heart one believes, resulting in righteousness, and with the mouth one confesses, resulting in salvation" (Romans 10:9–10).

The love God extends toward us is the ultimate definition of a gift—something totally undeserved. It is unattainable in any other way. His grace freely gives it. May this be the same love you promise—and freely give—to your mate.

⚜ GO DEEPER ⚜

Read John 4:7–14. Notice how Jesus offered the gift of eternal life and forgiveness to someone who desperately needed it but clearly did not deserve it. Jesus told her, "If you knew the gift of God . . . then you would have asked" for it. Do you know it's a gift? Have you humbly asked for it?

DAY 189
Love leads to God

No one has ever seen God. If we love one another,
God remains in us and His love is perfected in us.

1 John 4:12

When you have received God's love as your own, you are free to love in ways you've never been capable of doing before. He is able to perfect in you a love that can only come supernaturally, only as it flows from Him through you. You exchange your best attempts at loving for His flawless, unfailing love—but not until you've experienced it for yourself.

"This is how we know what love is: Jesus Christ laid down his life for us. And we ought to lay down our lives for our brothers" (1 John 3:16 NIV). He was willing to love you even though you didn't deserve it, even when you didn't love Him back. He was able to see all your flaws and imperfections and still choose to love you. His love made the greatest sacrifice to meet your greatest need. As a result, you are able by His grace to walk in the fullness and blessing of His love. Giving and receiving. Now and forever.

QUESTIONS

What are you willing to die for? If someone were to watch you from a distance for a few weeks, what would they say you love the most? Is this what you would want them to see?

189

Love follows Christ

Now this is His command: that we believe in the name of His Son Jesus Christ, and love one another as He commanded us.

1 John 3:23

Once you are established in the love of God, you can now share this same love with your spouse. You can love them even when you're not loved in return. You can see all their flaws and imperfections and still choose to love. And though you can't meet their needs the way God can, you can become His instrument to keep them face-to-face with His care. As a result, he or she can walk in the fullness and blessing of your love. Now and till death.

Commit yourself to loving your wife or husband in this new, unbreakable way. Promise them afresh that your love is not conditional; it is for anything that could possibly happen in life. They are as safe in your love as you are in God's.

True love is found in Christ. And nowhere else. And after you have received His gift of new life by accepting His death in your place and His forgiveness for your sins, you are finally ready to live the dare.

⤳⤳ THIS WEEK'S DARE ⤳⤳

Dare to take God at His Word. Dare to pray, "Lord Jesus, I'm a sinner. But You have shown Your love for me by dying to forgive my sins, and You have proven Your power to save me from death by Your resurrection. Lord, change my heart, and save me by Your grace."

DAY 191
Love gives of itself

"As the Father has loved me, I have also
loved you. Remain in My love."

John 15:9

Jesus came to Earth with a purpose and a plan. Specifically,
He came to do what pleased His Father (John 8:29), always
conforming Himself to God's will. "For whatever the Father
does, the Son also does these things in the same way" (John
5:19). "These things" included teaching the multitudes as
well as His closest followers, healing those who were sick
and in need, serving to the point of exhaustion, and remaining obedient to the point of death. He came to bring the love
of God within reach of His people, "so that the love with
which You loved Me may be in them" (John 17:26 NASB).

Jesus is the perfect example of how love gives of itself, not
counting the risk too great or the cost too high. Whatever is
required by the Father's will is not considered too much to
ask. It's the kind of love that can change a person's heart for
all eternity, and can also equip us with the ability to love our
spouses in the same unselfish manner. Jesus' love enables us
to give as He gives.

⮞ GO DEEPER ⮜

Read John 15:12–17 and consider the depth of
Christ's love expressed in this passage. No greater
love has ever been known. Think about the purpose
and calling that He gives to us along with His great
love.

Day 192

Love is often undeserved

*May the Lord direct your hearts to God's love
and Christ's endurance.*

2 Thessalonians 3:5

Your spouse won't always deserve your love. For many, that's the reason they don't give it. However, you still freely receive love from God, even though you don't deserve it. And that brings a whole new light to your circumstance.

Looking at it this way, you can see a selfish, uncooperative mate through new eyes. For in your relationship with God, your sin reveals that *you* have often been the one being selfish and uncooperative.

The reason you can give undeserved love to your spouse is because God gives undeserved love to you. Repeatedly, enduringly. Love is often expressed the most to those who deserve it the least. Ask Him to fill you with the kind of love only He can provide, then give it to your mate in a way that reflects your gratefulness to God for loving you. That's the beauty of redeeming love. That's the power of faithfulness.

THIS WEEK'S DARE

Dare to take God at His Word. Dare to pray, "Lord Jesus, I'm a sinner. But You have shown Your love for me by dying to forgive my sins, and You have proven Your power to save me from death by Your resurrection. Lord, change my heart, and save me by Your grace."

Love seeks to serve

"For even the Son of Man did not come to be served,
but to serve, and to give His life—a ransom for many."

Mark 10:45

The love of Jesus is so full and complete, He was able to empty Himself of rightful access to His heavenly throne and leave behind His option to use it "for His own advantage" (Philippians 2:6–7). His love is one that totally dies to self in order that His beloved can live.

He made this clear during His years of earthly ministry. "I have come down from heaven, not to do My will, but the will of Him who sent Me" (John 6:38). "I can do nothing on My own . . . because I do not seek My own will" (John 5:30). "My food is to do the will of Him who sent Me and to finish His work" (John 4:34). When He took the basin and towel to wash His disciples' feet, He was giving both them and us an "example" to follow (John 13:15). If we are to love like Jesus, we must remember that life and love is not about *us*, but rather about the one we love. In serving God and others, we experience the fullest life a person can know.

⊙≈⊚ PRAYER ⊙≈⊚

"Lord, help me remember that I am to serve my mate out of love. Remind me that You served us with forgiveness and hope, and that my life should reflect my gratefulness to You by my actions."

DAY 194
Love is bigger than we are

"For the Father Himself loves you, because you have loved Me and have believed that I came from God."

John 16:27

As much as you may want to be everything your wife or husband needs, you can't. Even if you were able to keep yourself in perfect health throughout their whole lifetime and could be with them every minute of every day, they would still be left with unmet needs no person is capable of filling. The only love great enough to satisfy the human heart is Jesus' love.

But thankfully as a believer in Christ, He resides in you by means of His Holy Spirit (Romans 8:9), where you are being "conformed" to His image day by day (Romans 8:29). This means even though your spouse's love tank will always be too big for you to completely top off, Jesus' love can come pouring out of you to touch the heart of your spouse, filling them with His joy, encouragement, and refreshment (Philemon 6–7). This should hardly leave you feeling inadequate as a person. In fact, nothing should please you more than knowing that Christ is alive and working through you to fulfill your mate.

✎ THIS WEEK'S DARE ✎

Dare to take God at His Word. Dare to pray, "Lord Jesus, I'm a sinner. But You have shown Your love for me by dying to forgive my sins, and You have proven Your power to save me from death by Your resurrection. Lord, change my heart, and save me by Your grace."

Love is satisfied in God

The Lord will continually guide you, and satisfy your desire.

Isaiah 58:11 NASB

You have hopefully realized by now that nothing in your toolbox of talents and resources can repair the damage sin has left behind in your heart. Jesus is the only one who can supply what you've been missing. If you've received Him by faith and have turned your life over to Him to manage and lead, then His Holy Spirit is renewing your heart. His wisdom, grace, and power can now be released into everything you do. Including, not the least, your marriage.

But whether this is new territory for you, or if you've been a follower of Jesus for quite a while, now is the time for you to firm up one thing in your mind: you need God every single day. You are as dependent on His grace and mercy right now and every day from now on as you were the hour you first believed. This is not a part-time proposition. That's because He alone can satisfy, even when all else fails you.

⮞⮞ GO DEEPER ⮜⮜

Read Matthew 5:1–3 to see the first words out of Jesus' mouth in His first sermon printed in the Bible. To be "poor in spirit" means to be spiritually bankrupt and totally dependent upon God at all times for all things. God's kingdom and power is at work in someone who lives like this. Will you live this way?

Day 196
Love trusts in God

I have learned to be content in whatever circumstances I am.

Philippians 4:11

You place expectations on your spouse every day. Sometimes they meet them. Sometimes they don't. But never will they be able to totally satisfy all the demands you ask of them. This is partly because some of your demands are unreasonable, and partly because your mate is only human.

God, however, is not. And those who approach Him in utter dependence each day for the real needs in their life are the ones who find out just how dependable He is.

Can your spouse give you an inner peace? No. But God can. Can your spouse enable you to be content no matter what life throws at you? No. But God can. That's why you need to seek Him every day. "Don't worry about anything, but in everything, through prayer and petition with thanksgiving, let your requests be made known to God. And the peace of God, which surpasses every thought, will guard your hearts and your minds in Christ Jesus" (Philippians 4:6–7). Release your spouse from the pressure of meeting needs that only God Himself can satisfy in you.

QUESTIONS

What expectations do you have for your spouse? Are your expectations healthy and honoring to God? Are you looking for satisfaction that God alone reserves the right to fulfill?

Love delights in God

Take delight in the LORD,
and He will give you your heart's desires.

Psalm 37:4

Do you trust God to supply what you need? When we are seeking Him first, loving Him first, and making our relationship with Him top priority, He promises to supply us with what we really need. When He is our true delight, we come to realize the inadequacy of every other substitute.

Jesus once spoke to a woman at a Samaritan well, a woman who had tried getting her needs met through a string of failed relationships. With both her life and her water bucket empty, she had come to this place broken and hardened. But in Christ, she found what He called "living water" (John 4:10)—a supply that wasn't just for quenching temporary thirst. What He offered her was a drink of soul satisfaction that never quits giving and refreshing.

This is what's available to you, no matter who your spouse is or what they've done to you. God is your everyday supply. Of everything you need.

THIS WEEK'S DARE

Be intentional this week about making a time to pray and read your Bible. Try reading a chapter out of Proverbs or the gospels each day. As you do, immerse yourself in the love God has for you.

Love stays supplied by God

*My God will supply all your needs
according to His riches in glory in Christ Jesus.*

Philippians 4:19

There are needs in your life only God can fully satisfy. Though your husband or wife is able to complete some of these requirements now and then, only God is able to do it all. People who claim that their spouse is not making them happy are disappointed because they are drawing from the wrong well. It's time to stop expecting somebody or something to keep you functioning and fulfilled. Only God can do that as you learn to depend on Him. But He wants to do it His way.

Your need for love, peace, and adequacy are real. No one is saying you shouldn't have them. But rather than plugging into things that are unstable at best and will always be subject to change—your health, your money, even the affections and best intentions of your mate—plug into God instead. He's the only One in your life that can *never* change. His faithfulness, truth, and promises to His children will always remain. Look to Him when you feel empty. Never be deceived into thinking that anyone or anything else can supply what you ultimately need.

⤜ GO DEEPER ⤛

Read John 4:7–19. The woman had been with six men and was still unsatisfied. What did Jesus' offer in verse 14? Are you letting God satisfy you, or are you demanding it from your mate?

Love must be received

*We have come to know and to believe the love
that God has for us. God is love, and the
one who remains in love remains in God.*

1 John 4:16

We keep wanting to earn God's love. We keep wanting to think that if we worked a little harder, He would love us more. And when we haven't been living for Him as we should, we have a hard time believing He loves us like He used to.

But God bases His love, not on our performance, but on His own unchanging character. Instead of doing our Christian duties hoping to attract His notice and to soften His anger, we should know that He delights in rescuing us. He doesn't need our good deeds. He has enabled us to obey Him so we can experience the freedom of pure hearts and motives, the joy of serving others, and the authenticity of living with confidence in His care.

This is not a love we've gotten for nothing. Jesus has done the hard work for us—a job we could never have completed. Our job now is to enjoy a love that makes us want to work hard out of gratitude, not out of a desperate desire to win His favor.

∽ THIS WEEK'S DARE ∾

Be intentional this week about making a time to pray and read your Bible. Try reading a chapter out of Proverbs or the gospels each day. As you do, immerse yourself in the love God has for you.

DAY 200
Love must be experienced

Dear friends, if God loved us in this way,
we also must love one another.

1 John 4:11

When people comment on the beauty of trees in autumn or go shopping for flowers, they don't pay much attention to the trunks, stems, and root structures. The appeal of a growing plant is what's happening along its shoots and branches. The colors and textures that give a shrub its distinctive shape are what draw our eye to it. And yet if not for their attachment to a main source of life and nutrients, the blooms would never have a chance to exist or open.

Jesus described our relationship with Him as being like branches attached to a vine. We depend on Him. We can do nothing without Him. If real, authentic, unconditional love is ever to flow from us, we must experience it flowing through us from Christ.

This is why the love we have for our spouses can never reach its full flower until we are abiding in Him through faith. And it will continue to sag and underperform whenever we try to live without staying connected to the Vine. "The one who remains in Me and I in him produces much fruit" (John 15:5).

PRAYER

"Lord, keep us in Your love. Don't let us stray from You, and do what You need to do to keep us from ruining our witness as Your followers. Teach us to guard our hearts. In Jesus' name, amen."

Love is equipped for happiness

*"But seek first the kingdom of God and His righteousness,
and all these things will be provided for you."*

Matthew 6:33

Life comes with many hardships and challenges. And the person inclined to be more focused on his lack than his supply will find reasons for complaining, sure that God owes him something. In reality, however, "His divine power has given us everything required for life and godliness" (2 Peter 1:3). Even in the toughest of circumstances, the person who truly longs to love more completely will find that God has given—and continues to give—all that is needed to make life a joyful experience.

King David, after being told by God that he would not be the one to build the first temple, could have given himself over to self-pity. Instead, he sat down and said, "Who am I, Lord God?" (2 Samuel 7:18). Even in disappointment, he was convinced "there is no one like You" (2 Samuel 7:22). From food and clothes, to forgiveness of sins, to His Word that speaks to us, and His church that surrounds us, even to our hope of coming glory with Him, He has supplied all we need and more. The love we share can flow out of our sheer abundance.

∾ THIS WEEK'S DARE ∾

Be intentional this week about making a time to pray and read your Bible. Try reading a chapter out of Proverbs or the gospels each day. As you do, immerse yourself in the love God has for you.

DAY 202
Love finds refuge in God

God, Your faithful love is so valuable that people
take refuge in the shadow of Your wings.

Psalm 36:7

Too many people live on the edges of Christ's love. Having received Him and His forgiveness by faith, they continue to flirt with the idea that something better is available somewhere else. When they're tired, frustrated, discouraged, or angry, they turn to old pleasures that used to keep them company, forgetting that running from these things is how they always end up back in Jesus' arms.

How much better (and less time-consuming) to find our satisfaction in God from the beginning. Instead of chasing our various escapes in hopes of finding love, joy, and peace, why not go directly to their source, the only place they can be found? A life given over to Christ yields the fruit of "patience, kindness, goodness, faith, gentleness, and self-control" (Galatians 5:22–23). How many pleasures of this world can give us that?

The person you really want to be, and the love you really want to know, is found by seeking refuge in God and being satisfied by His plenty. Then you are free to really live and love.

➤ QUESTIONS ➤

Do you find your satisfaction in God first, or in the things of the world? Do you yearn for more of God than anything else? What is He incapable of giving you that you need?

Love finds fullness in God

In Your presence is fullness of joy;
in Your right hand there are pleasures forever.

Psalm 16:11 NASB

One of God's purposes in creation is to reveal His character through the things He has made (Romans 1:20). So when a songbird gathers nesting material from your yard, you are also seeing the care and goodness of God on visible display. "All eyes look to You," the Scripture says, "You open Your hand and satisfy the desire of every living thing" (Psalm 145:15–16). But how much greater this applies to us, for we are "worth more than many sparrows!" (Luke 12:7).

Every day gives us fresh examples of how God meets all our needs. But beyond necessities, God knows how to satisfy our deepest longings better than we do. When the psalmist discovered this, he noted that God's "love is better than life" (Psalm 63:3). He went on to say, "You satisfy me with rich food; my mouth will praise You with joyful lips" (Psalm 63:5). Underneath the disappointments around you, the ground of your life is covered with blessings. In marriage and in life, God satisfies our mouths with good things and invites us to taste and see that He Himself is good.

❧ GO DEEPER ❧

Read Psalm 34. Enjoy this testimony of God's ability to do all things. What does He do to our fears and troubles? What needs does He not meet? What do we lack if we fear Him, if we show Him reverence and awe?

DAY 204
Love is faithful

For Your faithful love is before my eyes, and I live by Your truth.

Psalm 26:3

As Christians, love is the basis of our whole identity. It is the root and ground of our existence, something we are to be "firmly established" in (Ephesians 3:17). It is a quality we are to "abound" in more and more, filled to "overflow" (1 Thessalonians 3:12), always getting better at it, becoming increasingly defined by our love. Then we will not become "useless or unfruitful in the knowledge of our Lord Jesus Christ" (2 Peter 1:8), and the love we receive from Him will replenish us to love our spouses at greater depths of blessing.

Love is what we were created to share. It is a lifestyle of love that makes the gospel message even more attractive to those who are far away from God. Learning to love and expressing our love should be a lifelong ambition. In fact, we are to show love even when we are rejected. As difficult as that may sound, it is something we must commit to do, just as Christ did for us. Our "love for one another" is how people distinguish us as Christ's disciples (John 13:35).

◁◦◦ THIS WEEK'S DARE ◦◦▷

Love is a choice, not a feeling. Choose to be committed to love even if your spouse has lost their interest in receiving it. Say to them, "I love you. Period. I choose to love you even if you don't love me in return."

Love is a picture of God

"I will take you to be My wife in faithfulness,
and you will know the LORD."

Hosea 2:20

The account of the prophet Hosea is one of the most remarkable in the Bible. Against all logic and propriety, God instructed him to marry a prostitute. He wanted Hosea's marriage to show what heaven's unconditional love toward us looks like.

Hosea's wife Gomer was unfaithful. So Hosea was left to deal with abandonment and a broken heart. He had loved her, but she had spurned his love. She had been disloyal and adulterous, rejecting him for the so-called love of total strangers.

Time passed, and God spoke to Hosea again. He told him to go and reaffirm his love for this woman who had been repeatedly unfaithful and to buy her off the slave block. Yes, she had treated Hosea's love with contempt, but he welcomed her back into his life, expressing an unconditional love. This is a true story, but God used it as a dramatic picture of His faithful love for us.

GO DEEPER

God's heart for marriage, even in cases of adultery, is that we find reconciliation. When we are unfaithful to God, it is like committing spiritual adultery. Yet He calls us to Himself and seeks to restore our walk with Him. Read Hosea 6:1–3 and let it encourage you to draw closer to the Lord. Look at the blessings that follow one who does.

Love is dedicated

In Him, we have redemption through His blood, the forgiveness of our trespasses, according to the riches of His grace.

Ephesians 1:7

God's love is dedicated no matter what. He showers His favor on us without measure, though in return we often don't pay attention. At times we have acted shamefully and deemed His love an intrusion, as if it's keeping us from what we really want. We have rejected Him in many ways—even after receiving His gift of eternal salvation—and yet He still loves us. He stays dedicated.

The ancient Israelites are a prime example of this experience. God heard their cries in bondage and liberated them with His mighty power. But they longed to go back to slavery in Egypt at the first sign of difficulty. Yet God repeatedly forgave them and restored them on their road to the Promised Land.

Even so, His righteous love doesn't keep Him from calling us to account for our mistreatment of Him. We pay more of a price for our rejection than we often realize. And yet He still chooses to respond to us with grace and mercy. In Him we have the model of what rejected love does. It remains dedicated.

THIS WEEK'S DARE

Love is a choice, not a feeling. Choose to be committed to love even if your spouse has lost their interest in receiving it. Say to them, "I love you. Period. I choose to love you even if you don't love me in return."

Love chooses to bless

*"Love your enemies, do good to those who hate you,
bless those who curse you, pray for those who mistreat you."*

Luke 6:27–28

From the vantage point of the wedding altar, you would never have dreamed that the person you married might become to you a kind of "enemy," one you would need to love as an act of almost total sacrifice. And yet far too often in marriage, the relationship does indeed dwindle down to that level.

For many, this is the beginning of the end. Some respond by rapidly moving toward a tragic divorce. Others, more protective of their reputation than even their own happiness, decide to keep the charade going. But they have no intention of liking it—much less of loving each other again.

This is not the model for the follower of Christ. If love is to be like His, we must love even when its overtures are returned unwanted. We must bless regardless of the response. And for your love to be like that, it must be His love to begin with.

⮞⮞ PRAYER ⮜⮜

"Lord, help us to love one another with Your love. Teach us to forgive quickly and not to be easily offended. Remind us to keep no record of wrongs. In Your name we pray, amen."

DAY 208

Love counteracts anger

Man's anger does not accomplish God's righteousness.

James 1:20

Anger can be poisonous. Think of all the bad things it can do. It brings words to our lips that cause harm to others. It steals love, joy, and peace out of any environment it penetrates. It leads us to violence and destruction. It sets us up to make foolish, rash decisions based on little more than raw emotion. It stirs up strife and division, separating people who once walked in close fellowship—even those who once knelt at an altar together and promised their love for life.

Jesus said that anger is all it takes to be guilty of the same offense as murder (Matthew 5:21–22), because anger is the starting point for all kinds of wicked behaviors. But love is where it stops. Love steps into this high-risk, hot-tempered atmosphere and offers protection against the deadly results of anger. When you make the choice to love, it's like hunting down destructive anger, locking it in a room, and throwing away the key.

❧ THIS WEEK'S DARE ❧

Love is a choice, not a feeling. Choose to be committed to love even if your spouse has lost their interest in receiving it. Say to them, "I love you. Period. I choose to love you even if you don't love me in return."

Love walks through the valley

May my prayer reach Your presence; listen to my cry.

Psalm 88:2

Most marriages will encounter times when a spouse struggles with depression. And yet when you are the one going through it, life can feel like a dark, lonely place.

While depression can easily lead to sinful thoughts and behaviors, it is not a sin to feel low and discouraged, even to be immobilized by it. Godly people in the Bible went through down cycles after big, emotional events, such as Elijah in 1 Kings 19:1–4. That's important to remember, especially if you're the one trying desperately to minister to your suffering spouse. This is not a time to blame and criticize, or to question why they can't merely snap out of it.

But because depression is fertile soil where lies can grow, try reading the Psalms and other Scriptures aloud to your mate. Counteract their sense of gloom and unworthiness with the bright and living truths of God. If they won't listen, read these verses as prayers on their behalf. But never give up, and beg God to take any anger toward them out of your heart. You are here to love them through it.

QUESTIONS

Do you seek the Lord when life seems unfair and frustrating? Who better understands your situation and experience? Can you not trust Him with your struggles?

Love won't quit

"I hate divorce," says the LORD God of Israel. . . .
So guard yourself in your spirit, and do not break faith.

Malachi 2:16 NIV

God hates divorce. And those who know its stabbing pain firsthand, and who have cried out to Him for mercy and forgiveness, understand why. The evil of dealing "treacherously" with your wife or husband (Malachi 2:14), or having been left behind by a spouse who would not choose to love you, leaves a gaping hole in your life. Those guilty of causing or contributing to a divorce have felt the distance God allows to grow between us and Him when we reject His best for our own demands.

If your marriage is in crisis right now, and divorce remains a possibility in the back of your mind, remember that Jesus said divorce only exists today because of our hard hearts—"It was not like that from the beginning" (Matthew 19:8). Even though it is biblically permitted after adultery, should we not hate what He hates? God's heart is for reconciliation and resurrection. Even after an affair—as heroic and impossible as it seems—God can make your marriage a trophy of forgiveness and grace. His love is a conquering, victorious love. It never quits. Ours is held to the same standard.

⤙ GO DEEPER ⤘

Read God's thoughts on divorce and its consequences in Malachi 2:13–16. How does divorce affect our worship, lives, and children? How is it treacherous? Do your conclusions line up with God's?

Love takes five

"The LORD will fight for you; you must be quiet."

Exodus 14:14

Sometimes the tension in our homes can become nearly impossible to defuse. Too much has been said already, and any more words—even words of apology and promise—are not going to smooth things over. Not right now. That's when love does the bravest thing, and backs off for a while.

No, a few hours of quiet aren't likely to fix everything that's wrong, but it will at least lower the heat and give time for reflection. It will keep you from turning your thoughts into careless words that your spouse will have a hard time forgetting.

It's easy to despair for the future of your marriage when things are stirred up into a shouting match. When you're both entrenched on the battlefield, it's hard to imagine that you and your mate have much hope of finding common ground, now or ever. But call a time out. Go to your corners. Announce a cease-fire. Suspend hostilities. You may find that when you come together again at a lower heat index, you're able to see a glimmer of hope emerge.

◈ THIS WEEK'S DARE ◈

Talk with your spouse about honoring each other, even in times of frustration or disagreements. Commit to seek godly counsel for any critical issue that is causing ongoing friction in your marriage.

Love takes charge

Do you not know that the saints will judge the world?
And if the world is judged by you, are you unworthy
to judge the smallest cases?

1 Corinthians 6:2

Paul established the church in the Greek city of Corinth. Then he labored with them for many years through his letters, straining to help them break their ties to the culture's way of thinking, convincing them to see things God's way.

When they would get into heated disagreements, they would do what Corinthians always did—run to the courts for a judgment on the matter. It's not much unlike the way many Christians act today, running to a divorce attorney when their marriages seem unworkable, irreconcilable.

But if anyone has less reason to turn their lives over to a secular divorce proceeding, it is the believer in Christ, who has God's Spirit, and who the Bible says will one day have a hand in judging the world. Surely we ought to *at least* embrace this role when it comes to our own marriages. Make a commitment ahead of time that divorce will never be an option on the table. Remember who you are and work through this. Do whatever it takes to do things God's way.

GO DEEPER

Read Jesus' words about marriage, divorce, and adultery found in Matthew 19:3–9. Verse 5 is the theology of marriage. Verse 6 is Christ's conclusion. Why do people pursue divorce according to verse 8?

Love learns from the wise

Can it be that there is not one wise person among you who will be able to arbitrate between his brothers?

1 Corinthians 6:5

One of the keys to divorce prevention is keeping yourselves from ever entering the legal machine to start with, which runs these matters through the courts like cattle in a butchery. If you cannot settle your disputes on your own, make your next stop—not the lawyer's office—but a wise and godly family member or friend that you both trust. Surely among all the people you know, there are some godly men and women who will hear you out, seek His will, and offer sound advice. And if not, find some.

It may feel much less threatening or embarrassing to take your problems to someone who doesn't have such a history with you. But if you are having serious struggles in your relationship, God will put loving, perceptive people into your life to walk with you through this. Rather than working to bring something as sacred as your marriage to a point of quick closure, they will be there to offer long-term solutions from the Word of God that will help you preserve the treasure God has entrusted to you.

⟶ THIS WEEK'S DARE ⟵

Talk with your spouse about honoring each other, even in times of frustration or disagreements. Commit to seek godly counsel for any critical issue that is causing ongoing friction in your marriage.

Day 214
Love is hard to offend

Why not rather put up with injustice?
Why not rather be cheated?

1 Corinthians 6:7

In most marital difficulties, there's usually enough blame to go around. But we can plant ourselves so deeply on our side of an argument that we're not willing to do much in the way of compromise. To give in is to accept defeat. And we've got too much pride invested to back down now.

Obviously, some situations can escalate to a level of fear and violence that warrant removing yourself from danger. But in most cases, what's the worst that could happen if you decided to be the first one to give in? What if instead of trying to win your point, you just took one for the team? *Being* wronged is better than *doing* wrong. What do you think your spouse would do if you shouldered your part of the blame, forgave them for theirs, and agreed to start again.

Dead people are hard to offend, and so are those who die to self, those who make a habit of overlooking their mate's mistakes and letting God take responsibility for being their defender. Deny your right to hold your spouse in judgment. Lay down your arms, and wait on the Lord.

❧ PRAYER ❧

"Jesus, help us to love and forgive, no matter the issue. Convict us when needed, and give us tender hearts toward You. Build in us a faithful commitment to You and to each other. In Your name, amen."

DAY 215
Love always protects

You hide them in the protection of Your presence;
You conceal them in a shelter from the schemes of men.

Psalm 31:20

Marriage is made up of many things, including joys, sorrows, successes, and failures. But when you think about what you want marriage to be like, the furthest thing from your mind is a battleground. However, there are some battles you should be more than willing to fight. These are battles that pertain to protecting your spouse.

Unfortunately, your marriage has enemies out there. They come in different forms and use different strategies, but nonetheless, they will aid in destroying your relationship unless you know how to ward them off. Some are clever and seem attractive, only to undermine your love and appreciation for one another. Others try to lure your heart away from your spouse by feeding you unhealthy fantasies and unrealistic comparisons. It's a battle you must wage to protect your marriage. That's when love puts on armor and picks up a sword to defend its own.

◈ THIS WEEK'S DARE ◈

Talk with your spouse about honoring each other, even in times of frustration or disagreements. Commit to seek godly counsel for any critical issue that is causing ongoing friction in your marriage.

Day 216
Love monitors influences

That He may guard the paths of justice and protect the way of His loyal followers. Then you will understand righteousness, justice, and integrity—every good path.

Proverbs 2:8–9

Your mate and your marriage need your constant protection. There are many things from which to guard your relationship. One of those is harmful influences.

Are you allowing certain habits to poison your home? The internet and your television can be productive and enjoyable additions to your life, but they can also bring in destructive content and drain away precious hours from your marriage and family. The same thing goes for work schedules that keep you separated from each other for unhealthy amounts of time. But you can't protect your home when you're rarely there, nor when you're relationally disconnected. You have to fight to keep the balance right. And no level of business success is worth failing at home. As the steward of your marital relationship, you must make sure your values are guided by a biblical worldview. Any influence that tarnishes or weakens this perspective must be prevented.

✑ GO DEEPER ✑

Read 1 Corinthians 5:6–8. Paul is challenging this church to remove some ungodly influences from their lives. He uses the term "leaven" to explain how a little wickedness can contaminate other areas. Is there something that is weakening your marriage or your walk with God?

DAY 217
Love is a true friend

A righteous man is careful in dealing with his neighbor,
but the ways of wicked men lead them astray.

Proverbs 12:26

Not everyone has the material to be a good friend. Not every man you hunt and fish with speaks wisely when it comes to matters of marriage. Not every woman in your lunch group has a good perspective on commitment and priorities. In fact, anyone who undermines your marriage does not deserve to be given the title of "friend." And certainly, you must be on guard at all times from allowing opposite-sex relationships at work, the gym, or even the church to draw you emotionally away from the one you've already given your heart to.

Love seeks healthy, God-honoring relationships. Be grateful for those friendships or acquaintances that add value to your marriage. Be wary of those that do not. Having a true friend is a rare blessing, but a spouse who is also a true friend is priceless. Being a friend to your mate will deepen your relationship and sweeten your fellowship.

∾ QUESTIONS ∾

Do you invest as much time into the friendship you share with your mate as you do for other friends? Who would your spouse say is most important to you?

Love covers fault

Whoever conceals an offense promotes love,
but whoever gossips about it separates friends.

Proverbs 17:9

Everyone deals with some level of inferiority and weakness. And because marriage has a way of exposing it all to you and your mate, you need to protect your wife or husband's vulnerability by never speaking negatively about them in public. Their secrets are your secrets (unless, of course, these involve destructive behavior that's putting you, your children, or themselves in grave danger). Generally speaking, love hides the fault of others. It covers their shame.

This is not to say that it is irresponsible, or that it avoids dealing with crucial issues. Rather, love understands that the process of maturing takes time, knowledge, and experience. And sometimes this experience comes from weaknesses or failures. But love will not announce those failures to the world. Instead it provides a shelter from shame in which to get honest, learn together, and grow.

❧ THIS WEEK'S DARE ❧

Remove anything that is hindering your relationship, any addiction or influence that's stealing your affections and turning your heart away from your spouse.

Love guards the heart

Above all else, guard your heart, for it is the wellspring of life.

Proverbs 4:23 NIV

Watch out for parasites! A *parasite* is anything that latches onto you or your partner and sucks the life out of your marriage. They're usually in the form of addictions, like gambling, drugs, or pornography. They promise pleasure but grow like a disease and consume more and more of your thoughts, time, and money. They steal away your loyalty and heart from those you love. Marriages rarely survive if parasites are present. If you love your spouse, you must destroy any addiction that has your heart. If you don't, it will destroy you.

The Bible speaks plainly about this protective role, often using the analogy of a shepherd. God warned, "My flock has become prey and food for every wild animal." How so? For "they lack a shepherd" (Ezekiel 34:8).

You must pay attention to your marriage, guarding it from anything that tries to feed off the time and attention that only belongs to God and your spouse.

❧ GO DEEPER ❧

Read John 8:31–37. Jesus uses the idea of slavery to describe what sin does to our lives. How does He say that we can be set free from its bondage according to verses 31, 32, and 36? Are you enslaved to anything?

Love defends the heart

*"If the homeowner had known what time the thief was coming,
he would have stayed alert and not let his house be broken into."*

Matthew 24:43

You are responsible for the safety of your marriage relationship.

Wives—you have a role as protector in your marriage. You must guard your heart from being led away through novels, magazines, and other forms of entertainment that blur your perception of reality and put unfair expectations on your husband. Instead, you must do your part in helping him feel strong, while also avoiding talk-show thinking that can lure your attention away from your family. "Every wise woman builds her house, but a foolish one tears it down with her own hands" (Proverbs 14:1).

Husbands—you are the head of your home. You are the one responsible before God for guarding the gate and standing your ground against anything that would threaten your wife or marriage. This is no small assignment. It requires a heart of courage and a head for preemptive action. This role is yours. Take it seriously.

ᴥ THIS WEEK'S DARE ᴥ

Remove anything that is hindering your relationship, any addiction or influence that's stealing your affections and turning your heart away from your spouse.

Day 221
Love fights addictions

"You will know the truth, and the truth will set you free."

John 8:32

Jesus said the above words while encouraging His followers to realize that "everyone who commits sin is a slave of sin" (John 8:34). You can struggle long and hard with your most daunting temptations. You can give them permission to defeat and enslave you. But be confident of this—Christ can free you of them all. He can grow in you the courage and self-control to deny your flesh for the purpose of glorifying Him.

But you must embrace "the truth." Any addiction, whether it be for drugs or comic books, is destructive to your time, your money, and your heart. It's anything you rotate your life around, planning how to accommodate its demands, which have now become your desires. They promise to fill a need, but all they actually do is take. And given enough time and room to expand, they can grow to the point of stealing your marriage.

If you have any kind of addiction, then get honest and get help. Open up with someone you can trust to keep you accountable. Christ can win this battle in you and help you win back the heart and soul of your marriage.

❧ PRAYER ❧

"Father God, don't let any addiction capture our hearts or lives. Do whatever it takes to free us, and heal us from this poison. Give us Your view of these enemies, and help us to act wisely in our healing."

DAY 222
Love doesn't gamble

A greedy man is in a hurry for wealth;
he doesn't know that poverty will come to him.

Proverbs 28:22

Gambling is based upon greed, poor stewardship, and irresponsibility. It's also mathematically designed against you. It may yield a periodic payout, but you will lose in the end. Even if you are the one in a million to come out ahead, it will steal from you things money can't buy back. Winning takes money from others that you did not earn—money they don't want you to take.

Money is not to be a love or primary concern for the believer, knowing how often it makes wings for itself and flies away (Proverbs 23:5). God calls you to work hard using the abilities He's given you and to contribute to the well-being of your family and society. The wealth He entrusts to you is not meant to be treated lightly and squandered, but rather to fulfill your responsibilities and help others. Stewarding your money well is an honor to God.

The Bible says we are "receiving a kingdom that cannot be shaken" (Hebrews 12:28). We get a foretaste of it on Earth when we put our trust in Him, not in risking our families to get rich.

✐➵ THIS WEEK'S DARE ☙✐

Remove anything that is hindering your relationship, any addiction or influence that's stealing your affections and turning your heart away from your spouse.

DAY 223
Love is good to your body

Wine is a mocker, beer is a brawler,
and whoever staggers because of them is not wise.

Proverbs 20:1

Whether it be drugs and alcohol, overeating or starving yourself, any number of addictions can work against your overall health. But love recognizes these things for what they are—thieves intent on taking not only years from your life, but also destroying your ability to invest well in your relationships. When your heart is given over to overindulgence, each day becomes all about you and your so-called needs, with little energy left in reserve to contribute to God and your marriage.

Part of dealing with the truth means realizing this: the hunger that leads you to abuse alcohol, food, or prescription medication is actually a hunger for love, joy, and peace. And though these pleasure providers are good at faking temporary fulfillment, they actually get their strength by failing to satisfy. If you hope to achieve victory in these weakened areas, it will begin by understanding that true love, joy, and peace are exclusive by-products of living in honest fellowship with God. He knows your real need. He has your health at heart, and He is able to deliver you.

QUESTIONS

What has a hold on you that is not honoring to the Lord and your spouse? What are you doing to deal with this addiction? What is your highest priority?

DAY 224
Love doesn't accept substitutes

*Why, my son, would you be infatuated
with a forbidden woman?*

Proverbs 5:20

Pornography is primarily an issue for men. It creates unrealistic expectations and dissatisfaction in your marriage, leading to its destruction. And those who have the greatest struggle with it hate that they feel too weak to stop. The lust that fuels it is like an "arrow that flies by day" and a "plague that stalks in darkness" (Psalm 91:5–6). Though it embarrasses them to say it, the temptation never seems far away.

But pornography is proof that we don't conquer sin by stamping out desire. We conquer sin by letting God *change* our desires. We let Him give us such a deep hunger to honor Him and to bless our spouses, we refuse to allow a passing rush of sexual fantasy to reroute us from the place we're *choosing* to lead our hearts.

Ask Him to keep the lies of lust so thoroughly exposed in your mind that you will label pornography as sexual cocaine—highly addictive, dangerous, and ultimately deadly. Every glance is a slap in the face to the wife God has given you. Turn your heart toward her again, and away from *anything* that threatens your love for her.

GO DEEPER

Read Proverbs 5. Solomon counsels us to see the fuller consequences of immorality. Follow his contrast of living by lust or following God's loving plan. Begin applying verses 15–19.

Day 225
Love fights to stay pure

What a desire to clear yourselves, what indignation, what fear,
what deep longing, what zeal, what justice! In every way
you have commended yourselves to be pure in this matter.

2 Corinthians 7:11

Make up your mind that you and pornography have seen the last of each other—not just print and online images, but every billboard, TV show, and movie trailer that fires your imagination to have sexual feelings for another woman other than your wife. It is over.

The Bible is clear when it says, "Flee from sexual immorality" (1 Corinthians 6:18). That's because halfhearted resistance only makes the temptation stronger. But more than just shielding your eyes and running away, keep heading in the direction of God's Word and good accountability. More than just filtering your internet access, memorize verses that can trigger your confidence in God's ability to rescue, such as Job 31:1; 2 Timothy 2:22; 1 Corinthians 10:13; and 1 John 2:15–17. Turn times of temptation into immediate prayers for God's protection. Be reminded how exhilarating it feels to experience His "faithful love in the morning" and His "faithfulness at night" (Psalm 92:2). This is serious. No going back. Not now. Not ever.

THIS WEEK'S DARE

End it. Now. Identify every object of lust in your life and remove it. It must be killed and destroyed—today—and replaced with the sure promises of God, and with a heart filled with His perfect love.

Love is unhindered

*You were running well. Who prevented you
from obeying the truth?*

Galatians 5:7

Love is strong. It can withstand any challenge life hurls against it. But we make its job much harder when we allow our minds to be saturated by philosophies and opinions that run counter to God's clear teaching on marital love and faithfulness.

You may have friends that go back many years, but who don't share your trust in God and often encourage you toward activities and time commitments that tax your marriage. The Bible says you are to "come out from among them and be separate" (2 Corinthians 6:17), not allowing their influence to keep up the tension between you and your promises. Limit your contact with people who work against God's will for your life.

The same goes for pagan, unwholesome advice that comes from TV talk shows, or even the subtle worldviews that pervade popular film and fiction. Let the law of the Lord be your delight. Meditate on it "day and night" (Psalm 1:2). That's how a person learns to love, unhindered.

⌘ GO DEEPER ⌘

Read Psalm 1:1–6. Are you following the spiraling progression of verse 1? According to this chapter, what is the end result of following God's Word versus ungodly counsel?

DAY 227
Love guards your time

Pay careful attention, then, to how you walk—not as
unwise people but as wise—making the most of the time.

Ephesians 5:15–16

Many of the decisions that will have the greatest impact
on your marriage won't be between right and wrong, but
rather between good and best. Your unquestioned desire to
watch your favorite sports team on television, or to have a
standing lunch date with your friends, will always need to be
weighed against what's best for your wife or husband.

This may mean placing boundaries on yourself in terms
of your time on the phone, your hours at work, or even your
slowness at putting the children to bed in a timely manner.
Your spouse needs to know they come first to you—over
shopping, over hunting, and over church committees that
expect you to drop what you're doing any night of the week
to meet again.

There will always be other options for finding pleasure
than in your marriage, and always another person who'll
make you feel appreciated and important for giving time to
them. A well-rounded life includes balance, of course, but
you must keep the pendulum swinging in the direction of
your marriage.

✎ THIS WEEK'S DARE ✎

End it. Now. Identify every object of lust in your life
and remove it. It must be killed and destroyed—
today—and replaced with the sure promises of God,
and with a heart filled with His perfect love.

Day 228
Love is affair-proof

Stay away from every form of evil.

1 Thessalonians 5:22

Unfaithfulness obviously ranks near the top of the greatest stressors you can place on your marriage. Sadly, you may know this from personal experience. Regardless, this is the day for you to drive your promise into fresh, new ground. Your love will be for your spouse, and for your spouse alone.

We all know that few people go out looking for ways to put themselves into sexual compromise. Casual words become intriguing thoughts that become private conversations and then playing with fire. But only a fool—someone who has allowed their heart to stray from God's wisdom and be confused by selfish desire—thinks they can "embrace fire" and their "clothes not be burned" (Proverbs 6:27). The pleasure of a moment becomes an anchor of regret for a lifetime.

Don't think it couldn't be you. If David could fall (the man after God's own heart), and Solomon (known for his great wisdom), and Samson (known for his great strength), anyone is capable of sinning in this way. Keep your emotional distance from those of the opposite sex. Love always forsakes all others.

PRAYER

"Lord Jesus, do whatever it takes to prevent us from being unfaithful to each other, and burn in our hearts the same devotion we had at the altar. Give us the wisdom to guard this marriage at all costs."

DAY 229
Love vs. lust

*The world with its lust is passing away,
but the one who does God's will remains forever.*

1 John 2:17

God's blessings are far beyond our fundamental needs. Yet like Adam and Eve, we still want more. So we set our eyes and hearts on seeking worldly pleasures. We try to meet legitimate needs in illegitimate ways. For many, it's seeking sexual fulfillment in another person or in pornographic images. And once our eyes are captured by curiosity, our hearts become entangled.

Lust is in opposition to love. It means to set your heart and passion on something forbidden, and it's the first step in falling out of fellowship with God and others. That's because lust represents a lie. This person or thing that seems to promise sheer satisfaction is more like a bottomless pit of unmet longings.

It's time to expose lust for what it really is: a misguided thirst for satisfaction that only God can fulfill. When our eyes and hearts are on God, our actions lead us to lasting joy, not to endless cycles of regret and condemnation.

✎ THIS WEEK'S DARE ✎

End it. Now. Identify every object of lust in your life and remove it. It must be killed and destroyed—today—and replaced with the sure promises of God, and with a heart filled with His perfect love.

DAY 230
Love is content

Be satisfied with what you have, for He Himself has said,
"I will never leave you or forsake you."

Hebrews 13:5

Adam and Eve were supplied with everything they needed in the Garden of Eden. They also had fellowship with God and intimacy with one another. But after Eve was deceived by the serpent, she saw the forbidden fruit and set her heart on it. Before long, Adam joined in her wishes, and against God's command, both of them ate. That's the progression. From eyes to heart to action. And then follows shame and regret. It's the same progression David experienced in his sin with Bathsheba, even though God had made him king over Israel and met all his needs. God even said to him, "If that was not enough, I would have given you even more" (2 Samuel 12:8).

We, too, have been supplied with everything we need for a full, productive, enriching life. "For we brought nothing into the world, and we can take nothing out" (1 Timothy 6:7). So having the basics of "food and clothing," we should "be content" (1 Timothy 6:8). And Jesus promised these two things would always be provided to God's children.

GO DEEPER

Read 1 Timothy 6:6–8. What does this passage say we need in order to find contentment? What does Philippians 4:19 say that God will supply to His children? Where does it come from?

Love fills, lust empties

But those who want to be rich fall into temptation,
a trap, and many foolish and harmful desires,
which plunge people into ruin and destruction.

1 Timothy 6:9

Lust is like a warning light on the dashboard of your heart, alerting you to the fact that you are not allowing God's love to fill you. We can lust after possessions, power, or prideful ambition. We see what others have, and we want it. Our hearts are deceived into saying, "I could be happy if I only had this." Then we make the decision to go after it.

But lust only breeds more lust. It will make you dissatisfied with your husband or wife. It breeds anger, numbs hearts, and destroys marriages. Rather than fullness, it leads to emptiness.

Are you tired of being lied to by lust? Then begin setting your eyes on the Word of God. Let His promises of peace and freedom work their way into your heart. Daily receive the unconditional love He has already proven to you through the cross. And let His fullness be the perfect fit for the empty places in your heart.

QUESTIONS

Is there something that has taken hold of your heart through lust? How is it hurting your relationship with your spouse and with God? What are you planning to do about it?

DAY 232
Love leads to satisfaction

Do not love the world nor the things in the world.
If anyone loves the world, the love of the Father is not in him.

1 John 2:15 NASB

Are you fed up with believing that forbidden pleasures are able to keep you happy and content? Then be grateful for everything God has already given you rather than choosing discontentment. You'll find yourself so full of what He provides, you won't be hungry anymore for the junk food of lust.

Also while you're at it, set your eyes and heart on your spouse again. "Let your fountain be blessed, and take pleasure in the wife of your youth. . . . Why, my son, would you be infatuated with a forbidden woman or embrace the breast of a stranger? For a man's ways are before the Lord's eyes, and He considers all his paths" (Proverbs 5:18, 20–21). You'll never be as happy or satisfied as you could be in your own home, with your own mate, loving God's way, and living with a pure heart.

Lust may seem like the best this world has to offer, but love offers you the best life in the world.

❧ THIS WEEK'S DARE ❧

As a way to lead your heart toward your mate, give your mate something that says, "I love you," even when no special occasion exists. Make the gift something as nice as you can reasonably afford.

Love leads the heart

The one who trusts in himself is a fool,
but one who walks in wisdom will be safe.

Proverbs 28:26

Feelings can be shallow. They fluctuate depending upon circumstances. In an effort to follow their hearts, people have abandoned their jobs to pursue get-rich-quick schemes, or taken off for Hollywood believing they are the next big star, or left their mate in order to chase an attractive coworker. This selfish philosophy is also the source of countless divorces. It leads many to excuse themselves from their wedding vows because they no longer "feel in love."

The truth is, our hearts are basically selfish and sinful. Jesus said that evil thoughts, adultery, and lies come out of the heart (Matthew 15:18–19). So until our heart is genuinely changed by God, it will continue to choose wrong things. Instead of following your heart, the Scriptures communicate a much stronger message: *Lead your heart.* This means to take full responsibility for your heart's condition and direction. Instead of chasing whatever you feel will make you happy in the moment, Scripture says, "Delight yourself in the Lord; and He will give you the desires of your heart" (Psalm 37:4 NASB).

GO DEEPER

What does Proverbs 28:26 say about trusting your heart? What does verse 25 say that we should trust instead?

Day 234
Love molds the heart

For as he thinks in his heart, so is he.

Proverbs 23:7 NKJV

Your heart is the most important part of who you are. It is the center of your being where "the real you" resides. It is your identity. All your real thoughts, beliefs, values, motives, and convictions start in your heart. Because of this, every area of your life is impacted by the direction of your heart.

The world says, "Follow your heart!" This is the philosophy of new age gurus, self-help seminars, and romantic pop songs. Because it sounds romantic and noble, it sells millions of records and books. But there's something wrong with this philosophy. It can be very foolish.

The problem is that following your heart usually means chasing after whatever feels right at the moment. People use this as an excuse for sin. They say, "I was just following my heart." But we cannot allow the world to mold our hearts. We are given the charge to guard it and to lead it. And when we lead it to follow God, it becomes more and more like Him.

THIS WEEK'S DARE

As a way to lead your heart toward your mate, give your mate something that says, "I love you," even when no special occasion exists. Make the gift something as nice as you can reasonably afford.

Love seeks lasting treasure

"For where your treasure is, there your heart will be also."

Matthew 6:21

Your heart follows your investments. Whatever you pour your time, money, and energy into will draw your heart. This was certainly true before you were married. You wrote letters, bought gifts, and spent time together as a couple . . . and your heart followed. But if you stopped investing as much in the relationship and started pouring yourself into other things, your heart followed those. If you are not in love with your spouse today, it may be because you stopped investing in your spouse yesterday.

Ask yourself what has your heart right now? What's become important to you? You can tell by looking at where your time, money, thoughts, and energy have been spent recently. Are you still putting these things into your mate? How about the things of God? As you draw closer to God, the Holy Spirit will act as your spiritual GPS. When you begin to veer off course, His still, small voice will redirect you—if you'll listen—back toward your real treasure.

PRAYER

"Lord, remind us to invest in our marriage whether our emotions are there or not. Help us to love each other regardless of our feelings, but we ask You to renew our love for one another as we obey You."

Day 236
Love sets the course

Set your hearts on things above,
where Christ is seated at the right hand of God.

Colossians 3:1 NIV

It's time to identify where your heart needs to be and then choose to set your heart on those things. If you do not, your lust or pride will take over by default. Remember, lust is when your heart is set on something that is wrong and forbidden. But with God's help, you can choose to take your heart off of the wrong things and set it on something that is good and honorable. Like your relationship with God. Like your marriage.

Don't wait until you feel like doing the right thing, or until you fall in love with your spouse to invest in your relationship. Start pouring into your marriage and investing where your heart is supposed to be. Spend time with your spouse. Buy him or her gifts. Write letters. Go on dates. Intentionally communicate! The more you invest, the more your heart will value your relationship. And you just might be surprised at how much your love is rekindled.

❧ THIS WEEK'S DARE ❧

As a way to lead your heart toward your mate, give your mate something that says, "I love you," even when no special occasion exists. Make the gift something as nice as you can reasonably afford.

DAY 237
Love protects the heart

The Lord is my strength and my shield;
my heart trusts in Him, and I am helped.

Psalm 28:7

When something unhealthy tempts your heart, it is your job to guard against it. That's one responsibility that God has given each of us. And it's a duty that requires action on a regular basis.

When an unhealthy desire for money or possessions draws your heart, you must recognize it and check your priorities. When a wrong relationship threatens the health of your marriage, you must guard against it. If your job begins commanding your focus and time to the detriment of your family, then something has to give. And that something cannot be the marriage you vowed to protect.

You must take responsibility for setting your heart on godly things and turning your heart to the Lord. Invest your time, money, and energy into things that please God (your spouse, your kids, the Word of God). Then let God provide you with the fulfillment that comes only when we set our hearts on Him. Proverbs 4:23 says, "Guard your heart above all else, for it is the source of life."

⟶ QUESTIONS ⟵

What is the most important priority in your life? Does this priority honor God? If so, how are you doing at guarding it and keeping it at the forefront?

Day 238
Love chooses forgiveness

For what I have forgiven, if I have forgiven anything,
it is for you in the presence of Christ.

2 Corinthians 2:10

Counselors who deal with broken couples on a regular basis will tell you that unforgiveness is the most complex problem of all, a rupture that is often the most difficult to repair. Forgiveness cannot just be considered but must be deliberately put into practice. It has to happen, or a successful marriage won't.

If someone hurt you, it may have been very wrong, whether they admit it or not. They may not even be sorry about it. They may feel perfectly justified in their actions. They may continue to cause you pain by repeating offenses and opening new wounds. But forgiveness doesn't absolve anyone of blame. It doesn't clear their record with God. It just clears you of having to worry about how to punish them. When you forgive another person, you're not merely turning them loose. You're just turning them over to God, who can be counted on to deal with them His way.

⟨⟨⟨ GO DEEPER ⟩⟩⟩

Unforgiveness is a useless attempt at punishing someone and paying them back. It is returning evil for evil. Instead, we should let go and let God handle any vengeance. Read Romans 12:17–21 and observe God's better alternative to bitterness.

Love cancels debts

"This is how my heavenly Father will treat each of you unless you forgive your brother from your heart."

Matthew 18:35 NIV

Jesus painted a vivid picture of the need to forgive in His parable of the ungrateful servant. A man who owed an enormous sum of money was surprised when his master heard his pleas for mercy and totally canceled his debt. But upon being released, he went to another man who owed him a much smaller amount and demanded immediate payment. When the master heard of it, he was enraged at the man's hypocrisy and threw him into prison.

Torture. Prison. When you think of unforgiveness, these are the pictures that should come to your mind. This is what those who withhold forgiveness should expect to experience. When God has forgiven us of so much, how can we refuse to forgive others who have wronged us? This is especially true for your spouse. Great marriages are not created by people who never hurt each other, only by people who daily choose to "not keep a record of wrongs" (1 Corinthians 13:5).

THIS WEEK'S DARE

Whatever you haven't forgiven in your mate, forgive it today. Let it go. Just as we ask God to "forgive us our debts" each day, we must ask Him to help us "forgive our debtors" each day as well. Say from your heart, "I choose to forgive."

Day 240
Love frees others

"Forgive us our debts, as we also have forgiven our debtors."
Matthew 6:12 NIV

Imagine finding yourself in a dark, prison-like setting. As you look around, you see a number of cells with people who have wounded you. This prison, you discover, is a room in your own heart. But not far away, Jesus is standing there, extending to you a key that will release every inmate.

But these people have hurt you too badly, so you resist and turn away. Yet as you try to leave, you discover that there is no way out. You're trapped inside with the other captives. Your anger and bitterness have made a prisoner of you as well. Your freedom is now dependent on your forgiveness.

That's why people who have genuinely forgiven say, "It felt like a weight being lifted off my shoulders." Yes, that's *exactly* what it is. It's like a breath of fresh air rushing into your heart. For the first time in a long time, you feel at peace. You feel free.

Whether it's your spouse or someone else, is there anyone you need to forgive?

⌘ GO DEEPER ⌘

Forgiving someone can be very difficult. Read Peter's question and Jesus' answer in Matthew 18:12–35. What happened to the person who refused to forgive? How do his consequences describe what bitterness does to us? How could he be released after finding himself in prison? Only by forgiving. His freedom depended on it.

DAY 241
Love trusts God to judge

*Never take your own revenge, beloved,
but leave room for the wrath of God, for it is written,
"Vengeance is Mine, I will repay," says the Lord.*

Romans 12:19 NASB

When you forgive someone of an offense, it's not about winning and losing anymore. It's about freedom. It's about letting go. You're saving yourself the trouble of scripting any more arguments or trying to prevail in a tense situation.

But how do you do it? You just release your anger and responsibility for judging this person to the Lord. You recognize that God is the judge, not you, and that He will deal with the offense in His time and in His way.

How do you *know* you've forgiven the offender? You know it when the thought of their name or the sight of their face—rather than causing your blood to boil—causes you to feel sorry for them instead, to pity them, to genuinely hope they get this turned around. You know it when you see their need for mercy and grace before a holy God. Love begins again where bitterness ends.

∼ THIS WEEK'S DARE ∼

Whatever you haven't forgiven in your mate, forgive it today. Let it go. Just as we ask God to "forgive us our debts" each day, we must ask Him to help us "forgive our debtors" each day as well. Say from your heart, "I choose to forgive."

Day 242
Love doesn't waste a day

From the rising of the sun to its setting,
let the name of the LORD be praised.

Psalm 113:3

Every day is like a package. You open it in the morning, the moment you wake up. Then at night, you close up all of its experiences—both the good and the bad—put them away, and prepare to open a new one again at sunrise. That's how the Bible teaches us to look at life. We ask only for our "daily bread" (Matthew 6:11), not worrying about tomorrow "because tomorrow will worry about itself. Each day has enough trouble of its own" (Matthew 6:34).

One of the implications of this approach is to keep your sins confessed on a daily basis, while also not letting any offense done against you go unforgiven overnight. People who live otherwise can wake up years later to find their hearts cluttered with piled-up resentment. The freedom and friendship they want in their marriage are obscured by tall stacks of wrongs, collected and cataloged by date and time.

If you want to keep the bitterness and rancor out of your relationship, take a moment tonight—and every night—to square your accounts with each other before going to bed.

✑ PRAYER ✑

"Lord, help us forgive each other quickly, so as not to give the enemy a foothold in our marriage. Remind us of Your love for us, that we would desire to love one another more."

Love leaves nothing unresolved

*"I walk along slowly all my years
because of the bitterness of my soul."*

Isaiah 38:15

Houses are built brick by brick, one upon the other until the entire structure is complete. It's the same way walls are built between a husband and a wife—one unresolved offense at a time, one upon the other, until neither person has a clear path for getting over or around it. Bitterness builds up between you, while tearing you both down at the same time.

This is why you cannot afford to keep any anger buried in your heart against your mate. Each time you hurt each other, you must deal with it. As soon as you realize you have said or done something to cause offense, go and apologize, even if they're not ready to accept it. Make sure they know you're brokenhearted about this. And whenever they come to you repenting, forgive without a trace.

The best marriages are those that force each other to talk it out and work it through—hurt by hurt—until all the bricks are gone.

THIS WEEK'S DARE

Whatever you haven't forgiven in your mate, forgive it today. Let it go. Just as we ask God to "forgive us our debts" each day, we must ask Him to help us "forgive our debtors" each day as well. Say from your heart, "I choose to forgive."

Love uproots bitterness

*See to it that no one falls short of the grace of God
and that no root of bitterness springs up,
causing trouble and by it, defiling many.*

Hebrews 12:15

Bitterness plants itself in your heart like a poisonous weed, taking up the same space that could otherwise be home to beauty and color. Hurts that at one time would have been fairly easy to pull up have now spread their root systems into other areas of your life, sprouting up as anger, touchiness, and loss of interest in spiritual things. It pollutes. It festers. This root of unforgiveness causes your marriage to rot from the inside out.

But like every sin, the chief problem is not what bitterness does to *you*, as dark and destructive as it can be. The main issue is that bitterness is an offense against Almighty God. It reflects a heart of ingratitude toward His grace and blessing. It reveals us as someone who has quit trusting Him to know what we need, even if what we need is a season of hardship that drives us closer to Him. Bitterness robs us of our willingness to walk with Him.

☙ QUESTIONS ❧

Is there any bitterness in your heart? If so, what is keeping you from turning it over to God? Are you the rightful judge, or is He? How long will you hold onto your bitterness?

Day 245
Love thinks clearly

Don't give the Devil an opportunity.

Ephesians 4:27

Most divorces would not happen if no one became bitter. When our heart has grown hard and bitter, it will eventually show up in our actions. Even worse, we will have found one of the surest ways for Satan to worm himself into our lives. It won't be long until we begin saying and doing things that are very much unlike us . . . and very much like him.

The devil operates by confusion. He twists meanings. He reads *into* things, filling in the gaps with negative assumptions. He paints beautiful pictures of the life we're missing out on, while smudging the portrait of the life we have. He works to convince us that our love should be earning a much greater return on investment than it's getting in our current marriage. He makes divorce look like a good alternative, a magic remedy.

Love knows better. It knows that when we scrub the bitterness from our minds, we toss the devil out in the process. Love knows that a heart good at housekeeping is much easier to keep clean.

⮜⮞ GO DEEPER ⮜⮞

Read Ephesians 4:26–32. When we disobey God's command in verse 26, we experience the consequences of verses 27 and 29–30. Instead, we should carry out the appeals of verse 31 by following the steps listed in verse 32? Have you?

DAY 246
Love looks good on us

A joyful heart is good medicine,
but a broken spirit dries up the bones.

Proverbs 17:22

Forgiveness shows on your face. Freedom from hatred and malice feels good all the way down to your toes. When you make the courageous choice to keep your heart emptied of anything that could clog it with anger, revenge, and entitlement, you keep a spring in your step. Love blesses you physically.

Bitterness, on the other hand, has a way of etching lines in your face long before age has called for them. It darkens the look in your eye and hardens your general expression. Smiles come slowly. Angry stares tighten your appearance. Research findings have even concluded that a bitter, ungrateful heart can make you more susceptible to disease, able to put up less resistance.

If God's will is to sanctify us completely—"spirit, soul, and body" (1 Thessalonians 5:23)—it stands to reason that Satan can use our interconnected natures against us by turning a heart of bitterness into something that's bad for our whole person. Let love have its way, and your whole body will thank you for it.

∽∼ THIS WEEK'S DARE ∼∽

Talk with your spouse about any issues of bitterness you have with them or anyone else. If your mate is willing, pray together and ask God for forgiveness. Purpose to release each issue to the Lord, then ask God to bless you and your marriage in a fresh way.

Love receives forgiveness

> "Whenever you stand praying, if you have anything
> against anyone, forgive him, so that your Father
> in heaven will also forgive you your wrongdoing."

Mark 11:25

Bitterness is spiritual poison. It eats away at the essence of your life with Christ—the forgiveness of sins through His perfect sacrifice. By holding back your willingness to forgive your spouse, your parents, or anyone who's mistreated you, you block the flow of God's forgiveness to you. "For if you forgive people their wrongdoing," Jesus said, "your heavenly Father will forgive you as well. But if you don't forgive people, your Father will not forgive your wrongdoing" (Matthew 6:14–15).

Some things are mutually exclusive, the Bible attests. "If anyone says, 'I love God,' yet hates his brother, he is a liar. For the person who does not love his brother whom he has seen cannot love God whom he has not seen" (1 John 4:20). It is impossible to walk in fellowship with God while also walking in unforgiveness. It attacks your spiritual fellowship. If you feel like God is far away, bitterness might be the source of your spiritual desert. Open your heart to forgive, and you will open the door for intimacy with God again.

GO DEEPER

Read Mark 11:24–26. Good prayer and fellowship are both connected to forgiveness. Is there anything that anyone has done to you that you have not fully forgiven? Your parents? Your spouse?

DAY 248
Love offers stability

"There the Lord will give you a trembling heart,
failing of eyes, and despair of soul."

Deuteronomy 28:65 NASB

Everyone gets hurt in life. The wound that first caused your heart to bleed may have happened in a moment. Perhaps it was spread out over a period of days or weeks. It was most likely a short amount of time. But in the weeks, months, and years since, you may have lost countless hours of sleep to your hurt and anger. You've had numerous conversations with yourself, behind the steering wheel or on the lawn mower, where you've hashed out an ironclad defense of your position, practicing lines you hope to use one day. You've decided there can only be one winner—and the loser is not going to be you!

It takes a lot of energy to stay mad at people. It wears on your emotions and exhausts your reserves. Life moves on with all its routines and responsibilities, yet simmering underneath is this ongoing drain on your emotional resources.

But the homework and extra study required to "win" in your anger ensures that everyone loses. The beating your emotions take from bitterness is always worse than the original offense.

❧ THIS WEEK'S DARE ❧

Talk with your spouse about any issues of bitterness you have with them or anyone else. If your mate is willing, pray together and ask God for forgiveness. Purpose to release each issue to the Lord, then ask God to bless you and your marriage in a fresh way.

Love forgives it all

*"This is how my heavenly Father will treat each of you
unless you forgive your brother from your heart."*

Matthew 18:35 NIV

There are levels of forgiveness. Some people claim they've forgiven, but it was only a surface exercise. They said the words. They went through the motions. But their anger is still easily aroused when they think of it. They may say, "I've forgiven, but I refuse to forget!" That's an indication their forgiveness was only skin deep.

When you have truly forgiven someone from the depths of your heart, you won't necessarily "forget" that it happened. You will probably continue to feel sorry the incident took place, but the anger will be gone. The hatefulness is over. If you've genuinely pulled up the "root of bitterness" (Hebrews 12:15), you'll be able to tell that you've moved on and feel free emotionally. You're not holding this over their head any longer. This is what heart-level forgiveness looks like.

You may question whether this is possible. But with God, all things are possible—even looking in the face of someone who hurt you more deeply than you've ever been hurt before, and forgiving "from your heart."

PRAYER

"Lord Jesus, help us totally forgive, as You have totally forgiven us. Don't let bitterness have any place in our hearts, but rather a clean slate for each other. Give us the desire to love no matter the cost."

DAY 250
Love seeks peace

"Blessed are the peacemakers,
because they will be called sons of God."

Matthew 5:9

Loving spouses make their homes a fortress of peace. They commit to it. They settle for nothing less. It becomes a hallmark their children long remember about them. They put a priority on peace. They always make a point of staying on speaking terms. They love being at peace more than they love being right.

Three times in Jesus' appearances to His disciples following the Resurrection, His greeting, spoken as a word of blessing, was simple: "Peace to you" (John 20:19, 21, 26). Paul's greeting to many of the churches in his New Testament letters was, "Grace to you and peace from God our Father and the Lord Jesus Christ" (Ephesians 1:2). The Bible declares our Lord to be "the God of peace" (Romans 15:30), who has torn down the "dividing wall of hostility" that keeps people from uniting under His name (Ephesians 2:14).

If your home has seen more than enough discord, promise today that you will let God's peace become a living reality in your marriage. Make peacemaking your lifestyle of choice.

✎ THIS WEEK'S DARE ✎

Talk with your spouse about any issues of bitterness you have with them or anyone else. If your mate is willing, pray together and ask God for forgiveness. Purpose to release each issue to the Lord, then ask God to bless you and your marriage in a fresh way.

Love is responsible

*For when you judge another, you condemn yourself,
since you, the judge, do the same things.*

Romans 2:1

Today is about personal responsibility. It's something we all agree others should have, yet struggle to maintain ourselves. We are so quick to justify our motives. So quick to deflect criticism. So quick to find fault—especially with our spouse.

But love doesn't pass the blame so easily or justify selfish motives. Love is not nearly as concerned with our performance as with others' needs. When love takes responsibility for its actions, it's not to prove how noble we've been, but rather to admit how much further we have to go.

Are you taking responsibility for this person you chose for yourself as the love of your life? How deliberate are you about making sure your spouse's needs are met? Or are you only concerned with your mate fulfilling yours? Love calls us to take responsibility for our partner in marriage. To love them. To honor them. To cherish them. That's responsibility.

❧ GO DEEPER ❧

Read Galatians 5:13–15. Freedom is not permission to do whatever we want, but rather the opportunity to do what we should. Focus on verse 13. Do you use your freedom at home to merely please yourself, or to serve others in your family?

Love doesn't make excuses

*Rebuke is more effective for a wise man
than a hundred blows on a fool.*

Proverbs 17:10 NKJV

We tend to believe that our views are correct, or at least more correct than our mate. And we don't believe that anybody, given our same set of circumstances, would act much differently than we have in relation to them. As far as we're concerned, we're doing the best we can. And our spouse just ought to be glad we're as good to them as we are.

However, love doesn't make excuses. Love keeps working to make a difference—in us and in our marriage. That's why, the next time you're in an argument with your spouse, instead of working up your comebacks, stop and see if there's something worth listening to in what your mate is saying. What might happen in your relationship if instead of passing the blame, you first admitted your own wrongs? This is how love is responsible. It is willing to admit and correct its faults and errors up front. It remains focused on reconciling rather than retaliating.

❧❧ QUESTIONS ❧❧

Do you have a tendency to make excuses rather than taking responsibility for your actions? Do you think others don't notice this fact about you? What do you want them to see about you in this area?

DAY 253
Love confesses faults

*If we confess our sins, He is faithful and righteous to forgive
us our sins and to cleanse us from all unrighteousness.*

1 John 1:9

Love makes you want to have a right relationship with
both God and your mate. Once these relationships are right,
the stage is set for other areas of your life to fall into place.
Pride is very resistant to responsibility, but humility and
honesty before God and your spouse is crucial if you want to
maintain a healthy heart.

This doesn't mean you're always wrong and your spouse is
always right. This is not a demand that you become a door-
mat. But if there is something that is not right between you
and God or between you and your spouse, something that
is separating you or straining your interaction, this matter
should be your first priority.

Are you taking responsibility for your own faults? Have
you said or done things to your spouse that are wrong? Or to
God? Make it your priority to confess your areas of sin first.
Then you'll be on better ground to work things out with
your spouse.

❧ THIS WEEK'S DARE ❧

Take time to pray through your areas of wrongdoing. Ask for God's forgiveness, then humble yourself
enough to admit them to your spouse. Ask your
spouse for forgiveness as well. No matter how they
respond, make sure you cover your responsibility in
love.

DAY 254
Love seeks forgiveness

Against You—You alone—I have sinned
and done this evil in Your sight.

Psalm 51:4

In order to enjoy the blessings of God's favor, you must stay clean before Him. This doesn't mean you can never stumble, but that you confess it to God and ask for forgiveness when you do. Admit it—you want and need God's forgiveness.

You also need the forgiveness of your spouse.

Can your spouse say that you have wronged or wounded them in any way and never made it right? Part of taking responsibility is admitting when you've failed and asking for forgiveness. It's time to humble yourself, correct your offenses, and repair the damage. It's an act of love. God wants there to be no unresolved issues between the two of you.

When you seek forgiveness, your spouse should forgive you, but your responsibility does not lie with their decision. If they have wronged you or they will not forgive you, leave that for them to deal with at another time.

⟶⟶ GO DEEPER ⟵⟵

Read Matthew 5:23–25. Is there anything you have done wrong against your spouse or another family member and never made it right? Have you considered how this is affecting your worship toward God? What steps will you take this week to take responsibility and seek forgiveness?

Love keeps its word

When you make a vow to God, don't delay fulfilling it,
because He does not delight in fools.

Ecclesiastes 5:4

Many of the problems that arise in marriage come from one of us promising to do something, then failing to do it. Often this is the fault of speaking without thinking and then forgetting what we've promised. Other times, we are forced to choose between who we're going to please—our spouse or someone else. We may find ourselves prioritizing the request of a friend or coworker over a promise we've made to our wife or husband.

Though situations can come up to prevent us from following through on a commitment, our spouse should know they can count on us if it's within our power. The loyalty we feel about keeping our word to them should be the same (or greater) as it is to our boss, our pastor, or a wealthy client. Jesus taught us to let our "yes" be "yes," and our "no" be "no" (Matthew 5:37). He warned us about the danger of speaking "careless" words (Matthew 12:36). If you hope to win the trust of your mate, start with the simple priority of doing what you said you would do.

☙ THIS WEEK'S DARE ❧

Take time to pray through your areas of wrongdoing. Ask for God's forgiveness, then humble yourself enough to admit them to your spouse. Ask your spouse for forgiveness as well. No matter how they respond, make sure you cover your responsibility in love.

DAY 256

Love does its job

*Know well the condition of your flock,
and pay attention to your herds.*

Proverbs 27:23

Irresponsible spouses put an undue strain on their marriage. Their lack of initiative in pulling their share of the weight drains others, leads to resentment, and lowers the level of respect in the home. By routinely expecting the other to do the work, they become poor stewards of the treasure God has given them in a mate.

Marriage is designed to be a prime setting for giving and sacrifice. We should always stay willing to lay our plans aside in order to help the other. But almost in the same breath as he reminded us to "carry one another's burdens," the apostle Paul made it clear that "each person will have to carry his own load" (Galatians 6:2, 5). The "burdens" we share represent weights that no person can handle without help. But to "carry your own load" means that you have responsibilities you are to shoulder alone without dumping it on others.

We alone are responsible for what God has given us to carry. When each of us is faithful to do our part, we are the most prepared to be the true help our spouse needs. Are you carrying your load?

∼ PRAYER ∼

"Lord, forgive us when we put unnecessary burdens on each other. Help us to carry out our responsibilities, and to serve one another whenever possible. In Jesus' name, amen."

DAY 257
Love works hard

Idle hands make one poor, but diligent hands bring riches.
Proverbs 10:4

If your spouse wasn't expecting anything of you, how much effort would you invest in your marriage? If no one was around who needed your help, or was watching to see what you do, how would you generally choose to fill your time?

Love should inspire us to hard work—love for God, as well as love for our spouse. Rather than needing constant reminders to stay on task, rather than requiring coercion to get off the couch, we should see what needs doing, and do it.

The Scriptures contain stern warnings for people who require supervision to perform their best work, humbling us enough to learn from the ant—"observe its ways and become wise" (Proverbs 6:6). Ants take initiative, keep working, and finish what they start—all without needing to be supervised. Those who are in the habit of making excuses, who never met an unpleasant chore they couldn't put off till later, will be "filled with craving all day long" (Proverbs 21:26). Love should keep you self-motivated. Your spouse needs your help, and your children need your example.

∽∾ THIS WEEK'S DARE ∽∾

Take time to pray through your areas of wrongdoing. Ask for God's forgiveness, then humble yourself enough to admit them to your spouse. Ask your spouse for forgiveness as well. No matter how they respond, make sure you cover your responsibility in love.

DAY 258
Love is willing to confront

*But speaking the truth in love, let us grow
in every way into Him who is the head—Christ.*

Ephesians 4:15

In marriage, you make the choice to be responsible for more than just yourself. Not only do you get the blessing of sharing your spouse's company, you also invite their questions, concerns, and baggage into your world.

So love must be willing to listen and be patient. And at times, love must be courageous enough to confront issues of sin, harmful behavior, and poor attitudes—not out of exasperation, but out of a pure desire to help the other through it. Jesus lovingly confronted His disciples. He also commanded us, saying, "If your brother sins, go and show him his fault in private" (Matthew 18:15 NASB). This is never fun, but it is necessary to help your relationship move forward. You should pray beforehand for your spouse's heart and response, even as you open up your own heart to their scrutiny and care.

Speaking the truth, even when it's hard to say and hear, can be so thoroughly covered in gentle kindness that your spouse will know your love for them is stronger than anything they're struggling with.

✺ GO DEEPER ✺

Read Luke 17:3–4. If irritations are not sin, they deserve discussion, but not rebuke. God calls us to lovingly rebuke one another when we are sinning. This should be balanced with the spirit of Galatians 6:1.

Love takes action

"Get up, for this matter is your responsibility,
and we support you. Be strong and take action!"

Ezra 10:4

It is normal to have problems. Even the strongest and most godly people you know recognize things in themselves that need to be improved. But sadly, the most normal way to respond to these matters is to deny they exist, or to conclude they can't be helped. Instead of dealing with problems head-on, we often decide to sweep them under the rug.

As a result, you see people going from church to church, from friend to friend, and from job to job, running from their problems rather than facing them down. But part of growing as a person—and as a couple—is to admit weakness, to confess sin, to clean up our own messes, and to work through our own resistance to submit ourselves to God and His Word. When we cry out to Him for help and embrace our responsibility, He saves us from leaving behind trails of destruction that can destroy not only ourselves but our marriages as well.

QUESTIONS

How are you doing with the responsibilities God has given you? Are you taking them seriously, and with the needed focus and attention? What would your spouse say about these areas?

DAY 260
Love walks in truth

But if we walk in the light as He Himself is in the light,
we have fellowship with one another.

1 John 1:7

God walks in the light and invites us to do so. The only thing easier than overreacting and getting angry at one another is to see an issue that needs dealing with in your marriage, and choosing to keep it in the dark or to act like it doesn't exist.

Your marriage will never thrive unless you allow total openness to exist between you. Love allows freedom of speech. No problem or concern should be off-limits. You should feel permission to talk about anything. Yes, some subjects will always require extra measures of gentleness and sensitivity. But if the fear of awkwardness or discomfort determines what you can discuss, your room will inevitably grow crowded with elephants. You will be left to ponder these matters alone, but rarely together. Frustration and suspicion will rule where unity is supposed to feel at home.

Love and honesty can do more to dispel shame, hurts, and irresponsibility than any other cure. True fellowship with each other only happens in the light.

THIS WEEK'S DARE

Eliminate the poison of unrealistic expectations. Think of areas where your spouse has told you you're expecting too much, and apologize for being so hard on them about it. Promise them you'll seek to understand, and assure them of your unconditional love.

Love encourages

*Guard me and deliver me; do not let me
be put to shame, for I take refuge in You.*

Psalm 25:20

Marriage has a way of altering our vision. We go in expecting our mate to fulfill our hopes and to make us happy. But this is an impossible order for any spouse to fill, no matter who they are. Unrealistic expectations breed disappointment. And the higher and more unreasonable your expectations, the more likely your spouse will fail you and cause you frustration.

Divorces are nearly inevitable when people refuse to allow their spouses to be human. There needs to be a transition that takes place in your thinking. You must choose to live by encouragement rather than by expectations. The way your spouse has been for the last few years is likely what he or she will be like in the future, probably for the rest of your life—apart from your loving encouragement and an intervention from God.

Love always puts the focus on personal responsibility and improving yourself rather than on demanding more from others.

GO DEEPER

Read 1 Thessalonians 5:11, 14–15. Examine Paul's specific challenge for each type of situation. Are you patient with everyone? Would your spouse say that you are encouraging, that you seek after what is good for them?

DAY 262
Love does not criticize

"How can you say to your brother, 'Let me take the speck out of your eye,' when all the time there is a plank in your own eye?"

Matthew 7:4 NIV

Does your spouse feel like they're living with a speck inspector? Are they routinely on edge, fearful of not living up to your expectations? Would they say they spend most days sensing more of your disapproval than your acceptance? Perhaps you'd respond by saying that the problem is not with you but with them. "If they really do come up short in a lot of areas, why is that my fault?"

The problem with this kind of attitude is that few people thrive in an environment filled with negative comments. When someone is constantly unhappy with you, it's hard for you not to take their displeasure personally. The truth must be spoken in love, but a cloud of criticism is depressing for anyone to live under. Especially in marriage.

Don't you want your married life to be a place where you can enjoy free expression of who you are? Don't you want to grow within a safe environment that encourages you even when you fail? Your spouse does too. And love gives them that privilege.

⤜◈⤐ THIS WEEK'S DARE ⤜◈⤐

Eliminate the poison of unrealistic expectations. Think of areas where your spouse has told you you're expecting too much, and apologize for being so hard on them about it. Promise them you'll seek to understand, and assure them of your unconditional love.

Day 263
Love builds

Therefore encourage one another and build each other up. . . .
Comfort the discouraged, help the weak, be patient with everyone.

1 Thessalonians 5:11, 14

People desire to please those who praise them the most. Your relationship with your spouse began with both of you bending over backwards to please the other. During the early days of marriage, we may be more inclined to listen and make subtle changes. But as the years go by, our spouse's disapproval only tends to entrench us. Rather than making us want to correct things, it makes us want to dig in even deeper.

Love is too smart for that. Instead of putting our mate in a position to rebel, love teaches us to give them room to be themselves. Marriage is a unique friendship designed by God Himself where two people live together in flawed imperfection, but who deal with it only by encouraging each other.

Make a daily commitment to let go of unrealistic expectations and to become your spouse's greatest encourager. As you do, the person God created them to be may emerge with a new confidence and love for you.

⚬⚬⚬ PRAYER ⚬⚬⚬

"Lord Jesus, help us to encourage one another and to support each other in each of our areas of work. Teach us to bless easily and to forgive easily, as you have forgiven us. In Your name we pray, amen."

DAY 264
Love finds the good

*Do not let any unwholesome talk come out of your mouths,
but only what is helpful for building others up.*

Ephesians 4:29 NIV

A word of encouragement can change a person's life forever. The Bible commands us to encourage one another daily and build each other up (Hebrews 3:13). There are a few key ways you can maximize this opportunity in you marriage.

Public adoration: Whether on a stage with a microphone or in a small room at a dinner party, you'll have prime opportunities to honor your spouse. It is vital that you take advantage of these moments to praise them in front of others.

Private appreciation: In daily conversations around family and friends, it's important to build up your spouse knowing they will eventually hear about it.

Personal admiration: Whether over a romantic dinner, or when whispering in bed, it's good for your spouse to hear you personally encourage them. Share how God uses them. Thank them for being who they are. Say the words they long to hear: "I'm so glad I married you. I'm still in love with you. I am so privileged to have you in my life."

◦◦◦ THIS WEEK'S DARE ◦◦◦

Eliminate the poison of unrealistic expectations. Think of areas where your spouse has told you you're expecting too much, and apologize for being so hard on them about it. Promise them you'll seek to understand, and assure them of your unconditional love.

DAY 265
Love is compassionate

"A priest happened to be going down that road.
When he saw him, he passed by on the other side."

Luke 10:31

Few people stir up a quicker image of hardness and lack of concern than the religious officials in Jesus' story of the Good Samaritan (Luke 10:30–37). Passing by a beaten man, too busy to stop and help, they stand as a symbol of coldness that is condemned by all people. Everyone knows that withholding compassion from a hurting person is in many ways a form of cruelty.

Then why do we so often fail to notice when our spouse is hurting? Even if we notice, why do we sometimes leave them to suffer alone? Is rolling over and going to sleep much different than the priest and Levite passing by on the other side?

Life brings pain. And pain makes our responses pivotal. If your spouse is ever suffering, know that your love is being tested and your future intimacy is on the line. Silence and avoidance are not options. You have to step in with overwhelming support and compassion. If you do, it will tie their heart to yours more deeply than before, and you will become a model for Christ's love.

QUESTIONS

How do you show compassion to your spouse?
Would they say you are there for them when they
need you? Are you a source of comfort and strength?
If not, why not?

DAY 266
Love feels the other's pain

Put on heartfelt compassion, kindness,
humility, gentleness, and patience.

Colossians 3:12

Experiencing compassion for your husband or wife is more than just feeling sorry for them. It's much deeper than mere pity. Love hurts when your spouse hurts. It gets you personally involved on a deep level. Even your body senses the pain they feel, especially when it's mixed with your desire to alleviate their suffering or to at least be a firm support through their trial. The original word for *compassion* in Scripture literally carries the idea of one's bowels aching in sympathy for another.

But true compassion doesn't stop at simple concern. It is not satisfied simply by being able to imagine what the other person is going through. Compassion works all the way through our hearts until it comes out in loving actions, in the sacrificial giving of our time and attention. "Is there anything I can do for you?" "What can I bring you?" "Would it help if I . . . ?"

Yes, it would. And yes, love does this all the time.

❧ GO DEEPER ❧

Read Matthew 20:29–34. What question did Jesus ask the two blind men? How did His compassion cause Him to respond to their need? What would happen if you began asking this question and responding with compassion?

266

Love learns from God

The LORD will indeed vindicate His people and have compassion on His servants when He sees that their strength is gone.

Deuteronomy 32:36

All the benefits we receive from God can be linked to His compassion. If it weren't for His loving care, there would be no forgiveness of sin, no escape from hell, and no healing of our spiritual and physical diseases. The only reason we have life and hope is because He has crowned us "with faithful love and compassion" (Psalm 103:4).

He led the weak-minded Lot away from destruction in Sodom because of His compassion (Genesis 19:16). He heard the cries of His people in Egypt and sent Moses to deliver them (Exodus 3:7). After watching Job's terrible ordeal, God restored him by His great mercy (James 5:11). And now He is "waiting to show you mercy, and is rising up to show you compassion, for the LORD is a just God" (Isaiah 30:18). He yearns deeply for you. He loves you with mercies that are new every morning.

Think of what God's compassion has accomplished in you. Think of what your compassion could mean to your spouse. Love learns wisely and willingly from God and courageously emulates Him.

⤜ THIS WEEK'S DARE ⤏

As a way to demonstrate compassion, find any area in your spouse's life where pain or suffering exists. Ask God to help you find ways to alleviate their pain and to minister to them in love.

Love lifts up the weary

When He saw the crowds, He felt compassion for them, because they were weary and worn out, like sheep without a shepherd.

Matthew 9:36

How do you serve your spouse when you can tell they are simply exhausted? What are some of the things they feel and think after a long day of corralling the children? What are some of the temptations your spouse faces after being run down by an exhausting season of work? What do you see in their eyes when they're not sure they can keep going at this pace?

Jesus saw people like that—people who were spiritually, physically, and relationally empty. He could recognize the signs of a person feeling depleted. And though He was probably tired Himself from the work of the day, the needs of the people, and the taunts of His critics, He stepped into the weary crowd. His words brought encouragement. His touch inspired them to believe that the promises of His love and eternal presence were sturdy and true.

Don't overlook your spouse's fatigue or take their efforts for granted. Don't consider it just part of what they signed up for in marriage. Look for ways to help ease their burden.

GO DEEPER

Read the account of Matthew 9:35–10:1. What did Jesus' compassion (9:36) lead Him to do (9:37–10:1)? Does your compassion get you thinking, planning, and acting in order to lessen the pain of others?

Love cares for the poor

He will have compassion on the poor and needy,
and the lives of the needy he will save.

Psalm 72:13 NASB

Part of Jesus' purpose in coming to Earth was to "preach good news to the poor" (Luke 4:18). This tells us that the greatest poverty a person can experience is spiritual poverty. Jesus met the physical needs of many people, and commanded us to do the same. But as devastating as hunger and physical lack can be, the pain of an empty heart is something that can do more than kill the body. It can lead to an eternity of craving but never being satisfied.

Christ has called you to minister to the spiritual lack in your mate—to care deeply for how they are missing the fullness of God's blessing by lacking faith and trust. What makes this role such a privilege is that we are lacking in many ways ourselves. So our responsibility to care for our spouse's spirit is also an invitation to receive their watchful, caring eye on ours too. Together we can find the richness of a growing relationship with Christ.

THIS WEEK'S DARE

As a way to demonstrate compassion, find any area in your spouse's life where pain or suffering exists. Ask God to help you find ways to alleviate their pain and to minister to them in love.

Love is eager to teach

He began to teach them many things.

Mark 6:34

Neither of you is an ignorant person. But there are certain things you don't know. And it is part of the blessing of marriage to be able to learn from each other.

You may have grown up in a Christian home, for example, receiving salvation at a much younger age than your spouse. In many ways you've each had experiences the other cannot relate to from firsthand knowledge, but your insight into these things can be valuable in rounding out both of you as a person.

The problem that frequently arises, however, is when we belittle our wife or husband for not understanding something that is in our expertise. Maybe you possess a good sense for directions, but your spouse does not. Maybe you are extremely discerning and can't understand why they don't pick up on cues that are so obvious to you. Rather than harping on the other's inadequacies, take opportunities to help them learn from you—gently, patiently. Make your marriage an example of what happens when two minds come together.

⟶⟶ PRAYER ⟵⟵

"Father God, expose any pride in us, that we would confess it and remove it from our marriage. Help us to bless and edify one another as a valuable part of this relationship. Help us to love. In Jesus' name, amen."

Love makes allowances

*"I have compassion on the crowd, because they've already
stayed with Me three days and have nothing to eat."*

Mark 8:2

Is one of you the absent-minded type? Does leaving the house usually involve a frantic search for car keys, followed by another mad dash inside for something you forgot? Is your menu planning often a call to the pizza shop? If you had to find the materials to wrap a gift, to hang a picture, or to clean the grill, would you know immediately where to look for them?

The spouse who is married to someone that struggles at staying organized has an interesting challenge—one that the devil can cleverly exploit to make things worse. His stock-in-trade temptation is to turn your frustration into an exasperated tirade. It's so easy to do. The proof is hard to refute. But as Jesus felt when seeing the overflow crowd milling around with no real clue about what to do next, you can choose to look with compassion on your discouraged mate. They're frustrated too. A kind word of patience and understanding from you would go a lot further to help them than another angry lecture. Take joy in helping your mate.

❧ THIS WEEK'S DARE ❧

As a way to demonstrate compassion, find any area in your spouse's life where pain or suffering exists. Ask God to help you find ways to alleviate their pain and to minister to them in love.

DAY 272
Love mourns losses

*When the Lord saw her, He had compassion
on her and said, "Don't cry."*

Luke 7:13

Seeing your spouse devastated or inconsolable over a loss is hard to watch. And sometimes in our desire to help, we go into problem-solving mode, doing our best to cheer them up and tell them it's not so bad. However, love is usually best served at times like these when we take our wife or husband in our arms, saying little—perhaps saying nothing—and just crying alongside them.

Those whose first inclination is to distract or look on the bright side are usually those who haven't yet been touched by loss or misunderstanding. Jesus was One who totally understood. He knew what it was like to be persecuted, to feel betrayed, to experience pain and have reason to give up. He knew suffering better than anyone. And Jesus' first reaction to seeing the widow in Luke 7 grieving another loss—the loss of her only son—was simply to express His sorrow. He was able to do more, of course—and did!—but He began where we should begin . . . with heartfelt compassion.

⟶ GO DEEPER ⟵

Read the full account of Jesus' compassion on the widow in Luke 7:11–17. According to Romans 12:15, what should we do when our spouse is weeping?

Day 273
Love receives sinners

"Go and learn what this means: 'I desire mercy and not sacrifice.' For I didn't come to call the righteous, but sinners."

Matthew 9:13

Each of us is born a sinner. The only difference is that some of us throw our sin load on the back of Christ, who carries them all away where they can no longer cause us eternal harm. We're free of sin's penalty and power.

We should certainly understand, however, what sin feels like. And when our spouse—whether a Christian or not—is exhibiting sinful behaviors and attitudes in the home, we of all people should look on them not with disdain or condemnation, but rather with deep compassion for what their sin is doing to them. Not to us. To them.

The reason sinners were comfortable in Jesus' presence was not because He went easy on their lifestyles, but because His main concern was to save them from what their immoral lifestyles were costing them. Pray that your mate will open their heart to Christ again "so He may have compassion" on them (Isaiah 55:7). And let it start with you . . . with your compassion.

❧ QUESTIONS ❧

Are you a person of compassion? Do you pray for your spouse's heart? Why not set some time aside to ask God to do a special work in the life of your mate?

DAY 274
Love reaches out

Moved with compassion, Jesus reached out
His hand and touched him.

Mark 1:41

Because you interact with each other on a daily basis, it's not hard to tell when something is wrong in your spouse's life. A tone of voice, a certain expression—you recognize it immediately as being a sign of disappointment, concern, or depression. Love understands that the most common answer to "What's the matter?" is "Nothing." Therefore, it does not stop at such an unconvincing response. Love keeps gently asking and then reaches out to help.

There are times when your mate is willing to admit that something is wrong, but they're not interested in talking about it. Not yet anyway. Love knows that waiting for a more conducive time is often a wise thing to do. But even if the mood clears and the subject isn't brought back up, don't let your aversion to conflict keep you from asking again later. Anything that's hurting another becomes less heavy when you carry it together. Be sure your wife or husband knows you consider it an honor to serve them with compassion when needed.

☙ THIS WEEK'S DARE ❧

What is one of the greatest needs in your spouse's life right now? Is there one you could lift from their shoulders by a daring act of sacrifice on your part? Whether the need is big or small, purpose to do what you can to meet the need.

Love sacrifices

He laid down His life for us.
We should also lay down our lives for our brothers.

1 John 3:16

Love makes sacrifices. It willingly goes the extra mile, pays the higher price, or endures the greater pain if that is what is required to meet the deeper need of another. Love keeps us so tuned in to what our spouse needs that we often respond without being asked. And when we don't notice ahead of time and must be told what's happening, love immediately responds to the heart of the issue. It has already answered the questions, "Does she deserve it?" or "Is he worth it?"

Commitment requires sacrifice. Love is less concerned about being misunderstood or taken advantage of than about meeting the needs of the other. Love inspires us to sacrifice what we want, in order to give our spouse what they need.

That's what Jesus did. "He laid down His life for us" to show us that "we should also lay down our lives" for others. He taught us that the best evidence for love is found in seeing a need in someone else, then doing all we can to satisfy it.

☙ GO DEEPER ❧

Read 1 John 3:16–19. The writer goes from the general (verse 16) to the specific (verses 17–18). Do you hesitate to help others in need, or are you leading the way to demonstrate love practically to those around you?

DAY 276
Love refreshes

A generous man will prosper;
he who refreshes others will himself be refreshed.

Proverbs 11:25 NIV

Life is hard. But usually what we mean by that is *our* life is hard. We're the first to feel it when *we're* the ones being mistreated or inconvenienced. We're quick to sulk when *we're* the ones who feel deprived or unappreciated.

But too often, the only way we notice that life is hard for our mate is when they start complaining about it. Then, instead of genuinely caring or rushing in to help, we might think they just have a bad attitude. Instead of rightly judging the situation, we turn a deaf ear to their concerns.

Not when love is at work.

Love doesn't have to be jarred awake by your mate's obvious signs of distress. Before worries and troubles have begun to bury them, love has already gone into action mode. It sees the weight beginning to pile up, and it steps in to help. That's because love calls us to be sensitive, proactive, and protective of our spouse.

❧ THIS WEEK'S DARE ❧

What is one of the greatest needs in your spouse's life right now? Is there one you could lift from their shoulders by a daring act of sacrifice on your part? Whether the need is big or small, purpose to do what you can to meet the need.

DAY 277
Love meets needs

"For I was hungry and you gave Me something to eat;
I was thirsty and you gave Me something to drink."

Matthew 25:35

There are needs you should be looking for in your wife or husband. Instead of sitting around upset that they're not treating you the way they should, let love turn your attention to *their* needs. Spend time asking and noticing what they may be lacking. Determine what you may be able to do to help fulfill them.

Is he "hungry"—needing you sexually, even when you don't feel like it? Is she "thirsty"—craving the time and attention you give to everyone else? Does he feel like a "stranger"—insecure in his work, needing home to be a refuge? Is she "naked"—frightened or ashamed, desperate for the warm covering of your affirmation? Is he feeling "sick"—physically tired and needing you to help guard him from interruptions? Does she feel in "prison"—fearful and depressed, needing some safety and intervention?

The words, "How can I help you?" need to stay fresh on your lips at all times.

◆ PRAYER ◆

"Lord Jesus, help us meet each other's needs in a way that shows love and value to one another. Teach us to take joy in delighting our spouse. In Your name we pray, amen."

Day 278
Love takes heed

Perfume and incense bring joy to the heart, and the pleasantness of one's friend springs from his earnest counsel.

Proverbs 27:9 NIV

When your mate is overwhelmed and under the gun, love calls you to set aside what seems essential in your own life to help, even if it's merely the gift of a listening ear. Often all they really need is just to talk the situation out. They need to see in your two attentive eyes that you truly care about what this is costing them and you're serious about helping them seek answers. They need you to pray with them about what to do, and then keep following up to see how it's going.

The solutions may be simple and easy, or they may be complex and require energy and great effort. Either way, you should do whatever you can to meet the real needs of this one that is a part of who you are. It's the kind of attention and support you'd love to know was waiting for you when you have a need. Be the one who takes the lead in taking heed.

⟶ THIS WEEK'S DARE ⟵

What is one of the greatest needs in your spouse's life right now? Is there one you could lift from their shoulders by a daring act of sacrifice on your part? Whether the need is big or small, purpose to do what you can to meet the need.

DAY 279
Love is ready to act

Don't neglect to do good and to share,
for God is pleased with such sacrifices.

Hebrews 13:16

When you help your spouse, you are also helping yourself. That's the beautiful part of sacrificing for your mate. Jesus did it for us. And He extends the grace to do it for others.

When the New Testament church began to walk in love, their life together was marked by sharing and sacrifice. Their heartbeat was to worship the Lord and to serve His people. "All the believers were together and had everything in common. So they sold their possessions and property and distributed the proceeds to all, as anyone had a need" (Acts 2:44–45). As Paul said to one of these churches in a later decade, "I will most gladly spend and be spent for you" (2 Corinthians 12:15).

Lives that have been raised from death by Jesus' sacrifice should be ready and willing to make daily sacrifices to meet the needs of others. And nowhere should this be more evident and exercised than in our own homes, in our own families, and in our own marriages.

QUESTIONS

How often would your spouse say you willingly make sacrifices for them? When you do, is it with a joyful attitude, or is it usually with strings attached? What would they say your motives typically are?

Love is free to serve

You are called to freedom, brothers; only don't use this freedom as an opportunity for the flesh, but serve one another through love.

Galatians 5:13

Jesus explained that the key to greatness and honor is to become a servant of others. It is possible, however, to serve in such a way that your spouse almost wishes you hadn't. When you spotlight the things you've been doing, and compare their inferior contributions to yours, you miss the whole point of having a servant's heart. It's hard for them to feel your love coming through when you serve everything with a side of martyr complex.

The beauty of service is in staying humble and viewing it as a privilege. Yes, you do have the freedom to watch television, work out, or take part in any number of self-serving activities. But love leads you to declare yourself free from having to cater to your own demanding wants and wishes. You are now free to serve your spouse with joy and gratitude—not because you have to or because they expect it. No more complaining or keeping a scorecard, not when serving is enjoyed as the "greatest" thing you can do (Matthew 23:11).

GO DEEPER

Read Matthew 23:1–12 and notice the disdain of Christ on those who serve hypocritically or for personal glory. What attitude should we maintain while we serve according to verse 12?

DAY 281
Love stays motivated

*Render service with a good attitude,
as to the Lord and not to men.*

Ephesians 6:7

It doesn't take much experience to discover that your mate will not always motivate your love. In fact, many times they will *de-motivate* it. More often than you'd like, it will seem difficult to find the inspiration to demonstrate your love. That's simply the nature of life, even in fairly healthy marriages.

Although moods and emotions can create moving motivational targets, one is certain to stay in the same place, all the time. When God Himself is your reason for loving, your ability to love is guaranteed. That's because it comes from Him—and flows through you.

The love that's demanded from us in marriage is not dependent on our mate's sweetness or suitability. The love between a husband and a wife should have one chief objective: honoring the Lord with devotion and sincerity. The fact that it blesses our beloved in the process is simply a wonderful, additional benefit.

⌾ THIS WEEK'S DARE ⌾

Pray for the needs of your spouse. Whether it comes easy for you or not, say "I love you," then express love to them in some tangible way. Thank God for giving you the privilege of loving this one special person—unconditionally, the way He loves both of you.

Day 282
Love has a single source

*Whatever you do, do it enthusiastically,
as something done for the Lord and not for men.*

Colossians 3:23

When you were a child, your parents established rules for you to follow. Your bedtime was at a certain hour. Your room had to be kept mostly clean. Your schoolwork needed to be finished before you could play. If you were like most people, you bent these rules as often as possible.

But if you met Christ along the way, you probably were exposed to this idea—"Children, obey your parents in everything, for this is pleasing in the Lord" (Colossians 3:20). Obedience was no longer a battle between you and your parents. It was now between you and God.

Knowing that God is your source and supply—of your own needs as well as those of your spouse—changes your whole reason for interacting with your mate. No longer does this imperfect person decide how much love you'll show. Rather, your omni-perfect God uses even a flawed person like yourself to bestow loving favor on another. In this way, your love is not determined by who your mate is, but who your God is.

⤺⤻ GO DEEPER ⤺⤻

Paul challenged believers to allow their relationship with Christ to become the motivation behind what they do. Read Ephesians 6:1, 5–9 and look for the words "in the Lord" or "as to Christ." Take note of the reward he mentions in verse 8.

DAY 283
Love has a goal

*Wives, be submissive to your husbands, as is fitting
in the Lord. . . . Husbands, love your wives, just as also
Christ loved the church and gave Himself for her.*

Colossians 3:18; Ephesians 5:25

Has your wife become hard to live with lately? Is her
slowness at getting over a disagreement wearing on your
patience? Don't withhold your love just because she thinks
differently. Love her "as to the Lord."

Is your husband tuning you out, apparently brooding over
something he's not interested in sharing? Do you feel hurt
by his unwillingness to open up? Don't battle back with a
double dose of silence and inattention. Love him anyway. As
to the Lord.

Love motivated by mere duty can never hold out for very
long. Only love that is lifted up as an offering to God is able
to sustain itself when all other reasons have lost their ability
to energize us. If you are committed to giving your spouse
the best love you possibly can, you need to shoot for love's
highest motivation. Love that has God as its primary focus is
love that doesn't yet know the heights it can attain.

❧ THIS WEEK'S DARE ❧

Pray for the needs of your spouse. Whether it comes
easy for you or not, say "I love you," then express love
to them in some tangible way. Thank God for giving
you the privilege of loving this one special person—
unconditionally, the way He loves both of you.

Love brings unity

"Holy Father, protect them by Your name that You have given Me, so that they may be one as We are one."

John 17:11

One of the most impressive things about the Bible is the way it is linked together from beginning to end. Though written more than approximately 1,600 years ago, composed by more than forty writers, God sovereignly authored it with one united voice.

Unity. Togetherness. Oneness. These are the unshakable hallmarks of our God.

From the very beginning of time, we see His unity at work through the Trinity—Father, Son, and Holy Spirit. They serve each other, love each other, and honor each other. Though distinct, they are One, indivisible.

Since this relationship is so special, He has chosen to let us experience an aspect of it as well. In the one unique relationship of husband and wife, two distinct individuals are spiritually united into "one flesh" (Genesis 2:24). And "what God has joined together, man must not separate" (Mark 10:9). It's easy to divide two. It's hard to divide one.

❧ PRAYER ☙

"Father God, keep us knitted together in love and purpose. Draw us closer in our marriage with each passing year, and guard our hearts for Your glory and Your use. In Jesus' name, amen."

DAY 285
Love defends unity

*Make every effort to keep the unity of the Spirit
through the bond of peace.*

Ephesians 4:3 NIV

The love between husband and wife is so intertwined and complete, God uses the imagery of marriage to explain His love for the church. The church (the bride) is most honored when its Savior is worshipped and celebrated. Christ (the bridegroom) is most honored when He sees her "as a radiant church, without stain or wrinkle or any other blemish, but holy and blameless" (Ephesians 5:27 NIV). Both Christ and the church love and honor the other. That's the beauty of unity.

What would happen in your marriage, husband, if you devoted yourself to loving, honoring, and serving your wife in all things? What would happen, wife, if you made it your mission to do everything possible to respect and support your husband? What if every threat to your unity was treated as a poison, to be eliminated by love, humility, and selflessness? What would that require of you? How would it change you?

The greater the health of your unity, the more immune you will be to the sickness of division.

⤖ THIS WEEK'S DARE ⤖

Pray for the needs of your spouse. Whether it comes easy for you or not, say "I love you," then express love to them in some tangible way. Thank God for giving you the privilege of loving this one special person—unconditionally, the way He loves both of you.

Love promotes unity

Over all these virtues put on love,
which binds them all together in perfect unity.

Colossians 3:14 NIV

The unity of the Trinity is evidence of the power of one-ness. It is unbreakable. It is unending. And it is this same spiritual reality that disguises itself at your home and mail-ing address. Though painted in the colors of work schedules, doctor visits, and trips to the grocery store, oneness is the eternal thread that runs through the daily experience of what we call "our marriage" and gives it a purpose to be defended for life.

Therefore, love this one who is as much a part of your body as you are. Serve this one whose needs cannot be sepa-rated from your own. Honor this one who, when raised upon the pedestal of your love, raises you up also in the eyes of God, all at the same time.

Ask the Lord to reveal anything in your own heart that is threatening oneness with your spouse. Pray that He would do the same for them. If appropriate, discuss this matter openly, seeking God for unity.

QUESTIONS

How unified are you and your spouse on important matters? Are you each willing to do what's best over your desire to get your way? If any issues have not been worked out in your relationship, are you willing to take them to God together in prayer?

DAY 287

Love cooperates

*Then God said, "Let Us make man
in Our image, according to Our likeness."*

Genesis 1:26

One of the qualities the Bible reveals about the Trinity is
that they always cooperate together. The work of Creation,
for example, was a collaborative effort. Inside the oneness of
their being, each of them—Father, Son, and Holy Spirit—
was involved in bringing forth life, as indicated by the "Us"
and "Our" pronouns in Genesis 1:26. The "Spirit of God" is
seen "hovering over the surface of the waters" (Genesis 1:2).
The Father is declared to have appointed the Son "heir of
all things," the One "through whom He made the universe"
(Hebrews 1:2).

This spirit of cooperation is also designed to exist in the
special relationship you share as husband and wife. God
has placed a calling on your life together, and it will require
both of you working in tandem to accomplish it through His
strength. Begin thinking of yourselves like this in more and
more aspects of your lives, from your praying to your child
rearing to your financial goals and record keeping. Join your
efforts in every way possible as you pursue God's purposes.

❧ GO DEEPER ❧

Read John 14:25–31. Observe how Jesus, the Holy
Spirit, and the heavenly Father all cooperate together
in loving interaction. How do they each support One
another?

Love honors each other

"May they all be one, as You, Father, are in Me and I am in You. May they also be one in Us."

John 17:21

The relationship between the members of the Trinity is one of perfect honor and respect. They bless each other. They find significant joy by being in each other's presence. They desire and appreciate the expressions of love and acceptance they receive, while giving glory to each other in a way that is deeply felt and fiercely loyal. They are one—and totally complete.

This is the model your marriage is to follow. Though your relationship may be colored by healthy elements of fun and lightheartedness, it is to be based on a genuine sense of honor. Compliments should come freely to your lips. When speaking about your mate to others in public, you should always refer to them in terms of gratitude and admiration. Your friends should be able to say, "They truly adore each other."

Those at Jesus' baptism had this feeling, after seeing the Spirit of God "descending as a dove" and lighting on Jesus, as the Father proclaimed, "This is My beloved Son, in whom I am well-pleased" (Matthew 3:16–17). Love with this kind of honor.

∼ THIS WEEK'S DARE ∼

Isolate one area of division in your marriage. Ask the Lord to reveal anything that is threatening oneness with your spouse. Pray that He would do the same for them. If appropriate, discuss this matter openly, seeking God for unity.

Love serves and submits

"I have glorified You on the earth
by completing the work You gave Me to do."

John 17:4

Submission may be a hot-button topic in marriage, but when we see it practiced within the Trinity, we lose some of our zeal to rebel against it. Jesus' life on Earth gives remarkable, almost surprising accounts of how He freely bent His will to the Father's. Though "He is before all things, and by Him all things hold together" (Colossians 1:17), even Jesus—with His supreme stature over all creation—submits His will within the Trinity. Likewise the Spirit, sent to us by the Son, serves by carrying out Jesus' desired ministry today.

We are meant to learn from this model. Our marriages are designed to reflect this kind of deference toward one another as we yield our rights in order to serve each other. Obviously neither of you is God. You are not able to trust completely, as the Trinity can, that your mate knows all, sees all, or is incapable of error. But we honor God and each other when we set our goals high and strive to follow the example He has placed before us.

GO DEEPER

Read how Jesus prayed for His followers in John 17:20–26. He used the loving dynamic of the Trinity as the basis for His prayer. When a husband and wife both seek to honor God together, it will bring them into a loving unity.

DAY 290
Love handles money well

"So if you have not been trustworthy in handling worldly wealth, who will trust you with true riches?"

Luke 16:11 NIV

Countless divorces are related to money problems. That's because money is a double-edged sword. It enables us to meet our family's needs and advance God's kingdom, but it can deeply wound us if we set our hearts on it and chase it. Scripture says, "But those who want to get rich fall into temptation and a snare and many foolish and harmful desires which plunge men into ruin and destruction" (1 Timothy 6:9 NASB).

People spend their lives working countless hours to get money. Our pride is fed by the status it brings, the pleasure it promises, and the power it gives. But it can easily become an idol and passion if we are not careful. It can take the place of God and be seen as our "provider."

Jesus spoke carefully about seeking God first in your life and not letting fear, greed, or money worries dictate your decisions. Everything we possess is a gift from God (James 1:17). He's our true Provider. By managing money as His—not ours—we take the first big step toward handling it properly.

◦◦◦ THIS WEEK'S DARE ◦◦◦

Isolate one area of division in your marriage. Ask the Lord to reveal anything that is threatening oneness with your spouse. Pray that He would do the same for them. If appropriate, discuss this matter openly, seeking God for unity.

DAY 291
Love believes in giving

Honor the LORD with your possessions
and with the first produce of your entire harvest.

Proverbs 3:9

God reveals Himself as One who gives—freely and abundantly. Christ's offering of His life is sacrificial giving at its absolute best and deepest. If we are to be like Him, then, we must be giving people. From the Old Testament (Malachi 3:10) through the New (Matthew 23:23), the standard of giving was established as the tithe—10 percent—taken not from the leftovers, but rather as an offering from the first of our income. No, God doesn't need our money. But in tithing, we guard our hearts from greed while worshipping Him as the giver of all 100 percent. It is a way to exercise our faith while also blessing others. But the tithe is merely a starting place. The nature of grace is to go beyond.

To prove how giving He is, God responds to the giving of our money and resources with the giving of His great provision. He knows our hearts naturally doubt that we can do more with less, so He invites us to test Him: "See if I will not open the floodgates of heaven and pour out a blessing for you without measure" (Malachi 3:10). Try it yourself. Let Him prove Himself faithful. You'll discover that you can't out-give God.

❧ PRAYER ❧

"Lord, forgive us for failing to be generous with what You have given us. Lead us to boldly obey You in this, knowing that it honors You and blesses others. In Jesus' name, amen."

DAY 292
Love avoids debt

The one who loves money is never satisfied with money,
and whoever loves wealth is never satisfied with income.

Ecclesiastes 5:10

Greed never stays within its banks. It can lead to mounting debt that eats away at the peace and harmony in your marriage. Even if the financial strain is less about greed and more the result of trying to survive on meager funds, the outcome is the same. Debt is a drain on your life. It heightens your anxiety, enslaves you, and activates blame and unrest.

That's why love leads us to avoid financial debt. The Bible says, "If you have nothing with which to pay, why should he take away your bed from under you?" (Proverbs 22:27 NKJV). When we owe more than we make, the basic, loving elements of marriage that are supposed to keep our sails full are replaced by overwork and fatigue. We become touchy and preoccupied. Marriage becomes more of a business endeavor, a moneymaking operation, rather than the sharing of love and life together.

When you choose to add more debt to your life—whether through impatience, greed, or worry—you are multiplying long-term stress to your time, commitments, and marriage.

◔ THIS WEEK'S DARE ◔

Isolate one area of division in your marriage. Ask the Lord to reveal anything that is threatening oneness with your spouse. Pray that He would do the same for them. If appropriate, discuss this matter openly, seeking God for unity.

DAY 293
Love makes decisions together

Let us judge for ourselves what is right;
let us decide together what is good.

Job 34:4

Many of the arguments that arise over money come from one spouse making a decision without consulting the other. When you show up at home with a major purchase, or over-rule your mate's sense of caution about an investment or house-buying negotiation, you break down the trust in your relationship. You declare yourself more capable at making these calls alone than with help. And when one of these decisions proves unsound—and it will—you open up your marriage for blame and resentment.

One of you is likely more adept than the other at balancing the checkbook and organizing a bill payment system. But even though you've opted to let him or her take the lead in managing your money, this doesn't mean you can afford to forfeit the other's insight in making financial decisions. God has given you one another to balance out your strengths and weaknesses. By teaming up and listening to each other's judgment, you'll do a better job of keeping your account balances and your marriage out of the red.

⟡ QUESTIONS ⟡

Are you a good listener? What would your spouse say? Would you be willing to make some "unity rules" with your spouse the next time you have a big decision to make?

Day 294

Love serves God, not money

"No one can be a slave of two masters, since either he will hate one and love the other, or be devoted to one and despise the other. You cannot be slaves of God and of money."

Matthew 6:24

One of life's most significant Love Dares is this: the choice to love and serve God rather than money. "For the love of money is a root of all kinds of evil, and by craving it, some have wandered away from the faith and pierced themselves with many pains" (1 Timothy 6:10).

In life, you will have many opportunities to put "getting more money" above your marriage, your family, and God. You will be given chances to orient your life around how to pay for the next big purchases you desire. Either way, it all comes down to the priority of your heart. Jesus said that we can serve God or money, but not both. Therefore, don't promote money into a management position. Don't submit to it as your boss. Rather, force your money to submit to you, to play by your rules. God promises to take good care of those who seek Him first. Therefore, let money become a *tool* of worship, not an *object* of worship.

∽ GO DEEPER ∽

Read Matthew 6:19–21. Will you use money as a tool of worship? How will the warning in verse 24 affect your life and decisions? Which master will you serve?

Love and marriage

"For this reason a man will leave his father and mother
and be joined to his wife, and the two will become one flesh."

Matthew 19:5

God has a blueprint for how marriage is supposed to work. It involves a tearing away and a knitting together. It reconfigures existing relationships while establishing a brand new one. That's why couples who don't take this "leaving" and "cleaving" message to heart will reap the consequences down the line. That's when the problems are much harder to repair without hurting someone.

Leaving means that you are breaking a natural tie. Your parents step into the role of counselors to be respected but can no longer tell you what to do. The purpose of "leaving" is not to abandon all contact with the past, but rather to preserve the unique oneness that marriage is designed to capture. *Cleaving* carries the idea of catching something or someone by pursuit, clinging to them as your new rock of refuge and safety.

Leave. And cleave. And dare to walk as one.

❧ THIS WEEK'S DARE ❧

Is there a "leaving" issue you haven't conquered yet? Confess it to your spouse today, and resolve to make it right. Follow this with a commitment to your spouse and to God to make your marriage the top priority over every other human relationship.

DAY 296
Love values oneness

"So they are no longer two, but one flesh.
Therefore what God has joined together, man must not separate."

Matthew 19:6

When a young person gets married, a parent may not be ready to release him or her from their control and expectations. Whether through unhealthy dependence or inner struggles over the empty nest, parents don't always embrace their new role and responsibility. In such cases, the grown child—now married—has to make "leaving" a courageous choice of their own. It may be one of the hardest things you've ever done, but it honors God's design, and it will only get harder the longer you put it off.

If you're too tightly connected to your parents, the independent identity of your marriage will not be able to flower. You will always be held back, and roots of resentment and division will send up new shoots into your relationship. For without "leaving," you cannot do the "cleaving" you need, the joining of your hearts that's required to experience oneness. Unity is a marriage quality to be guarded at great cost. Only in oneness can you become all that God means for you to be.

◦◦◦ PRAYER ◦◦◦

"Father God, if we have any unresolved issues that are preventing us from experiencing the oneness you designed for us, please expose them and teach us to trust You with them. In Jesus' name, amen."

Love comes with a blueprint

*To sum up, each one of you is to love his wife as himself,
and the wife is to respect her husband.*

Ephesians 5:33

After your wedding ceremony, you are free to become everything God meant when He declared you "one flesh." You are able to achieve oneness in your decision making, even when you begin from differing viewpoints. You are able to achieve oneness in your priorities, even though you may have come together from vastly different backgrounds. You are able to achieve oneness in your sexual affections toward each other, even if either or both of you live with memories of impurity in your premarital past.

The man is now the spiritual leader of your new home, tasked with great responsibilities. He is to cherish and love his wife just as "Christ loved the church and gave Himself for her" (Ephesians 5:25). The wife is now in union with him, called to support his leadership and "see to it that she respects her husband" (Ephesians 5:33 NASB). When a couple follows God's blueprint for marriage, they begin building a love that can truly last a lifetime.

⤜⤳ THIS WEEK'S DARE ⤜⤳

Is there a "leaving" issue you haven't conquered yet? Confess it to your spouse today, and resolve to make it right. Follow this with a commitment to your spouse and to God to make your marriage the top priority over every other human relationship.

DAY 298
Love lives by design

"May they be one as We are one."

John 17:22

It's not unusual for couples of all kinds to ignore God's design for marriage, thinking they know better than He does how their relationship is supposed to work. Genesis 2:24 may have sounded nice and noble when it was wrapped around the sharing of vows at the wedding. But as a fundamental principle to be put into practice, this leaving and cleaving and becoming one flesh just seems too difficult to do. Though life may pressure us to go against the flow of God's plan, the reality is that He sees the bigger picture and is testing our faith while asking us to trust Him.

If you'll continue to keep God's passion for oneness forefront in your mind and heart, your relationship—over time—will begin to reflect the inescapable "one flesh" design that is printed on its DNA. You don't have to go looking for it. It's already there. But you do have to live it, or there's nothing else to hope for but dishonor and disunity.

GO DEEPER

Jesus ordained one model for marriage in Matthew 19:3–6, which comes from Genesis 2:24. Based on these passages, answer the following questions: What is required in a marriage? What breaking is necessary? How is it consummated? Is marriage heterosexual or homosexual? Does it come from heterosexual or homosexual parents? How is the new union described?

DAY 299
Love understands its role

A time to plant and a time to uproot what is planted.

Ecclesiastes 3:2 NASB

When a man and woman enter their wedding ceremony, they are still under their parents' authority. The moms and dads are seated first, given a place of honor. The father of the bride traditionally gives his daughter away. Until that moment, she has been under his protection and care. But after the service, the new husband and wife leave before anyone else. They walked in under another's authority; they walk out under God's. In the space of less than an hour, their parents have transitioned from the role of authorities to counselors.

Some cultures teach against this changing of roles, expecting even grown, married children to submit to the will of their parents for life. Even in cultures where this is not the case in theory, it can sometimes become the case in practice, when parents continue to wield power over the new couple's decisions. But this is not God's established plan. "A man leaves his father and mother and bonds with his wife, and they become one flesh" (Genesis 2:24). This is where love is designed to leave in order to cleave.

∼ THIS WEEK'S DARE ∼

Is there a "leaving" issue you haven't conquered yet? Confess it to your spouse today, and resolve to make it right. Follow this with a commitment to your spouse and to God to make your marriage the top priority over every other human relationship.

DAY 300
Love delights

*Your land will not be called Desolate; instead,
you will be called My Delight is in Her.*

Isaiah 62:4

In your marriage relationship, you won't always feel like loving. It is unrealistic for your heart to constantly thrill at the thought of spending every moment with your spouse. Nobody can maintain a burning desire for togetherness just on feelings alone. But it's also difficult to love someone only out of obligation.

Left to ourselves, we'll always lean toward being disapproving of one another. She'll get on your nerves. He'll aggravate you. But our days are too short to waste in bickering over petty things. Life is too fleeting for that. Instead, it's time to lead your heart once again to delight in your mate.

Enjoy your spouse. Take her hand and seek her companionship. Desire his conversation. Remember why you fell in love with her personality. Accept this person—quirks and all—and welcome him or her back into your heart.

✐✐ GO DEEPER ✐✐

Read Song of Solomon 5:2–8 and consider the fickleness of their feelings for one another. Observe how she reignites her desires for her husband.

Love brings oneness

Let the peace of Christ rule in your hearts, since as members of one body you were called to peace. And be thankful.

Colossians 3:15 NIV

It's time to let love change your thinking. It's time to realize that your spouse is as much a part of you as your hand, your eye, or your heart. They too need to be loved and cherished. And if your wife or husband has issues causing pain or frustration, then you should care for them with the same measure of love and tenderness as you would use on a bodily injury. If your spouse is wounded in some way, you should think of yourself as an instrument that helps bring healing to their life.

In light of this, think about how you treat your spouse's physical body. Do you cherish it as your own? Do you treat it with respect and tenderness? Or do you make them feel foolish and embarrassed? Do you make fun and belittle?

Just as you treasure your eyes, hands, and heart, you should treasure your spouse as a priceless gift.

✎❧ QUESTIONS ❧✎

Have you ever criticized your spouse's body in a hurtful way? If so, have you ever asked for forgiveness? What are some ways you could honor and cherish the body of your husband or wife?

DAY 302
Love continues to honor

*Honor your father and your mother so that you may have
a long life in the land that the LORD your God is giving you.*

Exodus 20:12

Even though a wife and husband are out from under their
obligation to obey their parents' commands, the Bible gives
clear instruction that honoring one's parents is a lifelong
duty.

Be free and generous with your expressions of thanks
toward your mom and dad. Give weight to their advice and
counsel, respecting their judgment and not rashly ignoring
what they have to say. Communicate with them about the
things that are happening in your life, knowing that many of
the blessings you enjoy are a derivative of their investment
in you. As they age, commit to caring for them in any way
possible, even if it becomes sacrificial and inconvenient.

It's true that some parents have been (and perhaps continue to be) cold, harsh, and uncivil toward you. And even
though you cannot honor their attitudes and actions, your
choice to live an exemplary, godly life will be a testament of
gratitude to them for giving you birth. "A wise son brings joy
to his father" (Proverbs 10:1). The greatest honor anyone can
give their parents is the honor of a life well lived.

∽ THIS WEEK'S DARE ∽

If possible, invite either of your parents (or an older
godly couple) out on a double date with you. Use the
"Treasure Hunters" list of questions in the appendix
to learn from their life experiences.

DAY 303
Love gives freedom

Where the Spirit of the Lord is, there is freedom.

2 Corinthians 3:17

In dealing with parents and in-laws, there is a world of difference between honoring and obeying. *Honoring* means rewarding them with your concern and respect. But they are not allowed to run your life or make demands on you. Your wedding tied the knot and permanently broke the umbilical cord. They, too, are called upon by God to show respect by letting you be the authority over your new family unit.

If this boundary is breached and violated, the grown child should go to his mother or father—with honor—and insist on a respect for privacy and the freedom to make decisions without fear of offending. These loving reminders may or may not be well received. But your allegiance to your spouse must take precedence over your desire to please your mom and dad.

If you are the parents of married children, you may be the first to notice when they are making mistakes, or you may have a hard time relating with your son-in-law or daughter-in-law. But you must be as aware of the boundaries as they are, showing loving restraint and trusting God for their care and future.

⮞⮞ GO DEEPER ⮜⮜

Jesus kept a balance in His teaching on honoring parents (read Matthew 15:1–6) while not getting out of bounds in your loyalty to them (read Matthew 10:37; 12:46–50).

DAY 304
Love establishes guidelines

Look, I am about to do something new; even now it is coming.

Isaiah 43:19

Some couples enter marriage trying to replicate what they experienced growing up and observed in their parents. Others, whose upbringing was far from the best, swing the pendulum and do as many things different from their parents as they can. Sometimes, the best lessons children learn from their parents are what *not* to do.

The truth is, even the best of parents make mistakes in raising their family. There may be much to emulate in your mother or father, and you are wise to learn from their good example and build upon their strengths. But your calling is not to become a mirror image of their marriage, as loving as it may be. God did give you the parents who raised you, but He wants you to build upon their successes while avoiding their failures. You must break the chains of generational sins by completely forgiving your parents and then moving on in faith. Most important, you are to submit your life to the Lordship of Christ and the guidance of His Word. Draw up the rules for your own family by following His. He is your standard and greatest ideal.

✿✦✦ THIS WEEK'S DARE ✦✦✿

If possible, invite either of your parents (or an older godly couple) out on a double date with you. Use the "Treasure Hunters" list of questions in the appendix to learn from their life experiences.

Love meets sexual needs

*Marriage should be honored by all,
and the marriage bed kept pure, for God will
judge the adulterer and all the sexually immoral.*

Hebrews 13:4 NIV

The biblical foundations of marriage were originally expressed in the creation of Adam and Eve. She was made to be "a helper suitable for him" (Genesis 2:18 NASB). The unity of their relationship and physical bodies was so strong, they were said to become "one flesh" (Genesis 2:24). This same oneness is a hallmark of every marriage. It's so sacred that we are not to share this same experience with anyone else.

"You were bought at a price," God declares in His Word (1 Corinthians 6:20). He set His affections on you and went to every length to draw you into desiring Him, just as He spoke to Israel, saying, "Behold, I will allure her . . . and speak kindly to her" (Hosea 2:14 NASB). Now it is your turn to win the heart of your mate. When you do, you will enjoy the pure delight that flows when sex is expressed for all the right reasons. You will also have the opportunity to "glorify God in your body" when you come together (1 Corinthians 6:20). How beautiful.

PRAYER

"Lord, give us the delight in our intimacy that You designed us to have. Help us love unselfishly and yearn to please one another in a way that pleases You. In Jesus' name, amen."

Love blesses intimacy

A husband should fulfill his marital duty to his wife,
and likewise a wife to her husband.

1 Corinthians 7:3

Some people think the Bible has nothing good to say about sex, as though all God seems concerned about is telling us when not to do it and who not to do it with. In reality, however, the Bible has a great deal to say about sex, and about the blessing it can be for both husband and wife. Even its boundaries and restrictions, in fact, are God's ways of keeping our sexual experiences at a level far beyond any of those advertised on television or in the movies. By enjoying sex in its appropriate place, we enjoy the freedom of letting it draw us into greater purity, rather than the shame of feeling it draw us away from His blessing and purposes.

In Christian marriage, romance is meant to thrive and flourish. After all, it was created by God. It's all part of celebrating what God has given, becoming one with our mate while simultaneously pursuing purity and holiness. He delights in us when this happens.

❧ THIS WEEK'S DARE ❧

If possible, invite either of your parents (or an older godly couple) out on a double date with you. Use the "Treasure Hunters" list of questions in the appendix to learn from their life experiences.

DAY 307
Love is designed to give

A wife does not have authority over her own body,
but her husband does. Equally, a husband does not have
authority over his own body, but his wife does.

1 Corinthians 7:4

Inside the boundaries of your marriage, it is biblically healthy to build sexual needs. Desire is not a reason for guilt or an urge to be resisted, but rather an opportunity for our oneness to be enjoyed, preserved, and celebrated. When this legitimate need goes unmet—when it's treated as selfish and demanding by the other—our hearts are subject to being drawn away from marriage, intent on filling this longing somewhere else, some other way.

This is why, to counteract this tendency, God established marriage with a "one flesh" mentality. Sex is not to be used as a bargaining chip. It is not something God allows us to withhold from the other without consequence. Though there can certainly be abuses to this divinely designed framework, the heart of marriage is one of giving ourselves to each other to meet the other's needs. Sex is one God-given opportunity for us to fulfill that purpose.

⟨⟨⟨ GO DEEPER ⟩⟩⟩

Read 1 Corinthians 7:1–5. God's desires for purity and oneness are met in a godly, healthy marriage. What does verse 5 say about the potential consequences of not being together sexually?

DAY 308
Love does not deprive

Do not deprive one another—except when you agree, for a time, to devote yourselves to prayer. Then come together again; otherwise, Satan may tempt you because of your lack of self-control.

1 Corinthians 7:5

You are the one person designated by God to meet your spouse's sexual needs. If you allow distance to grow between you in this area, you are taking something that rightly belongs to your spouse, leaving him or her to fight an inner war with frustration and sin. If you let your mate know that sex doesn't need to be any more than you want it to be, you rob your spouse of the biblically mandated honor and endearment that should be present in your relationship. You violate the "one flesh" unity of marriage by making it more about you.

So whether you are being deprived, or depriving the other, know that God's plan for you is to come to agreement with your spouse on this. Love is the only way to re-establish loving union between each other. All the things the Love Dare entails—patience, kindness, selflessness, thoughtfulness, protection, honor, forgiveness—will play a role in renewing your sexual intimacy.

✎ QUESTIONS ✎

How can you demonstrate to your spouse that you desire to meet their sexual needs with the right attitude? Would you say God is pleased with your view in this area?

Day 309
Love is pure

To the pure, everything is pure, but to those
who are defiled and unbelieving nothing is pure.

Titus 1:15

God created sex as a pure and holy gift to be fully enjoyed in the beauty of marital intimacy. It is not merely for consenting adults to share, but is God's wedding gift to a husband and a wife as an ongoing celebration of their covenant of love.

In many homes, awkwardness has kept parents from painting sexual feelings in terms of God's blessing, leaving children to enter marriage still thinking of sex as a dirty word. If either of you sinned by experiencing sexual intimacy before marriage, you may continue to carry around a tainted perception of sex as being impure.

This is the devil's way—to distort the honor of God's design, then tempt us to pursue the fulfillment of our desires in unholy ways. But if his deceptions have blurred the pure image of sex in your mind, now is the time to confess the sins of your past, embrace the cleansing mercy of God, and direct your thinking in accordance with His Word. God has given you a precious gift to enjoy with your spouse. Do so with pure, perfect freedom.

THIS WEEK'S DARE

If at all possible, try to initiate sex with your husband or wife. Do this in a way that honors what your spouse has told you they need from you sexually. Ask God to make this enjoyable for both of you as well as a path to greater intimacy.

DAY 310
Love accommodates

I belong to my love, and his desire is for me.
Song of Solomon 7:10

You and your mate are undoubtedly wired differently when it comes to what stirs your feelings of romance. In general, men are microwaves, quickly turned on and ready in a matter of seconds. Women, as a rule, are more like Crock-pots. Slow cookers. It takes time and patience to draw them out. Being sexually aroused requires planning and thinking ahead.

Like any gift you give to each other, it's important to know what your spouse enjoys—his likes and dislikes, her tastes and preferences. It should be part of the fun of marriage to talk to each other privately about what kindles sexual feelings within you. Some of the answers you hear may surprise you. Not everything that stimulates passion is necessarily silk and candles. A husband who offers to clean up the kitchen and bathe the kids may stir a woman's desire to be with him sexually. A wife taking her husband's hand and praying for him could make him want her even closer in his arms. Take the time to learn what engages your mate in this area. Then enjoy the intimacy that God designed just for the two of you.

✤✥ GO DEEPER ✤✥

How might the biblical principles of mutual submission (Ephesians 5:21) and mutual ownership (1 Corinthians 7:1–3) translate into loving accommodation in the marriage bed?

Day 311

Love recognizes value

"Don't give what is holy to dogs or toss your pearls before pigs."
Matthew 7:6

Holy matrimony is more than wording on a marriage license. Seeing your relationship in these sacred terms is one of the things that covers it in security and honor. It changes the way you treat or speak about your spouse and causes you to avoid doing anything that would make a mockery of this holy union. Treating marriage as anything less than holy would be like using your fine china to feed the pets, or mowing the grass in your wedding clothes.

This is why love leads us to lift our marriage up to a place of honor. We then openly praise and defend our mates in public, never criticizing them or making fun at their expense. We guard their honor and protect them as much as humanly possible from any harm that could come to them. We don't use vulgar language around them or entertain ourselves with forms of media that are unbefitting of the holy relationship we share. Love pursues what holiness is and seeks to preserve its sacredness even on the most ordinary of days.

❧ THIS WEEK'S DARE ❧

If at all possible, try to initiate sex with your husband or wife. Do this in a way that honors what your spouse has told you they need from you sexually. Ask God to make this enjoyable for both of you as well as a path to greater intimacy.

DAY 312
Love doesn't build weapons

This is my love, and this is my friend.

Song of Solomon 5:16

God has commanded husbands and wives to meet each other's sexual needs (1 Corinthians 7:3–5). This is not a suggestion; it is a command. Part of your promise when you agreed to enter into marriage was to lovingly tend to the needs of your mate. You also gave them your body as their holy possession.

It is quite possible that your spouse has not upheld their part of this commitment. They may not deserve to be treated with tenderness and acceptance. But even if your romantic desire for them is low or nonexistent, withholding affection will only deepen the divide between you. You may even find in returning to the marriage bed that this one concession could spark a renewal in your love for one another.

So if you are refusing your body to your spouse, using sex as a weapon to force your agenda and punish wrongs, you are joining them in disobedience. Love them as unto the Lord, in accordance with His Word and His love for you. If any tactics are needed in your marriage, let them be ones God uses to heal and restore.

～⌒⌒ PRAYER ⌒⌒～

"Lord, give us Your view of our bodies, that our intimacy is shared in joy and fulfilling love. Bind us together in heart, that we truly enjoy the gift You have given us to experience. In Jesus' name, amen."

DAY 313
Love treasures children

*"As for you, be fruitful and multiply;
populate the earth abundantly and multiply in it."*

Genesis 9:7 NASB

The Bible is written proof that God places a high value on children. His very first words to the newly created man and woman was to "be fruitful, multiply, fill the earth, and subdue it" (Genesis 1:28). His closing words of the Old Testament, leading up to Christ's coming, was to prophesy that He would "turn the hearts of fathers to their children and the hearts of children to their fathers" (Malachi 4:6). Jesus Himself obviously had high regard for children, as opposed to His disciples, who considered them a bother and interruption to Christ's more important work. "Let the little children come to Me," Jesus defended them. "Don't stop them, for the kingdom of God belongs to such as these" (Mark 10:14).

Our Lord is looking for "godly offspring" (Malachi 2:15). The Creator of life has designed marriage to be the nutrient-rich ground where His family can be born, grow, and thrive as a testimony to His power and righteousness. To love like God is to love children.

❧ THIS WEEK'S DARE ❧

If at all possible, try to initiate sex with your husband or wife. Do this in a way that honors what your spouse has told you they need from you sexually. Ask God to make this enjoyable for both of you as well as a path to greater intimacy.

DAY 314
Love longs for children

Sons are indeed a heritage from the LORD, children, a reward.

Psalm 127:3

Generations go through cycles where large families are either valued or discouraged. Some cultures place restrictions on the number of children a couple is expected to have. But the Bible is always our determiner of truth and wisdom. God declares through His Word that children are a blessing and gift from His hand. Most of us want all the blessings we can get.

When God speaks of children in Scripture, He often uses analogies of things that we generally want to possess a lot of, as much as we can hold. "Like arrows in the hand of a warrior" (Psalm 127:4)—does a fighting man in battle wish for only a limited amount of ammunition? Like fruit from a "fruitful vine" (Psalm 128:3)—do we prefer lots of fruit, or a little fruit? "A heritage from the Lord" (Psalm 127:3)—do most people hope for a small inheritance?

Whether through procreation or adoption, don't let your decisions about children be dictated by the world's standards, any more than by your own opinions and preferences. Let God's Word be your guide as you trust Him to build your family and grow the next faithful generation.

☙ QUESTIONS ❧

Have you asked the Lord how many children you are to have? Are your reasons biblical? Are you willing to trust Him in this area?

DAY 315
Love is best for the children

But I fear that, as the serpent deceived
Eve by his cunning, your minds may be corrupted
from a complete and pure devotion to Christ.

2 Corinthians 11:3

Though your love and loyalty to each other is instructed by Scripture to be as strong as death, it must always be subject to your higher devotion to Christ. And in the same way, as valuable as children are in the sight of God and His people, your marriage ultimately takes precedence. Parents are charged with making great sacrifices of themselves for their children. Personal getaways aren't to be expected every weekend. But parents who habitually ignore their one-on-one relationship for the sake of the children will suffer as a couple, and even cause their children to suffer from the indulgence.

One of the most commonly heard excuses for divorce is that it's "best for the children." But what's best for the children is seeing their mom and dad demonstrate unconditional love for each other, keep their commitments, work things out, and preserve a legacy of endurance. What's best for the children is when parents remember that loving each other is a gift they give not only to each other, but also to future generations.

☙ GO DEEPER ☙

Parents are commanded to train up their children (Ephesians 6:4) and meet their needs (1 Timothy 5:7–8), but successful children come from parents who stick together and avoid divorce (Malachi 2:13–15).

DAY 316
Love completes each other

Also, if two lie down together, they can keep warm;
but how can one person alone keep warm?

Ecclesiastes 4:11

God creates marriage by taking a man and a woman and uniting them as one. This "completing" aspect of love was revealed to mankind from the beginning.

God originated the human race with a male and a female—two similar but complementary designs meant to function in harmony. Our bodies are made for each other. Our natures and temperaments provide balance for each other, enabling us to more effectively complete the tasks at hand. Our oneness can produce children, and our teamwork can best raise them to health and maturity.

Where one is weak, the other is strong. When one needs building up, the other is equipped to enhance him, to encourage her. We can multiply one another's joys and divide one another's sorrows. Although our differences can frequently be the source of misunderstanding and conflict between us, they have been created by God and can be ongoing blessings if we respect them.

❧ THIS WEEK'S DARE ❧

Your spouse is integral to your future success. Let them know that you desire to include them in your upcoming decisions, and that you need their perspective and counsel. If you have ignored their input in the past, ask forgiveness.

DAY 317
Love multiplies effectiveness

For if either falls, his companion can lift him up;
but pity the one who falls without another to lift him up.

Ecclesiastes 4:10

Your two hands don't just coexist together. They multiply the effectiveness of the other. They cooperate together to accomplish tasks that neither could do without both of them working in harmony. And to continue succeeding at this level, each hand must be seen as incomplete without the other.

The same truth applies in marriage. One of you may be better at cooking, while the other is more thorough at cleaning the dishes. One may be more gentle and able to keep peace among family members, while the other handles discipline more effectively. One may have a good business head but needs the other to help him remember to be generous.

When we learn to accept the unique distinctions in our mate, we can bypass criticism and go straight to helping and appreciating one another. Take advantage of the uniqueness that makes each of us more effective, and be grateful for the benefits this adds to your marriage.

✧✦ GO DEEPER ✦✧

Read the amazing truths found in Ecclesiastes 4:9–12. Do you and your spouse recognize the value that the other one adds to your life? Study this passage and seek to become a living example of it. Let God become the third strand of your marriage.

DAY 318
Love receives insight

While he was sitting on the judge's bench, his wife sent word to him, "Have nothing to do with that righteous man."

Matthew 27:19

Pontius Pilate, the Roman governor who presided over the trial of Jesus, was unaware of who Christ was. And against his better judgment, he allowed the crowd to influence him into crucifying Jesus. But the one person who was more sensitive to what was really happening was Pilate's own wife, who came to him at the height of the uproar and warned him he was making a mistake.

Pilate's dismissal of his wife's intuition reveals an unfortunate side to man's nature. God made wives to complete their husbands, and He gives them insight that in many cases is kept from their men. If this discernment is ignored, it is often to the detriment of the man making the decision. We are always in a better position to see all angles of a situation when we work together, bringing our various perspectives and insights to bear on the matter. When husbands "live with [their] wives in an understanding way" (1 Peter 3:7 NASB), they are honoring their brides and guarding their marital unity.

☙ THIS WEEK'S DARE ❧

Your spouse is integral to your future success. Let them know that you desire to include them in your upcoming decisions, and that you need their perspective and counsel. If you have ignored their input in the past, ask forgiveness.

Day 319
Love asks for help

Plans fail when there is no counsel,
but with many advisers they succeed.

Proverbs 15:22

The effectiveness of your marriage is dependent upon both of you working together. Do you have big decisions to make about your finances? Are you having a real problem with a coworker? Are you absolutely convinced that your educational choices for the children are right, no matter what your spouse thinks?

Don't do all the analysis yourself. Don't deny your spouse's right to voice an opinion on matters that affect both of you. Love realizes that God has put you together on purpose. And though you may wind up disagreeing with your mate's perspectives, you should still give their views respect and strong consideration. This honors God's design for your relationship and guards the oneness He intends. The process of sharing and listening keeps your mutual respect and trust level high. Joined together, you are greater than your independent parts. You need each other. You complete each other.

PRAYER

"Father God, we need You to remind us to keep our spouse involved in our lives. Make us even more of a team. Make us partners in what You've called us to do. Bless us in Jesus' name, amen."

Love steps up

Then the LORD God took the man and put him into the garden of Eden to cultivate it and keep it.

Genesis 2:15 NASB

Adam had many jobs in the Garden. He was commissioned to tend and bring to flower the vegetation God had placed there. He was tasked with naming and giving identity to the creatures who shared this ideal living space. He was given a woman to love and lead, uniting with her as one flesh and honoring her as his wife.

These same goals and commands exist for men today. They are called to courageously lead their families in total submission to the Father, "from whom every family in heaven and on earth is named" (Ephesians 3:15). They are called to establish their wife and children's identity, helping them walk in the confidence of being beloved. They are called to bloom the hearts of their family members, to guard and protect them, to work and provide for them, to teach and train them in faithful love and truth. By fearing God and loving Him wholeheartedly, a man can confidently say, "As for me and my house, we will serve the Lord" (Joshua 24:15 NASB).

♔ THIS WEEK'S DARE ♔

Your spouse is integral to your future success. Let them know that you desire to include them in your upcoming decisions, and that you need their perspective and counsel. If you have ignored their input in the past, ask forgiveness.

DAY 321
Love is a blessing

*A house and wealth are inherited from fathers,
but a sensible wife is from the LORD.*

Proverbs 19:14

Just as men are given biblically ordained roles in marriage, women also are called with duties and responsibilities that are significant. The woman was created by God to be a "helper" or "helpmeet" to the man (Genesis 2:18). She comes alongside to support him in his work and position, enabling him to succeed by giving of herself. She is equipped to serve with him as a friend, and to be the only lover who ministers to his needs. "A capable wife is her husband's crown" (Proverbs 12:4).

As a mother, she provides for the needs of her children and family, expending herself to ensure they are clothed, fed, and nurtured. "She opens her mouth with wisdom" to counsel with her godly insight, and "loving instruction is on her tongue" (Proverbs 31:26). Though a companion to her husband, she is also a sister in Christ and co-heir of God's grace (1 Peter 3:7), encouraging her spouse to remain true to his calling in the Lord. She blesses God by blessing those around her.

QUESTIONS

Husbands, do you honor your wife as an invaluable helpmate to your life? If not, would you be willing to ask God to give you His perspective?

DAY 322
Love is respectful

Do this with gentleness and respect,
keeping your conscience clear.

1 Peter 3:16

All men deeply long to be respected. It's hard to underestimate the value of respect in a man's heart, the strength that quickens in his backbone when his wife gives him honor for who he is and what he does. There's a reason why God sums up His instructions on marriage by commanding the wife to "respect her husband" (Ephesians 5:33). It resonates with his manhood and becomes like adrenaline in his bloodstream. He can feel his confidence begin to surge. No matter how ashamed or defeated he may be, a wife's gentle respect begins the process that rallies him back into action.

Men simply tend to gravitate toward environments where they are respected more and held in higher honor. This is not to say that failure to treat him with high regard is an excuse for him to abandon the home or make himself scarce. Neither does it mean that everything he does is respectable or worthy of admiration. But there are ways to graciously confront your husband that will leave him feeling loved and encouraged. Like it or not, your constant respect is the secret to his heart.

☙ GO DEEPER ❧

Read Ephesians 5:33 and 1 Peter 3:1–2. God is explaining the key to a wife's success. The command to respect remains regardless of whether her husband is a believer or not.

Love is to die for

*"No one has greater love than this,
that someone would lay down his life for his friends."*

John 15:13

Few men live for something worth dying for. But every husband has that in his wife. Some challenge the notion that wives owe respect to their husbands. But what could be more daunting than being commanded by God to love someone to death—literally, to consider your spouse worthy of sacrificing your life for?

That's what God's Word declares. "Husbands, love your wives, just as also Christ loved the church and gave Himself for her" (Ephesians 5:25). And though defending your wife in love is not likely to come to physical death, she is worth your life every day—worth a deliberate, ongoing decision to die to yourself and lay down all that you are in serving her.

She doesn't have to be loving in return for this to remain your mission. Our love was certainly not a prerequisite for Christ's love of us. God has created her with a deep need in her heart to be loved and cherished. And He created you as the one she needs to receive it from. Love her first. Love her courageously. Love her sacrificially.

∽ THIS WEEK'S DARE ∽

Find a specific, recent example when your spouse demonstrated Christian character in a noticeable way. Verbally commend them for this at some point this week.

Love is wise

Don't abandon wisdom, and she will watch over you;
love her, and she will guard you.

Proverbs 4:6

You would not do anything in your right mind to intentionally dishonor your marriage. But when foolishness reigns in your home, then pride and disgrace follow close behind. Unfortunately, foolishness is the by-product of a life lived without wisdom, which comes from God, His Word, thoughtful listening, and keen observation.

Few things are more richly satisfying to possess in marriage than wisdom, and it yields a much greater return on your investment. In fact, wisdom is always connected to other noble qualities like humility and honor, which go a long way in helping your marital relationship.

Foolishness, on the other hand, is permanently connected with pride and shame. It always leads to disharmony and dishonor. A wise person builds their house, "but a foolish one tears it down with her own hands" (Proverbs 14:1). With wisdom, you get honor. With foolishness, you get disgrace. One is priceless, and the other worthless. And the one you spend your time pursuing will reflect the kind of person you really are.

❧ GO DEEPER ❧

Read Proverbs 11:2; 14:1; and 18:12. Each of these encourage us to embrace a lifestyle of wisdom. Wisdom is the correct application of knowledge, resulting in good decisions.

Day 325
Love celebrates godliness

[Love] finds no joy in unrighteousness, but rejoices in the truth.

1 Corinthians 13:6

From the moment you close your Bible in the morning, nearly everything else you'll encounter throughout the day will be luring you away from its truths. The opinions of your coworkers, the news on television, your typical Web sites—all of these and more will be working to shape your perceptions of what's true and most desirable in life.

They'll say a lot of things. And they'll say them loudly and frequently enough that if you're not careful, you can start believing them. You can begin valuing what everybody else values. Thinking the way everybody else does.

But the meaning of "real life" changes dramatically when we understand that God's Word is the ultimate expression of what real life is. The teachings it contains are not just good guesses at what should matter to us. They are principles that reflect the way things really are and the way God created life to be. His ideals and instructions are the only pathways to real blessing. And when we see people following them in obedience to the Lord, it should cause us to rejoice.

THIS WEEK'S DARE

Find a specific, recent example when your spouse demonstrated Christian character in a noticeable way. Verbally commend them for this at some point this week.

DAY 326
Love is influential

I have no greater joy than this:
to hear that my children are walking in the truth.

3 John 4

What makes you the proudest of your husband? Is it when he comes home with a trophy from the company golf tournament, or is it when he gathers the family before bed to pray together and read the Word?

What overjoys you the most in your wife? Is it seeing her try a new painting technique in the children's bedrooms, or is it seeing her forgive the neighbor whose dog dug up some of her flowers?

You are one of the most influential people in your spouse's life. Have you been using your influence to lead them to honor God, or to dishonor Him? Love rejoices most in the things that please God. When your mate is growing in Christian character, persevering in faith, seeking purity, and embracing roles of giving and service—becoming spiritually responsible in your home—the Bible says we should celebrate it. The word *rejoices* in 1 Corinthians 13:6 carries the idea of being absolutely thrilled, excitedly cheering them on for what they're allowing God to accomplish in their lives.

❧ PRAYER ❧

"Lord, give us eyes to see the value in the mate You have blessed us with, and the voice to encourage them to seek You and to do Your will with passion. In Your name, amen."

Day 327
Love exhorts one another

We must always thank God for you, brothers,
which is fitting, since your faith is flourishing.

2 Thessalonians 1:3

The apostle Paul, who helped establish and minister to many of the first-century churches, wrote in his letters how delighted he was to hear reports of the people's faithfulness and growth in Jesus. He said, "Therefore we ourselves boast about you among God's churches—about your endurance and faith in all the persecutions and afflictions you endure" (2 Thessalonians 1:4).

This should be what energizes us when we see it happening in our mate. More than when they save money on the grocery bill. More than when they achieve success at work. When we catch our spouse displaying godly attributes, it should cause a joy to rise in our hearts that far outweighs any other success. And our verbal encouragement should be like wind in their sails, pushing them onward to become more like Christ. Make frequent use of your ability to bless your wife or husband as you notice them honoring the Lord and being a blessing to your family and others.

❧ THIS WEEK'S DARE ❧

Find a specific, recent example when your spouse demonstrated Christian character in a noticeable way. Verbally commend them for this at some point this week.

Day 328
Love rejoices in growth

The report of your obedience has reached everyone.
Therefore I rejoice over you. But I want you to be wise
about what is good, yet innocent about what is evil.

Romans 16:19

When we focus on the Word of God, we see life differently. The value of godly decisions begins to matter more
to us, and the standard of holiness becomes a strong desire.
Ultimately, the pursuit of godliness, purity, and faithfulness
is the only way to find joy and fulfillment. Being "wise" about
holiness while being "innocent" about sin is the way to win
in God's eyes. And what more could we want for our wife or
husband than for them to experience the best that life has
to offer, no matter what the world says should matter most
to us?

Life will give you and your spouse many opportunities
to respond to both success and hardship. And in most cases,
you will respond to them together. So be happy for any success your spouse enjoys. But save your heartiest congratulations for those times when they are honoring God with their
worship and obedience even in tough times, when their
maturity in Christ is most clearly on display.

❧❧ QUESTIONS ❧❧

Do you take note of spiritual growth in your spouse?
How have you encouraged them to go deeper with
the Lord in their personal studies? If you haven't,
would you be willing to start now?

Love prays for change

*For you, wife, how do you know whether you will save your
husband? Or you, husband, how do you know
whether you will save your wife?*

1 Corinthians 7:16

What if your spouse is not a believer? How can you champion godly behavior if they don't believe in God or refuse to submit to Him? All over the world, it's not uncommon for one spouse to express belief in Jesus as the Son of God, and be all alone in their newfound faith. This was as real an issue in Paul's day as it could possibly be in ours. He told believing spouses to stay true to their unbelieving mates, praying for them and living an exemplary life before them in reverence to God (1 Corinthians 7:10–16).

Yes, this may invite ridicule in some marriages. But when Christ takes over a man's heart, the long-term life change and spiritual transformation He brings is a powerful testimony that is hard to refute. Scripture exhorts wives to quietly use their submission, purity, and respectful behavior to win over their husbands (1 Peter 3:1–2). Sometimes it may seem that you are only making it more difficult for your spouse to see Jesus in you. But stay prayerful, respectful, and loving. God is not finished with them yet. He has placed a witness to Himself right in their bed next to them. Be encouraged.

⋙ GO DEEPER ⋘

Read 1 Corinthians 7:12–16. Pray for God to make you
a strong witness and to grant your spouse repentance
where sin or unbelief is occurring (2 Timothy 2:24–26).

DAY 330
Love leads toward godliness

He did this to present the church to Himself in splendor, without spot or wrinkle or any such thing, but holy and blameless.

Ephesians 5:27

The purpose of Christ loving His people, the church, is not to make us feel good, nor is it simply to give us gifts we can enjoy while we're here. His love for the church has an eternal aim—"to make her holy, cleansing her in the washing of water by the word" (Ephesians 5:26). We satisfy His purposes most—we receive His love the best—especially when it's resulting in a life that looks more like His.

The greatest purpose of *your* love should occur, not when your spouse is impressed with you, not when you're able to give them something that deeply pleases them, but rather when you are leading them to be more like Christ. By helping them deal with their fears, confess their sins, discover their value, and be inspired by the hope of heaven, both of you will grow in grace and in the vastness of what God has done for you. You will become "mature, attaining to the whole measure of the fullness of Christ" (Ephesians 4:13 NIV). Your love will be cooperating with God's plan for your mate for all eternity. What greater joy could there be than that?

❧ THIS WEEK'S DARE ❧

Find a Christian marriage mentor who will be honest and loving with you. If you feel that counseling is needed, take the first step to set up an appointment. Ask God to direct your decisions.

DAY 331

Love is accountable

Arrogance leads to nothing but strife,
but wisdom is gained by those who take advice.

Proverbs 13:10

Mighty Sequoia trees tower hundreds of feet in the air and can withstand intense environmental pressures. Lightning can strike them, fierce winds can blow, and forest fires can rage around them. But the Sequoia endures, standing firm, only growing stronger through the trials. One of the secrets to the strength of this giant tree is what goes on below the surface. Unlike many trees, they reach out and interlock their roots with the other Sequoias around them. Each becomes empowered and reinforced by the strength of the others.

The secret of the Sequoia is also a key to maintaining a strong, healthy marriage. A couple that faces problems alone is more likely to fall apart during tough times. However, the ones who interlock their lives in a network of other strong marriages increase their chances of surviving the fiercest of storms. It is crucial that a husband and a wife pursue godly advice, healthy friendships, and experienced mentors. This decision can make a world of difference in your lives and the longevity of your marriage.

⟶ GO DEEPER ⟵

Read Proverbs 13:20 and 27:17. What do these verses teach will happen to you by having wise friends around you? What strong, godly couple can you have dinner with soon?

DAY 332
Love listens to counsel

A fool's way is right in his own eyes,
but whoever listens to counsel is wise.

Proverbs 12:15

Everyone needs wise counsel throughout life. Wise people constantly seek it and gladly receive it. Fools never ask for it and then ignore it when it's given to them, not realizing that the time spent in listening and waiting can save them the loss of many months and years down the line. Gaining wise counsel is like having a detailed road map and a personal guide while traveling on a long, challenging journey. It can be the difference between marital success or failure.

Why waste years of your life learning painful lessons when you could discover those same truths during a few hours of wise counsel? Why not cross the bridges others have built? Wisdom is more valuable than gold. Not receiving it is like letting priceless coins pass through your fingers. It is vital that you invite strong couples to share the wisdom they have gained through their own successes and failures.

❧ THIS WEEK'S DARE ❧

Find a Christian marriage mentor who will be honest and loving with you. If you feel that counseling is needed, take the first step to set up an appointment. Ask God to direct your decisions.

DAY 333
Love seeks reconciliation

*"Reach a settlement quickly with your adversary
while you're on the way with him."*

Matthew 5:25

Life and marriage will prove to be fertile ground for conflict from time to time. But love seeks to make quick amends for any wrongdoing on its part, forgiving the other's offense before it grows into a sizable barrier between the two of you. Whether the issue is over a minor fallout or perhaps something much more severe, love promises to move toward reconciliation in a hurry.

The Bible is actually the ultimate, real-life story of an offended party seeking out the offender. Though man's sin committed against God is enormous, and the far easier solution would have been to keep us forever separated from Him, He chose through Christ Jesus to seek reconciliation with us. We were left without a leg to stand on, but He chose a cross to die on so that His love for us would result in a renewed relationship. What right do we have then, in light of this, to stand at odds with one another?

✎ PRAYER ✎

"Heavenly Father, reveal to me anyone I need to reconcile with. Give me the courage and humility to take the first steps in bringing about forgiveness and healing. In Jesus' name, amen."

DAY 334
Love understands influence

Each of us will give an account of himself to God.

Romans 14:12

You must guard yourself against the wrong influencers. Everyone has an opinion, but you must be cautious about listening to advice from people who don't have a good marriage themselves, or who don't place a high value on God's will and purposes. Be cautious of those who seem more concerned about appearing smart or being liked by you than they are about speaking the truth with humility and frankness.

If your marriage is hanging by a thread or already heading for a divorce, then you need to stop everything and pursue solid counseling as quickly as possible. Call a pastor, a Bible believing counselor, or a marriage ministry today. As awkward as it may initially be to open up your life to a stranger, your marriage is worth every second spent and every sacrifice you will make for it. Even if your marriage is fairly stable, you're in no less need of honest, open mentors—people who can put wind in your sails and make your marriage even better. It might just be the relational influence that takes your marriage from mediocre to amazing.

❧ THIS WEEK'S DARE ❧

Find a Christian marriage mentor who will be honest and loving with you. If you feel that counseling is needed, take the first step to set up an appointment. Ask God to direct your decisions.

DAY 335
Love seeks other believers

*Let us not give up meeting together, as some
are in the habit of doing.*

Hebrews 10:25 NIV

Love can only grow so far when we keep it contained
inside ourselves. We are not designed to be little islands of
families, seeking God on our own but never joining hearts
with others who share our faith in Christ. Our relationship
with Him knits us into relationship with our spiritual brothers and sisters—people like us who have run to Him in their
emptiness and embraced Him as Lord.

So love takes us to church. But not every church is necessarily a healthy place to be. The kind of church you need to
be part of is one that believes the Bible in all things and pro-
claims it faithfully in its preaching. Look for a place where
you can grow spiritually, but not without getting your toes
stepped on sometimes by biblical truth. You should feel free
to worship there, serve others, and use your gifts in minister-
ing. Your children ought to feel loved by its people and at
home in its care. When you are one with the people of God,
in a place where God's presence abounds, your love for each
other is able to grow even more.

✎ GO DEEPER ✎

Read Acts 2:37–47 to see what should happen in
a healthy church. A commitment to God's Word,
prayer, and service should result in loving fellowship
and fruitfulness.

Day 336
Love gets involved

*Every day they devoted themselves to meeting together
in the temple complex, and broke bread from house to house.*

Acts 2:46

If church was no more than a building and a worship bulletin, it could be a Sunday morning destination only. But the church is actually its people. And people are not Sunday-only commodities. We are a living, loving organism designed to edify one another through close interaction.

To grow in love and develop in Christ, church cannot be a place you merely attend. If you don't get involved, you won't be able to obey the "one anothers" of Scripture—serving one another, encouraging one another, praying for one another, bearing one another's burdens, provoking one another to good works, and meeting one another's needs.

The healthy church described in Acts 2 was marked by an everyday interaction of believers in the busyness of daily life. They shared life together, including their homes and possessions, just as they shared their sufferings and joys. Your marriage needs this kind of dynamic with other believers. Don't get stuck on a back pew. Involve yourself in the work of God's church and in the lives of God's people.

QUESTIONS

Are you as involved as you need to be in your church? Do you feel like you are using the gifts God has given you for His glory? If not, are you willing to start now?

DAY 337
Love is honest

We do not want you to be uninformed, brothers.
1 Thessalonians 4:13

You have probably learned that there are no perfect churches. Yes, there are many great ones whose leaders orient their ministries around solid biblical principles, but every church has its share of hypocrites and dysfunction. The only perfect things about Christianity are Christ and His Word. Everything else is subject to being tainted by sin and uncleanness. Even those who find pleasure in pointing out the church's problems are also imperfect people. Where people are, sinners are—in or outside the church.

Followers of Christ have received His forgiveness and promises of eternal life, but God has much work left to do in their hearts. Some still gossip. Some are still selfish and greedy. Even the pastor will make mistakes. This is why we need God and each other even more. Knowing our weaknesses should drive us closer together to help one another rather than separate us to fall even farther.

Avoid church burnout by going in with your eyes wide open. Put full and total confidence in Christ and His Spirit. When you let God be God, you can let people be people.

✿ THIS WEEK'S DARE ✿

Commit to reading the Bible every day—not just reading from this or another devotional book, but actually opening the Scriptures and letting God speak to you through them.

DAY 338
Love builds on the rock

*What good is it, my brothers, if a man
claims to have faith but has no deeds?*

James 2:14 NIV

Jesus talked about people who build their entire lives on sand—their own logic, their best guesses, the latest reasoning. When the storms of life begin to blow, foundations of sand will only result in total disaster. Their houses may light up and look nice for a while, but they are tragedies waiting to happen. They cannot sustain the weight of life's challenges, and cannot support themselves when the beams and girders they've chosen for their lives prove unstable and insufficient.

But Jesus said, "Everyone who hears these words of Mine and acts on them will be like a sensible man who built his house on the rock. The rain fell, the rivers rose, and the winds blew and pounded that house. Yet it didn't collapse, because its foundation was on the rock" (Matthew 7:24–25). When your home is founded on the rock of God's unchanging Word, it is insured against destruction. That's because God has the right plan for everything, and He's revealed these plans in His Word. They're right there for anyone who will read and apply them.

PRAYER

"Father God, build our marriage on the rock of Your
Son Jesus. Give us faith and endurance, and the
strength to follow Your Word. In Jesus' name we pray,
amen."

Love lives through Scripture

*But as for you, continue in what you have learned
and firmly believed, knowing those from whom you learned.*

2 Timothy 3:14

Those who practice a consistent pattern of reading the Bible soon discover it to be "more desirable than gold—than an abundance of pure gold; and sweeter than honey—than honey dripping from the comb" (Psalm 19:10). Each day, the Lord desires to speak to you and your spouse through Scripture in ways that help you see your lives against an eternal backdrop.

It's very important to be part of a church where the Word is faithfully taught and preached. Not only will you learn more, but you'll also get to join with others who are on the same journey you are, wanting to be fed by the truths of Scripture.

Unlike most other books, which are designed to be read and digested, the Bible is a *living* book. It lives because unlike the ancient writings of other religions, its Author is still alive. And it lives because it becomes a part of who you are, how you think, and what you do.

◈ THIS WEEK'S DARE ◈

Commit to reading the Bible every day—not just reading from this or another devotional book, but actually opening the Scriptures and letting God speak to you through them.

Day 340
Love led Jesus to the cross

He humbled Himself by becoming obedient
to the point of death—even to death on a cross.

Philippians 2:8

It's not uncommon, even for people who have been married a long time, to have an occasional, passing doubt about their wife or husband's love for them. Memories can surface or a harsh word can be said, and a person can allow themselves to wonder if they are really the one their spouse always wanted.

But believers in Christ never have to doubt their Savior's love. If we do, we need only to remember what He did for us. If He had wanted to escape the indignity of being mocked by rank soldiers, or blindfolded to keep from being hit by surprise blows, He could have stopped it with divine authority at any time. "Do you not think," He said, "that I cannot call on My Father, and He will provide Me at once with more than 12 legions of angels?" (Matthew 26:53). Yet He went through with His Father's painful will. He paid the ultimate sacrifice to meet your ultimate need. He loves you that much. And the cross never lets us forget it.

❧ GO DEEPER ❧

Read Matthew 27:27–31, where the writer vividly describes the ordeal Jesus went through leading up to His crucifixion. Don't rush through it. Read slowly, letting the scene come to life for you. This was real pain, real humiliation. This is what your Savior endured . . . for you. How great a love!

Love works in all areas

The words of the LORD are pure words,
like silver refined in an earthen furnace, purified seven times.

Psalm 12:6

If being a regular Bible reader is new for you, you'll be surprised how quickly you'll begin thinking differently and more eternally as you begin digesting its truth day by day. And if you are serious about establishing strategies for life based on God's way of doing things, He will guide you to make the connections between what you're reading and how it applies. It's an enlightening journey with fresh discoveries to be made all the time.

God has a plan for the way you handle your money. He has a plan for the way you raise your children. He knows how you should treat your body, and how you should spend your time. He has a plan for the way you handle conflict, and a plan for marital success. Most any issue that you will encounter in life can be taken to the counsel of Scripture and illumined by His perfect wisdom. After all, God designed life itself. Isn't it just like your Maker to know exactly what you need?

◈ THIS WEEK'S DARE ◈

Commit to reading the Bible every day—not just reading from this or another devotional book, but actually opening the Scriptures and letting God speak to you through them.

DAY 342
Love yields to God

As for God, his way is perfect; the word of the LORD is flawless.
He is a shield for all who take refuge in him.

Psalm 18:30 NIV

Every aspect of your life that you submit to God's principles will grow stronger and longer lasting over time. But any part you withhold from Him, choosing instead to try your own hand at it, will weaken and eventually fail when the storms of life hit you. It may, in fact, be the one area that hastens the downfall of your home and marriage. But like most regrets, it doesn't have to happen.

Wise couples build their houses on the rock of God's Word. They've seen what sand can do. They know how it feels when their footing gets soft and the foundation gives way. They remember the uncertainty of their own logic. They realize how deceptive and unfulfilling the paths of sin are, and have learned the hard way that God's path is the only sure one. That's why you must determine to build your life and marriage on the bedrock of the Bible, and then you can plan on a solid future—no matter how bad the storms get.

❧❧ QUESTIONS ❧❧

How much of an emphasis do you make on building your marriage on God's Word? Does your marriage reflect a healthy foundation? Would your spouse agree with your assessment?

Day 343

Love is seen in Scripture

The instruction of the Lord is perfect, reviving the soul.

Psalm 19:7

Nowhere is love more readily evident than in the Word of God. This is where He reveals Himself to us as the lover of our souls, One who has gone to incomprehensible lengths to reach out to sinful man.

Treat His Word like a lamp to hold before you, like a light for your path (Psalm 119:105), whose truths are able to set you free from sin and regret as Jesus works in you (John 8:32). Every word is pure (Proverbs 30:5) and will last forever, "firmly fixed in heaven" (Psalm 119:89). This makes it wholly profitable to us "for teaching, for rebuking, for correcting, for training in righteousness" (2 Timothy 3:16).

His Word is absolutely true, with no mixture of error, "promised before time began" (Titus 1:2). It is true about God, true about man, true about sin, and true about salvation. May your eyes and ears be open to receive its truth, your heart open to accept it by faith, and your mind open to be renewed in hope. Read it. Know it. Share it. Live it. "The entirety of Your word is truth" (Psalm 119:160).

❧ GO DEEPER ☙

Do you embrace the Scriptures as the authoritative and inspired Word of God? Read 1 Thessalonians 2:13–14 to see how we should view it. Then study 2 Timothy 3:16–17 to see what God's Word equips us to do.

Day 344
Love leads to obedience

Be doers of the word and not hearers only, deceiving yourselves.

James 1:22

The Bible is an awesome book, but it can seem overwhelming at first to navigate if you're not familiar with it. Yet most people want to know how to hear from God. They want to know what He says on all kinds of matters pertaining to their lives. There will always be specifics of your situation that will require a mature, devoted heart in order to ascertain God's direction. But the Scripture is already rich with His revealed truth and guidance, and it is right here for you to discover. It has warnings to heed, treasures to find, and knowledge about God to be revealed.

But revelation is only the beginning, because the Bible is also a living book. God's Word comes most alive in us as we put it into practice, letting Christ live His righteousness through us. The potential dangers or treasures within your marriage are tied to how faithfully you turn His Word into days and nights of holy and selfless living. Don't be one who reads and forgets, who learns but doesn't apply. Make sure your feet are as open to the Word as your eyes are.

THIS WEEK'S DARE

Ask your spouse if you can begin praying together. Use this time to commit your concerns, disagreements, and needs before the Lord. Don't forget to thank Him for His provisions and blessings.

DAY 345
Love takes God's Word to heart

I have treasured Your word in my heart
so that I may not sin against You.

Psalm 119:11

As powerful as the Scriptures are to read, their impact multiplies when the Holy Spirit can bring them quickly to mind at a moment of temptation or in a time of decision. The practice of memorizing Bible verses keeps them stored away for opportune occasions. You'll be surprised how quickly their truth will circulate through your system, and how God will honor your diligent efforts with a nearer sense of His presence.

Meditating on the Word is said to make you like a "tree planted beside streams of water" (Psalm 1:3). As your mind "chews" on the Scriptures, your spirit is continually nourished by God's refreshing truth. His strength shows itself throughout your entire life making you fruitful in every good work. It is a promise of spiritual growth and prosperity.

If you're not sure where to start, here are seven pivotal verses that can transform your marriage: Ephesians 4:32; John 15:9; Philippians 2:3–4; Genesis 2:24; James 1:19; Ephesians 5:33; 1 Corinthians 13:4–7. Invite these into your heart, and let them renew your mind.

❧ GO DEEPER ❧

Read Joshua 1:8–9. What is required to bring about success in all we do? True meditation is not clearing your mind, but engaging your mind in deep thought and carefully processing God's Word.

Day 346
Love agrees in prayer

*"If two of you on earth agree about any matter that you pray for,
it will be done for you by My Father in heaven."*

Matthew 18:19

Praying for your spouse leads your heart to care more deeply about them. But more important, God is pleased when He sees both of you humbling yourselves and seeking His face *together*. His blessing falls on us when we agree in prayer.

The word Jesus used, in fact, about "agreeing" in prayer has the idea of a harmonious symphony. Two different notes, when played together, can create a pleasing sound of harmony. Played one at a time, you can immediately tell the difference. But put them together in agreement, and you get a fuller, more complete sound than either of them can make on its own.

Agreeing in prayer—even in the midst of disagreeing about some of the situations you're currently facing—pulls you both back toward your real center. It places you on common ground, face-to-face before the Father. When a husband and a wife agree in unity, it sends a harmonious prayer up to heaven that is pleasing to the ears of the Lord. Those are prayers God takes note of.

❧ THIS WEEK'S DARE ❧

Ask your spouse if you can begin praying together. Use this time to commit your concerns, disagreements, and needs before the Lord. Don't forget to thank Him for His provisions and blessings.

DAY 347
Love encourages prayer

*"Now, my God, may your eyes be open and your
ears attentive to the prayers offered in this place."*

2 Chronicles 6:40 NIV

If someone told you that by changing one thing about
your marriage, you could guarantee with nearly one hundred
percent assurance that your life together would significantly
improve—you'd at least want to know what it was. And for
many godly couples, that "one thing" is the daily practice of
praying together.

To someone who tends to devalue spiritual matters, this
sounds fairly ridiculous. And if told that shared prayer is a
key ingredient in marital longevity and leads to a heightened
sense of sexual intimacy, they'd think you had really gone
too far. But actually, the unity that grows between a man
and a woman who regularly pray together forms an intense
and powerful connection. The openness they expose to
each other in sharing, and the oneness they sense as they
stand together before the Lord, draw them together in deep,
significant ways. Within the sanctuary of your marriage, it's
time to discover how praying together can work wonders on
every level of your relationship.

⟶❦⟵ PRAYER ⟶❦⟵

*"Lord, give us a burden to pray for one another. Con-
vict us when we stray from seeking You. Remind us
that faith prays, and unbelief does not. Draw us to
You. In Jesus' name, amen."*

Day 348

Love partners in prayer

Rejoice in hope; be patient in affliction; be persistent in prayer.

Romans 12:12

When you were joined together as husband and wife, God gave you a wedding gift—a permanent prayer partner for life. When you need wisdom on a certain decision, you and your mate can seek God together for the answer. When you're struggling with your own fears and insecurities, your prayer partner can intercede on your behalf. When you and your spouse can't get past a particular argument or sticking point, you can call a time-out and go with your partner into emergency prayer. It should become your automatic reflex action when you don't know what else to do.

It's hard to stay angry for very long with someone you're praying for. It's hard not to back down when you're hearing your mate cry out to God for mercy in the midst of your heated crisis. In prayer, two people remember that God has made them one. And in the grip of His uniting presence, disharmony blends into beauty.

∽ THIS WEEK'S DARE ∾

Ask your spouse if you can begin praying together. Use this time to commit your concerns, disagreements, and needs before the Lord. Don't forget to thank Him for His provisions and blessings.

Love prays for unity

*I call on You, God, because You will answer me;
listen closely to me; hear what I say.*

Psalm 17:6

The church can sometimes be a place where conflict
rules. The disharmony that can flare up over various matters
can derail the church from its mission and disrupt the flow
of worship and unity. At times, godly church leaders will
see what is taking place, break off discussions, and call the
people of God to prayer. Instead of continuing the discord
and allowing more feelings to be hurt, they will seek unity
by turning their hearts back to God and appealing to Him
for help.

The same thing happens in our homes when there is an
intervention of prayer, even at high points of disagreement.
It stops the bleeding. It quiets the loud voices. It pauses you
as you realize whose presence you're in.

Prayer is a privilege to be enjoyed on a consistent, daily
basis. Even if they're typically short and to the point, your
prayers will become a standing appointment you can orbit
your day around, keeping God in the middle of everything.

❧ QUESTIONS ❧

Why not make God the center of your priorities and
goals in life? Why not run your decisions by Him as
you pray together for direction and insight?

Day 350
Love looks to God

The Lord *is far from the wicked,*
but He hears the prayer of the righteous.

Proverbs 15:29

It's true that praying together as a couple can initially feel awkward and uncomfortable. Anything this powerful will surprise you with its weight and responsibility when you actually try doing it. But bear in mind that God wants and invites you to engage in conversation with Him. In fact, He will grow you as you take prayer seriously and push past those times when you don't know what to say. The more you do it, the more it will become a natural part of your time together. Your prayers of thanksgiving, worship, and petitions will not only bring you before the throne of God, but draw you closer to your mate.

You'll look back at this common thread that ran through every facet of your life from average Mondays to major decisions, and be so thankful for this "one thing" that changed everything. This is one area where it's imperative that you agree to agree.

✨ GO DEEPER ✨

Read Matthew 18:19–20. Humble unity and answered prayer ties our hearts together as we rejoice over God's providence in our lives. God's Spirit is also present when we join in His name. His presence brings liberty and the fruit of the Spirit in our lives. What benefits would this have on your marriage?

DAY 351
Love prays instinctively

Devote yourselves to prayer; stay alert in it with thanksgiving.

Colossians 4:2

Many people relegate prayer to standard moods and conditions. Church. Meals. Bedtime. Waiting rooms. But except for very general appeals to God for help, we typically respond to life's sudden challenges and crisis with worry, discussion, frightened silence, or despair. We pass up the opportunity to embrace the privilege God has given us to bring every need and concern to Him in immediate prayer . . . together.

As husband and wife, prayer should be your instant refuge at the first hint of indecision or doubt. Any crisis should call you to immediate prayer together rather than panic. When you hear of a national disaster, a family emergency, or a friend diagnosed with cancer, take each other by the hand and rush headlong to the throne of grace. Even at the discovery of good news, a united prayer of thanks will deflect any temptation to take credit for God's blessings. Start now, even in situations that are not particularly dire and dangerous—at home, in the car, on the phone—and prayer will become your initial response every time, for everything.

✎ THIS WEEK'S DARE ✎

Ask yourself what your mate would want if it was obtainable. Commit this to prayer, and start mapping out a plan for meeting some (if not all) of their desires, to whatever level you possibly can.

DAY 352
Love handles problems together

*Now if any of you lacks wisdom, he should ask God,
who gives to all generously and without criticizing,
and it will be given to him.*

James 1:5

You won't always see eye-to-eye on a decision that needs making. Your disagreeing positions can even lead you to attack one *another* rather than attacking the problem. But wise couples know the real enemy is not each other. The real enemy is Satan and the division he is trying to bring between you and your spouse.

The Bible teaches us to use prayer and the Word as our main tools for discerning God's direction on all matters, knowing that His sheep "recognize His voice" (John 10:4). We can sometimes determine His will by the presence of peace we sense (Colossians 3:15), by a door of opportunity that opens in a timely fashion (2 Corinthians 2:12), by a united awareness that one of the solutions bears hints of God's wisdom.

This is not a formula. The Spirit wants us to trust *Him*, not our procedures. But when we join together in dealing with our issues, we turn the focus off ourselves and onto what God desires from each of us. Make praying together before all major decisions a permanent rule in your marriage.

⤗⤗ GO DEEPER ⤗⤗

Read Jeremiah 33:3. This passage summarizes how God guides our decisions as we seek Him in prayer. Jesus prayed all night before choosing His disciples (Luke 6:12–13). Why not you?

DAY 353
Love overwhelms

*I, the LORD, am your God, who brought you up from the land of
Egypt; open your mouth wide and I will fill it.*

Psalm 81:10 NASB

What is something your spouse would really, really love?
Common sense tells us we can't give our wife or husband
everything they might like. Our budgets and account balances tell us we probably couldn't afford it anyway. And even
if we could, it might not be good for us. Or for them.

But perhaps you've let your "no" become too quick of a
response. Perhaps you've let this negative default become
too reasoned and automatic. What if instead of dismissing
the thought out of hand, you did your best to honor it. What
might happen if the one thing they said you'd never do for
them became the next thing you did?

Is love like this no longer on the menu after so many years
of marriage? Wouldn't it be disingenuous to indulge your
spouse if your heart's not in it? Well, how about *putting* your
heart in it. How about adopting a new level of love that actually *wants* to fulfill every dream and desire you possibly can.
It's certainly worth seriously praying about.

❧ THIS WEEK'S DARE ❧

Ask yourself what your mate would want if it was
obtainable. Commit this to prayer, and start mapping out a plan for meeting some (if not all) of their
desires, to whatever level you possibly can.

DAY 354
Love is extravagant

*My purpose is that they may be encouraged
in heart and united in love, so that they may have
the full riches of complete understanding.*

Colossians 2:2 NIV

Love sometimes needs to be extravagant. To go all out. It sometimes needs to set aside the technicalities and just bless because it wants to.

Hasn't God's love met needs in your heart that once seemed out of the question? You were living under such a load of sin and regret. But He looked at you with love and wanted you back. He wanted you to realize your need for Him. And as you repented and turned to Him, He loved and forgave you. It wasn't when you were behaving like an angel that God chose to pour out His love on you. "But God proves His own love for us in that while we were still sinners Christ died for us!" (Romans 5:8).

He's your model. He's the One your love is designed to imitate. "But where sin multiplied, grace multiplied even more" (Romans 5:20). Though you weren't a likely candidate for His love, He gave it anyway. He paid the price. Could you?

❧ PRAYER ❧

"Jesus, would You help us to show love to each other in extravagant ways? Let us bless one another in creativity and thoughtfulness. Give us a heart to love. In Your name we pray, amen."

DAY 355

Love is generous

God loves a cheerful giver.

2 Corinthians 9:7

Not everything your spouse wants has a hefty price tag. Not everything he or she desires can be bought with money. Your wife may really want your time. She may really want your attention. She may really want to be treated like a lady, to know that her husband considers her his greatest treasure. She may really want to see in your eyes a love that chooses to be there no matter what.

Your husband may really want your respect. He may really want you to acknowledge him as the head of the house in front of the children. He may really want you to put your arms around his neck for no apparent reason, to be surprised by a long kiss or a love note when there's not a birthday or anniversary to justify it. He may need to know that you still think he's strong and handsome.

What is something your spouse would really love? It's time you started living out the answer to that question.

❧ THIS WEEK'S DARE ❧

Ask yourself what your mate would want if it was obtainable. Commit this to prayer, and start mapping out a plan for meeting some (if not all) of their desires, to whatever level you possibly can.

DAY 356
Love finds opportunities

"Give, and it will be given to you; a good measure—pressed down, shaken together, and running over—will be poured into your lap. For with the measure you use, it will be measured back to you."

Luke 6:38

Dreams and desires come in all shapes and sizes. But love takes careful notice of each one. It calls you to listen to what your mate is saying and hoping for. It calls you to remember the things that are unique to your relationship, the pleasures and enjoyments that bring a big smile to your spouse's face. Love calls you to give when it would be a lot more convenient to wait. And it calls you to daydream about opportunities so regularly that your mate's desires become yours as well.

We dare you to think in terms of overwhelming your spouse with love. To surprise them by exceeding all their expectations with your kindness. Try to imagine what you could do or be working toward that would give undeniable evidence to your mate about just how much you treasure them. It may or may not be a financial sacrifice, but it needs to reflect a heart that is willing to express itself with extravagance.

⟡ QUESTIONS ⟡

What could you do to overwhelm your mate? How could you be a blessing to them, and make them feel loved and valued with your actions? Why not act on this thought?

Love never fails

Love never fails.

1 Corinthians 13:8 NASB

Of all the things love dares to do, this is the ultimate. Though threatened, it keeps pursuing. Though challenged, it keeps moving forward. Though mistreated and rejected, it refuses to give up. Love never fails.

Many times when a marriage is in crisis, the spouse who is trying to make things work will go to the other, declaring that no matter what has happened in the past, he or she is committed to this marriage. But not wanting to hear this yet, the other spouse holds their position. They still want out. The partner who has just laid his or her heart on the line can't handle the rejection. So they withdraw their statement. "Fine. If that's the way you want it!"

But if love is really love, it doesn't waffle when it's not received the way you hope. If love can be told to quit loving, then it's not really love. Love that is from God is unending, unstoppable. If the object of its affection doesn't choose to receive it, love keeps giving anyway.

❧ GO DEEPER ❧

Read 1 Corinthians 13:4–8 out loud. The reason love never fails (verse 8) is because it bears all things, believes all things, hopes all things, and endures all things (verse 7). Regardless of what's behind, presently near, or coming ahead, love can withstand. It comes from God to us, and it is who God is through us.

Day 358
Love is found in Christ

Jesus Christ is the same yesterday, today, and forever.

Hebrews 13:8

Jesus' disciples were nothing if not unpredictable. After their final Passover meal together, when Jesus told them they would all forsake Him before the night was over, Peter declared, "Even if everyone runs away because of You, I will never run away! . . . Even if I have to die with You, I will never deny You!" (Matthew 26:33, 35). All the other disciples echoed the very same promise.

But later that night, Jesus' inner circle of followers—Peter, James, and John—would sleep through Christ's agony in the garden. On the way to Jesus' crucifixion, Peter would deny Him three times in the courtyard. But at that precise moment, the Bible says Jesus "turned and looked" at him (Luke 22:61). His men had failed Him—again—within hours of their sworn promises. Yet He never stopped loving them, because He and His love are "the same yesterday, today, and forever" (Hebrews 13:8).

His love never fails. And He is the model for you.

⟫⟫⟫ THIS WEEK'S DARE ⟪⟪⟪

Spend time in prayer, then write a letter of commitment and resolve to your spouse. Include why you are committing to this marriage until death, and that you have purposed to love them no matter what. Leave it for them to find.

DAY 359
Love is unchanging

"Heaven and earth will pass away,
but My words will never pass away."

Luke 21:33

Of the nine "fruit of the Spirit" listed in Galatians 5, the first of all is love. And because the unchanging Holy Spirit is its Source, then the love He creates in us is unchanging as well. It is based on the *will* of God, the *calling* of God, and the *Word* of God—all unchanging things. The Bible declares them "irrevocable" (Romans 11:29).

Along this devotional journey, you have been dared to be patient, to be unselfish, to sacrifice for your mate's needs. These are not just loving ideas, existing in isolation. Each quality of love outlined in this book is based on the love of God, captured and expressed in the Word of God. The *unchanging* Word of God. No challenge or circumstance can occur that will ever put an expiration date on Him or His love. Therefore, your love—which flows from His heart and through yours—bears the same, unchanging characteristics.

❧ GO DEEPER ❧

Read Colossians 3:12–14 out loud today. While so many good things should be flowing from our lives, what is the one perfect bond that ties it all together and keeps us together in unity?

Day 360
Love is committed

The grass withers, the flowers fade,
but the word of our God remains forever.

Isaiah 40:8

Throughout this journey you have been dared to build your marriage on the Word of God. That's because when all else fails, the truth of God will still be standing.

So today, your dare is to put your unfailing love into the most powerful, personal words you can, to write them down, and to share them with your mate. This is your chance to declare that no matter what imperfections exist—both in you and in your spouse—your love is greater still. No matter what they've done or how often they've done it, you choose to love them anyway. Though you've been far from steady in your treatment of them over the years, your days of being inconsistent in love are over. You're communicating total acceptance of this one man or woman as God's special gift to you, and you promise to love them until death. You're saying, "Even if you don't like what you're reading—even if you don't like *me*—I choose to love you anyway. Forever."

Because love never fails.

❧ THIS WEEK'S DARE ❧

Spend time in prayer, then write a letter of commitment and resolve to your spouse. Include why you are committing to this marriage until death, and that you have purposed to love them no matter what. Leave it for them to find.

Day 361
Love is a covenant

"For wherever you go, I will go, and wherever you live,
I will live; your people will be my people,
and your God will be my God."

Ruth 1:16

As you view your marriage relationship from this point on, we challenge you to consider it a *covenant* instead of a *contract*. These words and concepts sound similar in meaning but in reality are much different. A contract is usually a written agreement based on distrust, outlining the conditions and consequences to be applied if it is broken. A covenant, on the other hand, is a verbal commitment based on total trust, assuring someone that your promise is unconditional and good for life. It is spoken before God out of love for another.

A contract is self-serving and comes with limited liability. It establishes a time frame for certain deliverables to be met and accomplished. A contract can be broken with mutual consent. But a covenant is unbreakable. A covenant is for the benefit of others and comes with unlimited responsibility. It has no expiration date or cut-off period. It is a "till death do us part" promise. It reflects the nature of true love.

PRAYER

"Lord, seal our hearts with an undying love for one another. Brand us with a desire to make our marriage a treasure You are pleased with. Thank You for this lifelong blessing. In Jesus' name, amen."

DAY 362
Love is a promise

Christ is the mediator of a new covenant, that those who are called may receive the promised eternal inheritance.

Hebrews 9:15 NIV

The Bible contains several covenants as part of the unfolding story of God's people. God made a covenant with Noah, promising never again to destroy all flesh with a worldwide flood (Genesis 9:12–17). He made a covenant with Abraham, promising that an entire nation of descendents would come from his line (Genesis 17:1–8). He made a covenant with Moses, declaring that the people of Israel would be God's permanent possession (Exodus 19:3–6). He made a covenant with David, promising that a ruler would sit on his throne forever (2 Samuel 7:8–16). And ultimately, He made a "new covenant" by the blood of Christ, establishing an unending, unchanging legacy of forgiven sins and eternal life for those who believe in Him.

And then there's marriage—the strongest covenant on Earth between two people, the pledge of a man and a woman to establish a love that is unconditional and lasts a lifetime.

❧ THIS WEEK'S DARE ❧

Spend time in prayer, then write a letter of commitment and resolve to your spouse. Include why you are committing to this marriage until death, and that you have purposed to love them no matter what. Leave it for them to find.

DAY 363
Love is strong

Set me as a seal on your heart, as a seal on your arm.
For love is as strong as death.

Song of Solomon 8:6

Covenants usually come with a sign to help them be kept and remembered. In marriage, your wedding ring represents your covenant vows. They were premeditated promises, publicly spoken and witnessed by others. Your covenant was bound legally by an official, bound physically by consummation, and most importantly bound spiritually by God (Mark 10:2–9).

Keeping this covenant is not something you can do in your own strength. There's good reason why God was the One who initiated covenants with His people. He alone is able to fulfill the demands of His own promises. But the Spirit of God is within you by virtue of your faith in His Son and the grace bestowed upon you in salvation. That means you now *can* exercise your role as a covenant keeper, no matter what may arise to challenge you. You "can do all things through Christ who strengthens you" (Philippians 4:13). You can live a life of love.

⧼ GO DEEPER ⧽

Read 1 Peter 4:7–11 out loud today. Think of your marriage as you meditate on this passage. Let it powerfully challenge you to be fervent in your love, hospitality, and service to one another. Above all, may your marriage be a living testimony of the awesome love of God, to whom belongs the glory and dominion forever and ever. Amen.

Day 364
Love never gives up

Having loved His own who were in the world,
He loved them to the end.

John 13:1

If your spouse is not in a place of receiving your love right now, the act of covenant keeping can be more daunting with each passing day. But marriage is not a contract with convenient escape clauses and selfish exception wordings. Marriage is a covenant intended to cut off all avenues of retreat or withdrawal. There's no going back. There's no opting out. There's nothing in the world that should sever what God has joined together. Your love is based on a covenant. And your covenant is based on the unchanging character of a covenant-keeping God.

The prophet Malachi wrote that one reason God withholds His blessing is that He hates divorce and is angered when husbands deal treacherously with their wives, breaking the covenant they made (Malachi 2:16). Seeing marriage as a *contract* is like saying to your spouse, "I take you for me, and we'll see if it works out." But realizing it as a covenant changes it around to say, "I give myself to you and commit to this marriage for life."

❧ QUESTIONS ❧

Have you committed to your marriage for life? Could you remind your spouse of your lifelong covenant with them? Why not renew your love in a creative way?

DAY 365
Love honors God

My lips will glorify You because
Your faithful love is better than life.

Psalm 63:3

God created marriage to be a covenant for a spiritual reason. Every marriage is called to be an earthly picture of God's heavenly covenant with His church. It is to reveal to the world the glory and beauty of God's unconditional love for us. Jesus said, "As the Father has loved Me, I have also loved you. Remain in My love" (John 15:9). Let His words inspire you to be a channel of God's love to your spouse. Ultimately, this glorifies God.

The time is now, man or woman of God, to renew your covenant of love in all sincerity and surrender. Love is too holy a treasure to trade in for another, and too powerful a bond to be broken without dire consequences. Fasten your love afresh on this one the Lord has given you to cherish, prize, and honor. Your life together is before you. Dare to take hold of it, and never let go.

❧ THIS WEEK'S DARE ❧

Write out a renewal of your vows and place them in your home. Perhaps, if appropriate, you could make arrangements to formally renew your wedding vows before a minister. Make it a living testament to the value of marriage in God's eyes and the high honor of being one with your mate.

Appendix

APPENDIX I
The Locks and Keys of Effective Prayer

The effective, fervent prayer of a righteous man avails much.

—James 5:16 NIV

 ## THE LOCKS: TEN THINGS THAT BLOCK PRAYER

1. **Praying without Knowing God through Jesus**
   John 14:6—Jesus said to him, "I am the way, and the truth, and the life; no one comes to the Father but through Me."

2. **Praying from an Unrepentant Heart**
   Psalm 66:18–19 NIV—"If I had cherished sin in my heart, the Lord would not have listened; but God has surely listened and heard my voice in prayer."

3. **Praying for Show**
   Matthew 6:5—"When you pray, you are not to be like the hypocrites; for they love to stand and pray in the synagogues and on the street corners so that they may be seen by men. Truly I say to you, they have their reward in full."

4. **Praying Repetitive, Empty Words**
   Matthew 6:7–8—"And when you are praying, do not use meaningless repetition as the Gentiles do, for they suppose that they will be heard for their many words. So do

not be like them; for your Father knows what you need before you ask Him."

5. **Prayers Not Prayed**
   James 4:2—"You do not have because you do not ask."

6. **Praying with a Lustful Heart**
   James 4:3—"You ask and do not receive, because you ask with wrong motives, so that you may spend it on your pleasures."

7. **Praying while Mistreating Your Spouse.**
   1 Peter 3:7—"You husbands in the same way, live with your wives in an understanding way . . . and show her honor as a fellow heir of the grace of life, so that your prayers will not be hindered."

8. **Praying while Ignoring the Poor**
   Proverbs 21:13—"He who shuts his ear to the cry of the poor will also cry himself and not be answered."

9. **Praying with Bitterness in Your Heart toward Someone**
   Mark 11:25–26—"Whenever you stand praying, forgive, if you have anything against anyone, so that your Father who is in heaven will also forgive you your transgressions. But if you do not forgive, neither will your Father who is in heaven forgive your transgressions."

10. **Praying with a Faithless Heart**
    James 1:6–8—"But he must ask in faith without any doubting, for the one who doubts is like the surf of the sea, driven and tossed by the wind. For that man ought not to expect that he will receive anything from the Lord, being a double-minded man, unstable in all his ways."

THE KEYS: TEN THINGS THAT MAKE PRAYER EFFECTIVE

1. **Praying by Asking, Seeking, and Knocking**
   Matthew 7:7–8, 11—"Ask, and it will be given to you; seek, and you will find; knock, and it will be opened to you. For everyone who asks receives, and he who seeks finds, and to him who knocks it will be opened. . . . If you then, being evil, know how to give good gifts to your children, how much more will your Father who is in heaven give what is good to those who ask Him!"

2. **Praying in Faith**
   Mark 11:24—"Therefore I say to you, all things for which you pray and ask, believe that you have received them, and they will be granted you."

3. **Praying in Secret**
   Matthew 6:6—"But you, when you pray, go into your inner room, close your door and pray to your Father who is in secret, and your Father who sees what is done in secret will reward you."

4. **Praying according to God's Will**
   1 John 5:14—"This is the confidence we have before Him, that, if we ask anything according to His will, He hears us."

5. **Praying in Jesus' Name**
   John 14:13–14—"Whatever you ask in My name, that will I do, so that the Father may be glorified in the Son. If you ask Me anything in My name, I will do it."

6. **Praying in Agreement with Other Believers**
   Matthew 18:19–20—"Again I say to you, that if two of you agree on earth about anything that they may ask, it shall be done for them by My Father who is in heaven. For where two or three have gathered together in My name, I am there in their midst."

7. **Praying while Fasting**
   Acts 14:23—"When they had appointed elders for them in every church, having prayed with fasting, they commended them to the Lord in whom they had believed."

8. **Praying from an Obedient Life**
   1 John 3:21–22—"Beloved, if our heart does not condemn us, we have confidence before God; and whatever we ask we receive from Him, because we keep His commandments and do the things that are pleasing in His sight."

9. **Praying while Abiding in Christ and His Word**
   John 15:7—"If you abide in Me, and My words abide in you, ask whatever you wish, and it will be done for you."

10. **Praying while Delighting in the Lord**
    Psalm 37:4—"Delight yourself in the Lord; and He will give you the desires of your heart."

SUMMARY OF THE LOCKS AND KEYS OF PRAYER

1. You must be in a right relationship with God.

2. You must be in a right relationship with other people.

3. Your heart must be right.

The Word of God in My Life

Let this proclamation help you to rightly approach the Word of God.

- The Bible is the Word of God.
- It is holy, inerrant, infallible, and completely authoritative. (Proverbs 30:5–6; John 17:17; Psalm 119:89)
- It is profitable for teaching, reproving, correcting, and training me in righteousness. (2 Timothy 3:16)
- It matures and equips me to be ready for every good work. (2 Timothy 3:17)
- It is a lamp to my feet and a light to my path. (Psalm 119:105)
- It makes me wiser than my enemies. (Psalm 119:97–100)
- It brings me stability during the storms of my life. (Matthew 7:24–27)
- If I believe its truth, I will be set free. (John 8:32)
- If I hide it in my heart, I will be protected in times of temptation. (Psalm 199:11)
- If I continue in it, I will become a true disciple. (John 8:31)
- If I meditate on it, I will become successful. (Joshua 1:8)
- If I keep it, I will be rewarded and my love perfected. (Psalm 19:7–11; 1 John 2:5)

- It is the living, powerful, discerning Word of God.
  (Hebrews 4:12)
- It is the Sword of the Spirit. (Ephesians 6:17)
- It is sweeter than honey and more desirable than gold.
  (Psalm 19:10)
- It is indestructible and forever settled in Heaven.
  (2 Corinthians 13:7–8; Psalm 119:89)
- It is absolutely true with no mixture of error.
  (John 17:17; Titus 1:2)
- It is absolutely true about God. (Romans 3:4;
  Romans 16:25, 27; Colossians 1)
- It is absolutely true about man. (Jeremiah 17:9; Psalm 8:4–6)
- It is absolutely true about sin. (Romans 3:23)
- It is absolutely true about salvation. (Acts 4:12; Romans 10:9)
- It is absolutely true about Heaven and Hell.
  (Revelation 21:8; Psalm 119:89)

Lord, open my eyes that I may see truth and my ears to hear truth.
Open my heart to receive it by faith.
Renew my mind to keep it in hope.
Surrender my will that I may live it with love.

Remind me that I am responsible when I hear it.
Help me desire to obey what You say through it.
Transform my life that I may know it.
Burden my heart that I may share it.

Speak now, Lord.
Give me a passion to know and follow Your will.
Nothing more. Nothing less. Nothing else.

APPENDIX III
Twenty Questions for Your Spouse

Either on a date or during a private conversation, try using the questions below to learn more about the heart of your spouse. Allow the topics to raise additional questions that you may want to explore, but keep the mood and focus positive. Listen more than you talk.

PERSONAL

- What is your greatest hope or dream?
- What do you enjoy the most about your life right now?
- What do you enjoy the least about your life right now?
- What would your dream job be if you could do anything and get paid for it?
- What are some things you've always wanted to do but haven't had the opportunity yet?
- What three things would you like to do before the next year passes?
- Who do you feel the most "safe" being with? Why?
- If you could have lunch with anyone in the world, who would it be and why?
- When was the last time you felt filled with joy?
- If you had to give away a million dollars, who would you give it to?

MARITAL

- ❧ What are three things that I do that you really like?

- ❧ What are three things that I do that drive you crazy?

- ❧ What have I done in the past that made you feel loved?

- ❧ What have I done that made you feel unappreciated?

- ❧ What are three things that I can work on?

- ❧ Of the following things, what would make you feel most loved?

    Having your body massaged and caressed for an hour.

    Sitting and talking for an hour about your favorite subject.

    Having help around the house for an afternoon.

    Receiving a very nice gift.

    Hearing encouragement about how appreciated you are.

- ❧ What things in the past do you wish could be erased from ever happening?

- ❧ What is the next major decision that you think God would want us to make as a couple?

- ❧ What would you like your life to look like five years from now?

- ❧ What words would you like to hear from me more often?

Offer encouragement and a listening ear. Refuse to allow this to become an argument or time for you to criticize. Let this be a time for your mate to express themselves.

APPENDIX IV
Treasure Hunting
Parent/Mentor Interview

QUESTIONS FOR YOUR DOUBLE DATE

God will uniquely use your parents and strong, older couples to help you be successful in life and in your family. Wise decisions they have made will help you learn what to do. Mistakes they have made will help you learn what to avoid. Interview your parents/mentors using the following list of questions. Write down what they share. This is not a time for criticizing or arguing, but for listening and showing value to what each person shares from their heart.

- What are some habits or decisions you made that really helped your marriage?

- What are ways your spouse has expressed love to you in the past that meant the most?

- In your opinion, what are the top things that will help our marriage stay strong?

- In your opinion, what are the top mistakes couples make that hurt their marriage?

- What are some things wives wish their husbands better understood about women?

- What are some things husbands wish their wives better understood about men?

- Share your most important tips regarding how we can have the following things:

  - Strong Conflict Resolution?
  - Wise Money Management?
  - Good Romance?
  - Honoring you as in-laws while also being our own independent family?

- Is there anything you have wanted to share with us but have not had the right opportunity, and would be willing to share it now?

- To your knowledge, do either of you have any bitterness or unresolved anger with either of us? (If so, make restitution and ask forgiveness.)

- Will you commit to pray for us, support us, and counsel us in the future? Thank them!

APPENDIX V
How to Have a Devotion

A daily time of devotion is part of a personal and intimate walk between God and you. As a person grows in Christ, they will gain a greater consciousness of God's abiding presence with them. They will become accustomed to praising Him, thanking Him, or praying for help from Him at a moment's notice (1 Thessalonians 5:16–18). It's about a loving relationship, not ritualistic religion.

In addition to this, it is vital to consistently get alone with God at some point each day and spend time with Him one-on-one. In the chaos of His mass popularity, Jesus modeled this and was consistent in guarding intimate time with His heavenly Father (Mark 1:32–37; Luke 5:16; 6:12). So should we.

WHAT IS A DEVOTION?

A devotion is a time when you get your heart and mind daily synced up with God's heart and mind. It is like a bride escaping away with her husband—two lovers spending time enjoying one another. It is like a boy crawling into the lap of his tender Father, finding safety, comfort, and encouragement. It is also like a soldier reporting in and bowing before his King, then requesting His wisdom and provision so he can carry out the day's duties. Though the devil and hell itself will constantly try to prevent you from doing this, your daily time with God should be prioritized and guarded.

How Does It Work?

While there is no set formula, many people have developed an effective system that involves the following simple steps:

1. Get alone with a Bible, pen, and paper.
2. Ask God to speak to you through His Word.
3. Read a few minutes in the Scriptures. (Use a devotional guide or book if desired.)
4. Jot down what God is telling you, as well as any key points of application.
5. Pray for a few minutes applying what you learned and pouring out your heart.
6. Go, apply, and live out His Word in obedience.

During your ending time of prayer (#5), it is good to keep a few things in mind. The Lord's model prayer (Matthew 6:9–13) is not a mantra to be repeated but a guide to be followed. Jesus didn't say this is *what* to pray, but *how* to pray. In it you learn that your prayers should be intimate, reverent, worshipful, humble, and surrendered.

As you pray, pour out your heart and seek God for everything that you need. Repentantly confess any sins you have committed and seek His merciful forgiveness. Receive by faith His love for you while also loving Him back. Cry out in desperation for the wisdom, strength, and guidance for the great and small decisions that lie before you. Thank Him for the good things He's done for you and praise Him for how awesome He is. As you then go into the day, live with expectancy of seeing your own attitude and thoughts improve while watching Him work mightily around you and lovingly through you for His glory!

NOTES

NOTES